"In this innovative book, Dr. Minhas closely examines the evidence regarding the impact of racial and prejudicial stereotyping on (i) investigative interviewing and (ii) the outcomes of criminal investigations. He notes that police officers are not immune to such effects and offers solutions to the problems that can arise both for the police and for members of stigmatised communities."

—**Professor Ray Bull,** *Emeritus Professor of Forensic Psychology, University of Leicester*

Racial and Prejudicial Stereotyping by Police

This book uncovers the influence of racial and prejudicial stereotyping during police investigation of suspects from stigmatised communities. The book examines the under-researched aspect of whether and how negative stereotypes appear to influence the police interviews, investigative decision-making, and outcomes of criminal investigations when officers investigate individuals from stigmatised communities as suspects of crime.

In the United Kingdom, the United States, and Europe, the war on terror has been argued to impact adversely on existing race relations policies in the aftermath of terrorist activity in both the United States and Europe. Recent research has suggested that changes in legislation and counter-terrorism measures have contributed to the construction and reinforcement of the Muslim community as a suspect, which, in turn, may result in police bias and prejudice towards members of Muslim communities. Based on novel and groundbreaking research studies, the author examines whether such police bias could influence the police investigation and interviewing processes concerning individuals from the suspect community as well as the outcome of a criminal investigation.

The author introduces the Minhas Investigative Interviewing Prejudicial Stereotyping Scale (MIIPSS), an instrument developed and used to assess the level of police interviewers' racial and prejudicial stereotyping towards suspects from stigmatised groups, and maintains that its use would serve to minimise the influence of racial and prejudicial stereotypes on investigation. It is further suggested that the training of police officers on the implications of such prejudicial (racial/religious) stereotyping is essential to improving interviewing performance, case outcomes, and community cohesion.

This book will benefit academics, researchers, police officers, lawyers, social policy officers, and probation officers across the globe.

Rashid Minhas is a distinguished criminologist and esteemed academic who has dedicated his career to the study of policing, racial and prejudicial stereotyping in criminal investigations, investigative decision-making, and police interviewing practices. He is currently affiliated with the University of West London's School of Human and Social Sciences. With a strong educational background, Rashid earned his PhD in Criminal Justice and Social Psychology, demonstrating his commitment to exploring the complex intersections between criminology, psychology, and the criminal justice system. Rashid's work has been widely published in reputable academic journals, earning him recognition and respect within the scholarly community. Rashid's insightful publications shed light on critical issues surrounding criminal justice, offering practical insights and recommendations to improve investigative processes and ensure fairness in the criminal justice system.

Directions and Developments in Criminal Justice and Law

www.routledge.com/Directions-and-Developments-in-Criminal-Justice-and-Law/book-series/DDCJL

The ways in which crime is constructed in society is of time-honoured interest to criminologists across the globe. The ever-changing landscape of what is criminal and what is not affects scholars and policymakers in their approach to the body of law defining prohibited conduct, how that law evolves, and the modes by which it is administered. Rule of law cannot exist without a transparent legal system, strong enforcement structures, and an independent judiciary to protect against the arbitrary use of power. Critical consideration of the mechanisms through which societies attempt to make the rule of law a reality is essential to understanding and developing effectual criminal justice systems. The *Directions and Developments in Criminal Justice and Law* series offers the best research on criminal justice and law around the world, providing original insights on a broadly defined range of sociolegal topics in law, criminal procedure, courts, justice, legislation, and jurisprudence. With an eye towards using innovative and advanced methodologies, series monographs offer solid social science scholarship illuminating issues and trends in law, crime, and justice. Books in this series will appeal to criminologists, sociologists, and other social scientists, as well as policymakers, legal researchers, and practitioners.

12. Forced Mobility of EU Citizen
Transnational Criminal Justice Instruments and the Management of 'Unwanted' EU Nationals
Edited by José A. Brandariz, Witold Klaus, and Agnieszka Martynowicz

13. Revisiting Juvenile Justice in India
A Study on Juvenile Justice (Care and Protection of Children) Act, 2015
Atul Jaybhaye

14. Racial and Prejudicial Stereotyping by Police
Its Impact on Investigative Interviewing and the Outcomes of Criminal Investigations
Rashid Minhas

Racial and Prejudicial Stereotyping by Police

Its Impact on Investigative Interviewing and the Outcomes of Criminal Investigations

Rashid Minhas

Routledge
Taylor & Francis Group
NEW YORK AND LONDON

First published 2024
by Routledge
605 Third Avenue, New York, NY 10158

and by Routledge
4 Park Square, Milton Park, Abingdon, Oxon, OX14 4RN

Routledge is an imprint of the Taylor & Francis Group, an informa business

Library of Congress Cataloging-in-Publication Data
Names: Minhas, Rashid (Criminologist), author.
Title: Racial and prejudicial stereotyping by police : its impact on investigative interviewing and the outcomes of criminal investigations / Rashid Minhas.
Description: New York, NY : Routledge, 2024. |
Series: Directions and developments in criminal justice and law |
Includes bibliographical references and index.
Identifiers: LCCN 2023047452 (print) | LCCN 2023047453 (ebook) |
ISBN 9781032432991 (hardback) | ISBN 9781032433387 (paperback) |
ISBN 9781003366836 (ebook)
Subjects: LCSH: Racial profiling in law enforcement. |
Racism in law enforcement. | Stereotypes (Social psychology)
Classification: LCC HV7936.R3 M56 2024 (print) | LCC HV7936.R3 (ebook) |
DDC 363.2/3089–dc23/eng/20231024
LC record available at https://lccn.loc.gov/2023047452
LC ebook record available at https://lccn.loc.gov/2023047453

ISBN: 9781032432991 (hbk)
ISBN: 9781032433387 (pbk)
ISBN: 9781003366836 (ebk)

DOI: 10.4324/9781003366836

Typeset in Sabon
by Newgen Publishing UK

This book is dedicated to my beloved parents and my family, whose boundless support, guidance, and love have been the foundation upon which I have built my life.

Contents

Chapter 1

Introduction

Background

The period from 1974 to the present is marked by two distinct eras of political violence in the United Kingdom. The first era emerged during the Irish Republican Army (IRA) bombing campaign, which occurred between 1973 and 1996, where the perpetrators were commonly perceived as 'Irish terrorists'. The second era is more recent, likely beginning around 2001. During this time, both in the United Kingdom and globally, the primary threat of political violence has been portrayed as originating from individuals allegedly motivated by extreme interpretations of Islam, often labelled as 'Islamic terrorists' (Nickels, Thomas, Hickman, & Silvestri, 2012).

This period is set apart by occasions which are relevant to Irish and Muslim communities that have affected common society. Such occasions include (i) bombing campaigns; (ii) the adoption of anti-terrorism legislation; (iii) wrongful arrests and imprisonments; (iv) the shooting of alleged terror suspects; (v) the broad resolution of the Northern Ireland conflict; and (vi) controversies relating to the place of Islam and Muslims in the United Kingdom (Hickman, Thomas, Nickels, & Silvestri, 2012). Collectively, these occurrences have contributed to the construction of both communities as potential threats to society. This, in turn, has led to negative stereotyping, intelligence profiling, and even the expression of anti-Irish or anti-Muslim sentiments (Nickels et al., 2012).

Recent research has shed light on the pervasive negative portrayal of Irish and Muslim communities in public discourse, notably in the media (Hickman et al., 2012; Awan & Rahman, 2016). These portrayals often associate members of these communities with extremism, terrorism, and social backwardness (Nickels et al., 2012; Poole, 2018; Poole & Richardson, 2010). A recurring theme in this body of research is the suggestion that institutionalised prejudice, stemming from both the media and the political establishment, plays a significant role in perpetuating these negative stereotypes (Downing & Husband, 2005; Fraser, 2018). This

DOI: 10.4324/9781003366836-1

institutionalised bias can contribute to the misrepresentation and stigmatisation of these minority groups.

Nickels et al. (2012) propose that the media's development of minority groups as suspect and threatening is influenced by a range of social structures, social relations, and regulated practices. These encompass factors such as (i) the schedules of news making, (ii) news values, (iii) the relationship between media outlets, (iv) media ownership, and (v) the predominant ideological climate of the time. In a related study, Hickman et al. (2012) delved into the extent and manner in which both Irish and Muslim communities were depicted as suspects within public discourse. Their research found striking parallels between the experiences of Irish individuals in the 1970s and those of Muslim communities today regarding their representation in public discourse and their interactions with law enforcement. These parallels illuminate the persistent and concerning patterns of portrayal and treatment faced by these minority groups.

In the past, communities have often been unfairly portrayed as suspects, leading to grave violations of human rights and devastating consequences, including miscarriages of justice. A notable example of this is seen in cases like the 'Birmingham Six' and the 'Guildford Four' in England and Wales, where individuals confessed to serious crimes under intense police pressure, only to later be exonerated when it was discovered they were innocent. These instances revealed a troubling bias within the criminal justice system. Individuals from Irish communities were unfairly targeted as bombing suspects solely based on their community affiliations (Pantazis & Pemberton, 2009). This highlights a critical issue—the potential for prejudicial stereotyping to result in investigative failures, particularly within the context of police interviews (Bull, 2018; Milne & Bull, 1999). Surprisingly, little attention has been devoted to the influence of such prejudicial stereotyping on the investigative interviewing of suspects. To date, no known research has systematically examined the impact of prejudicial stereotyping on the investigation processes, including the interviewing of suspects, within the suspect community. This book aims to examine whether prejudicial stereotyping influences the investigation and interviewing processes of suspects from the suspect community, ultimately affecting criminal investigation outcomes.

Construction of suspect communities in the United Kingdom

Construction of the Irish community as a suspect in the United Kingdom

The concept of the suspect community was first introduced by Hillyard (1993) in his seminal work on the 'secret state' and the impact of the

Prevention of Terrorism Act (PTA) of 1974 on the Irish community. Hillyard's research delved into the effects of the PTA during the turbulent period of the Northern Ireland conflict. He argued that one of the most notable outcomes of the PTA was its role in constructing what he termed a suspect community within the United Kingdom—specifically, the Northern Irish population. This suspect community was formed as a result of the PTA's institutional design and operation. It is worth noting that despite concerns over the draconian nature of the powers granted by the PTA, it passed through the Parliament with unanimous support just one week after the IRA's Birmingham pub bombing in 1974. Even then-Labour Home Secretary Roy Jenkins described the powers as draconian. This swift enactment underscores the urgency and perceived necessity of the legislation at the time.

Hillyard, citing Lord Donaldson, pointed out that under the PTA the requirement of 'reasonable suspicion' to justify stopping an individual was dispensed with. Indeed, Hillyard (1993) cites the earlier ideas of Boyle, O'Hare, and McAllister thus,

> An officer [...] does not have to have any grounds for thinking that they have the information, but merely that the person concerned shall be in a category.
>
> (Boyle, O'Hare & McAllister, Divisional Court, 30 October 1980 (unreported), cited in Hillyard, 1993, p. 19)

Hillyard, accordingly, explained the concept of suspect community as the process of identification of a threat and of a sign of abnormality which exemplified and legitimated the politics of exception put in place by the state. Thus:

> A person who is drawn into the criminal justice system under the PTA is not a suspect in the normal sense of the word. In other words, they are not believed to be involved in or guilty of some illegal act [...] people are suspect primarily because they are Irish and once they are in the police station they are often labelled an Irish suspect, presumably as part of some classification system. In practice, they are being held because they belong to a suspect community.
>
> (Hillyard, 1993, p. 7)

While the primary motivation behind the extensive 'trawling operations', which involved hunting, detaining, and excluding Irish suspects, was apparently to gather intelligence (Breen-Smyth, 2014), Hillyard's analysis pointed to a profound consequence of these measures. He argued that they gave rise to a dual system of justice, effectively creating two distinct realms within the legal system. In this dual system: (i) the established justice framework continued to function for individuals accused of conventional crimes such as burglary, murder, and rape, often referred to as 'ordinary decent criminals'; while (ii) a shadowy and more draconian system emerged to handle those suspected of Irish 'terrorism'. This bifurcation of the justice system, as described by Hillyard, had significant implications for how individuals were treated and for the protections afforded to them within the legal process.

Furthermore, this later system, as outlined by Hillyard (1993), presented wide-ranging discretionary powers to the police, immigration officers, and customs officers in the realm of terrorism-related investigations. Perhaps most significantly, the PTA enabled the potential detention and investigation of individuals without requiring any reasonable suspicion of an offence to be present (Pantazis & Pemberton, 2009). The discretionary nature of these powers sheds light on a striking statistic: between November 1974 and December 1991, during the successive PTAs, a staggering 86 per cent of the 7,052 individuals detained in the United Kingdom were subsequently released with no further action taken against them (Hillyard, 1993). Hillyard's assertion that such measures 'facilitated miscarriages of justice against Irish suspects, most notoriously the cases of the Birmingham Six and the Guildford Four' (1993, p. 31) underscores the gravity of these powers. Moreover, he contends that alongside these wrongful convictions, many others likely suffered wrongful arrests, detentions, or unrecorded instances of police harassment.

Moreover, while Hillyard's study provided valuable insights into the experiences of individuals detained or arrested under the PTA, it warrants scrutiny regarding its scope and potential biases. Hillyard's primary focus on those who were stopped, detained, or arrested raises questions about whether the study adequately captures the broader impact of the PTA on individuals going about their daily lives. Critics, including Greer (2010) and Hargreaves (2016), contend that Hillyard's study may have limitations stemming from its sample selection. Notably, the sample in his study was not randomly selected but rather self-selected. This choice, according to these critics, could potentially over-represent individuals who had particularly negative experiences within the broader phenomenon under investigation. Furthermore, self-selected samples might offer a cathartic platform for participants to express grievances. Additionally, Hillyard's study consisted of a relatively small sample, prompting concerns about its representativeness concerning the wider population. These critiques suggest that while Hillyard's work sheds light on specific aspects of the PTA's impact, it may not provide a comprehensive picture of the broader societal effects.

The focus on specific individuals following security threats linked to the Irish community led to the targeting of individuals based on their perceived 'Irishness' (Breen-Smyth, 2014). For instance, the tragic case of Harry Stanley, who was of Scottish origin, exemplifies this phenomenon. Stanley was fatally shot by the police outside a South Hackney public house while carrying a chair leg. The police officer who shot him mistakenly believed he was dealing with an armed Irishman (Independent Police Complaints Commission, 2007). While the police often saw the targeting of Irish individuals as justified (Breen-Smyth, 2014), Hillyard (1993) highlights several profound impacts stemming from this practice. These include (i) the widespread erosion of Irish individuals' civil liberties; (ii) the adoption of increasingly intrusive and intensified policing methods; (iii) the perception of the entire Irish community in Britain as suspect; and (iv) the potential encouragement of the public to adopt the same view, which could have contributed to the increased anti-Irish racism prevalent at the time.

Furthermore, the concept of a suspect community extends beyond the methods of policing imposed upon a particular group; it also delves into the transfer of formal suspicion by authorities to public suspicion (Abbas, 2019; Breen-Smyth, 2014). Hillyard (1993) emphasised the key role played by the public in fostering suspicion within the Irish community. This dynamic often led to non-Irish individuals reporting the presence of Irish individuals to the police, amplifying the pervasive atmosphere of suspicion. This public suspicion was further fuelled by the press, which frequently propagated the notion that all Irish people were inherently suspect (Hillyard, 1993). Such media influence served to reinforce and perpetuate these negative perceptions.

Hillyard's (1993) notion of the construction of the Irish community as suspect has not gone unchallenged. Greer (1994) contested Hillyard's perspective, arguing that it treated Irish people as a monolithic group, failing to differentiate between those who held intensely anti-Irish nationalist beliefs. However, Pantazis and Pemberton (2009) offer compelling arguments in support of Hillyard's framework. Pantazis and Pemberton contend that the mere enactment of legislation granting state officials the authority to question anyone travelling between Northern Ireland and the United Kingdom in connection with terrorist activities implied that anyone, regardless of their religious or political identity, could come under suspicion. This phenomenon was notably exemplified by the routine practice of police labelling individuals as 'Irish suspects' on forms used to record fingerprints (Hillyard, 1993).

Consequently, the powers granted by the PTA may have been wielded more rigorously against the Catholic/Republican community than against the Protestant/Unionist community. However, it is important to note that the latter group was not immune to such treatment, particularly at ports and airports, where they were also singled out simply due to their perceived 'Irishness'. Pantazis and Pemberton (2009) argue that this evidence lends support to Hillyard's overarching argument about the wholesale discriminatory nature of the PTA, which impacted the entire Irish community. Furthermore, Hickman and Walter (1997) suggest that Hillyard's concept of a suspect community was entrenched within a broader anti-Irish discourse. This discourse meant that, even though much of the British anti-Irish prejudice was rooted in anti-Catholic bigotry, Protestants were not exempt from disparagement, embarrassment, and degradation solely because of their Irish identity. This broader context highlights the far-reaching consequences of the PTA's discriminatory practices.

Moreover, Pantazis and Pemberton (2009) contend that Hillyard's observations about the PTA hold significant relevance for several reasons. Not only did they shed light on the destructive effects of the PTA on individuals and communities, but they also drew attention to the manner in which democratic values and practices could be compromised in the pursuit of heightened security. When Irish people were previously branded as a suspect community, whether within the United Kingdom or across wider Europe, Breen-Smyth (2014) argues that the criteria for such suspicion were remarkably broad. Merely possessing a Northern Irish accent was sufficient for an individual to be identified as suspicious. This blanket attribution meant that even Northern Irish Unionists and Loyalists, who may have held loyalty to the British Crown, were also swept into the suspect category.

Furthermore, Hillyard's notion of a suspect community has faced criticism from Greer (1994, 2008), who raises questions concerning the legal interpretation of criminal suspicion. Greer (2008) asserts that the process of information trawling, as elucidated by Hillyard (1993), does not equate to treating individuals as criminal suspects, particularly given that the majority of those detained were eventually discharged without facing criminal proceedings. Greer goes on to argue that state suspicion, in and of itself, may not necessarily constitute a violation of human rights. However, he posits that such suspicion does become a breach of these rights when it is 'groundless' and results in adverse consequences for those affected (Greer, 2008). Greer might well be correct in his argument if a strict lawful meaning of criminal suspicion is applied.

Nevertheless, Pantazis and Pemberton (2009) argue that legal understandings may have little significance in people's everyday experiences of the law and their interactions with state officials, as well as their interpretations of these occasions. Additionally, these authors assert that Greer has, in a general sense, misunderstood the nature of Hillyard's work. According to Pantazis and Pemberton, a suspect community serves as an empirical study, focusing on the subjective encounters of individuals whose lives were affected and disturbed by the PTA. In this context, it is more appropriate to view such a study as a sociological exploration of individuals' encounters with the law, rather than an inquiry into the application (and/or misapplication) of legal rules Pantazis & Pemberton, 2009).

'Home-grown terrorism' narrative and the construction of a new 'suspect' community

In the wake of Al Qaeda's devastating attacks on the United States in 2001, issues related to national security and transnational crime surged to the forefront of the political agenda (Mythen, Walklate, & Khan, 2009). In the United Kingdom, a series of high-profile terrorist attacks, including the London Underground bombings and the car bomb incident at Glasgow Airport, firmly established terrorism as a critical social problem. These events propelled terrorism to the centre stage of political discourse in the United Kingdom, shaping discussions about risk and human security (Mythen, Walklate, & Khan, 2013). This shift was driven by the perception that a new form of global terrorism had emerged (Gregory & Wilkinson, 2005). Referred to as 'new terrorism', this phenomenon was characterised by the actions of extreme Islamic fundamentalists and distinguished from previous forms of political violence practised by terrorist organisations, such as the Irish Republican Army (Morgan, 2004).

The terrorism narrative in the United Kingdom gained prominence following the July 2005 attacks in London. This tragic event sparked broader political debates, with discussions centring on the 'home-grown threat'. This concept was particularly unsettling, as it suggested that British citizens were acting as a 'fifth column' within the country (Croft & Moore, 2010). After the July 2005 attacks, one of the suicide bombers, Mohammed Siddique Khan, delivered his 'martyr's testimony' in a broad Yorkshire accent. In response to these events, a government adviser expressed concern, suggesting that as many as one in five British Muslims 'may' support militant jihadi violence (Croft & Moore, 2010). These incidents and statements seemed to coalesce into a broader perception, one that former British prime minister Tony Blair articulated as the presence of 'home-grown radicals', who

> 'may have been born here. But [...] [the] ideology wasn't. And that is why it has to be taken on, everywhere'.
>
> (Blair, 2010)

According to Blair, the ideology and operations of these home-grown threats were products of Al Qaeda Central. However, for others, it was impossible to separate the home-grown threat from the broader network threat (Croft & Moore, 2010). As noted by Roy (2011, p. 20), 'We have seen that young Westerners went to countries to fight the jihad and came back to Europe to commit terrorist acts.'

This period saw the enactment of controversial counterterrorism legislation aimed at addressing the 'home-grown threat', such as the CONTEST strategy. From 2001 to 2010, the UK witnessed a significant number of arrests related to terrorist offences, totalling over 237 individuals (Fenwick, 2013). In parallel, intervention programmes designed to counteract extremist threats, like the Prevent Strategy, resulted in the referral of 228 individuals to security agencies due to their perceived risk to national security (Fenwick, 2013). However, it's worth noting the scepticism expressed by Awan (2018), who argues that the Prevent Strategy may not effectively prevent extremism or individuals from becoming terrorists. Instead, there is a risk that it could label the Muslim community as suspect. A review conducted by the Equality and Human Rights Commission (EHRC, 2010) illustrates the adverse effects of counterterrorism practices on the Muslim community. These practices have contributed to a prevailing sentiment of being viewed as a suspect community, further deepening feelings of estrangement, segregation, anxiety, and vulnerability among Muslims. Intervention projects, notably the Prevent Strategy, are founded on a foundation of suspicion, perpetuating perceptions of both the police and the British criminal justice system as entities that are distrustful of their authority (Choudhury & Fenwick, 2011; Spalek, 2011).

In the context of countering the 'home-grown threat', there has been a significant rise in hostility towards Islam and Muslims, commonly referred to as 'Islamophobia' (Awan, 2018). Poynting and Mason (2008) have observed that when specific groups are targeted by counterterrorism measures, it can inadvertently grant society 'permission to hate' these groups. Consequently, this may provide a moral justification for anti-Muslim hate crimes. Awan and Rahman (2016) note that there is substantial evidence suggesting that Muslims have become the target of a surge in anti-Muslim hate crimes within contemporary UK society. These authors contend that news coverage has often generalised about Muslims in an overtly biased manner. They further argue that the negative portrayal of Muslims in public discourse carries the risk of exacerbating and perpetuating anti-Muslim prejudice in society.

The negative portrayal of Muslims can have detrimental effects on criminal investigations. A striking example occurred in June 2006 when the Metropolitan Police conducted a counterterrorist operation, raiding a house in Forest Gate, London, and arresting two Muslim brothers, one of whom was shot and wounded during the operation. Despite the intelligence reportedly held by the police, suggesting that the house was involved in manufacturing a chemical terrorist weapon, a week-long search yielded no evidence. Both brothers were subsequently released without any charges being filed. Another instance highlighting the potential repercussions of negative portrayals is the case of Rizwaan Sabir, a postgraduate student in counterterrorism studies. He was arrested under the TA for downloading extremist material but was later released without charges. Documents from the Professional Standards Unit of the West Midlands police revealed that officers had 'fabricated' crucial elements of the case against him (Awan, 2012; Miller, Mills, & Harkins, 2011). At the point when such an injustice occurs, it undoubtedly results in several social harms, affecting not only the victim of the original crime but also the criminal justice system (Hillyard et al., 2004). The studies outlined in this book, therefore, examine whether prejudicial stereotyping stemming from counterterrorism policies, including the Prevent Strategy, might influence the outcome of a criminal investigation. It is in relation to this issue that the chapter will now begin discussing these issues.

From the 'old' to a 'new' suspect community

In 2008, Gareth Peirce, renowned for her work and advocacy in high-profile cases involving allegations of human rights injustices, drew striking parallels between the Irish communities and the Muslim communities in the United Kingdom. She served as legal counsel for individuals wrongfully convicted in the Birmingham and Guildford bombings and represented the family of Jean Charles de Menezes (a Brazilian man tragically killed by Metropolitan Police officers due to mistaken identity in the aftermath of the London bombings on 7 July 2005), and worked on behalf of Moazzam Begg (detained extrajudicially at Guantanamo Bay detention camp for nearly three years). Her work highlighted the lawful injustices that contribute to the alienation of many Muslims from the authorities and the state. Interestingly, Peirce pointed out that while the Irish community had similar experiences, Muslims lacked advocates comparable to the Irish state and the Irish-American diaspora (Breen-Smyth, 2014).

Subsequently, the term 'suspect community' has become associated with Muslims, and comparisons have been made between the experiences of the Irish and Muslim communities (Hickman et al., 2012; Legrand & Lister, 2018). Hickman and his colleagues had previously conducted several studies, initially focusing on the Irish communities (Hickman & Walter, 1997) and more recently on both Irish and Muslim communities in the United

Kingdom (Hickman et al., 2012). Their research in 2012 revealed striking parallels between the experiences of individuals from the Irish community in the 1970s to the 1990s and those from the Muslim community today in terms of how they are treated by the police and portrayed in the media. Pantazis and Pemberton (2009) note that in the contemporary United Kingdom, the Muslim community has effectively replaced the Irish community as the suspect community, particularly in the aftermath of the 'war on terror'. These authors advance the relevance of Hillyard's notion of the 'suspect' community to the Muslim communities and their experiences in the contexts of the 'war on terror'. They defined the suspect community as:

> a sub-group of the population that is singled out for state attention as being 'problematic'. Specifically, regarding policing, individuals may be targeted, not necessarily as a result of suspected wrongdoing, but simply because of their presumed membership to that sub-group. Race, ethnicity, religion, class, gender, language, accent, dress, political ideology or any combination of these factors may serve to delineate the sub-group.
> (Pantazis & Pemberton, 2009, p. 649)

Furthermore, these authors acknowledge the existence of a dual system of justice, initially identified by Hillyard (1993), through the incorporation of many of the powers from the PTA into the Terrorism Act (TA) of 2000 and 2006. This is evident in the broader discretionary powers granted for stop-and-search, as well as arrest under the TA 2006. The extension of pre-charge detention to 28 days and the use of control orders to detain individuals without trial further exemplify this dual system. Pantazis and Pemberton assert that the modus operandi of the police came under intense scrutiny in the media following significant events such as the release of the Guildford Four and the Birmingham Six, similar to the attention it garnered after the De Menezes shooting and the failed terror raids in Forest Gate and Birmingham.

In their 2008 study, Moore, Mason, and Lewis conducted an extensive analysis of over 974 newspaper articles spanning from 2001 to 2008. They revealed a striking trend: approximately 36 per cent of these articles that focused on British Muslims during this period were exclusively centred on the theme of terrorism. Moreover, their findings demonstrated that many of these print media stories revolved around the societal and political experiences of Muslims in the United Kingdom. This emphasis on terrorism in media portrayal is not an isolated occurrence. Numerous studies examining stories related to Islam and Muslims in British newspapers, including works by Allen (2012), Awan and Rahman (2016), Baker, Gabrielatos, and McEnery (2013), as well as Poole (2006), consistently echoed the same pattern. These studies found that, especially in the post-'war on terror' era, media narratives concerning Islam and Muslims were overwhelmingly focused on terrorism, further perpetuating negative stereotypes about this community. Awan and Rahman (2016) note that such reporting and portrayal of British Muslims may have played a significant role in reinforcing a framework that 'others' these communities. Moreover, this kind of media coverage could potentially influence people's perceptions of Muslims, given the dominant headlines and narratives they encounter.

In their comprehensive 2012 study, Hickman and his colleagues conducted an extensive analysis encompassing 800 policy documents, 2,798 news items, 42 key informant interviews with community and religious leaders, and seven mixed Irish and Muslim discussion group events. Their research revealed striking parallels between the experiences of the Irish and Muslim communities in Britain, particularly concerning their interactions with the police. What Hickman and his team observed was the recurrent comparison of 'the innocent Irish' and 'moderate Muslims' to 'Irish terrorists' and 'Muslim extremists' in various contexts, whether it be in the media, political debates, or policy documents. This tendency to juxtapose the 'law-abiding' with 'extremists' created a blurred line between moderate individuals and those associated with violent extremist groups. The consequences of this blurred boundary were profound, contributing to a social and political environment that often resulted in serious human rights violations and tragic outcomes, a phenomenon that arguably persists in the treatment of Muslim communities today. The historical context of the Irish experience, including miscarriages of justice such as the Birmingham Six and the Guildford Four, finds eerie echoes in contemporary events involving the Muslim communities, like the 'Forest Gate' and 'Nottingham Two' incidents. Adding to these concerns, Awan (2012) argues that the United Kingdom's new legislation on terrorism offences has heightened the risk of wrongful convictions by lowering the burden of proof required under criminal law, as exemplified by Section 16(2)(b) of the TA 2006.

Furthermore, it is increasingly evident that the very powers intended to bolster security, such as those found in the TA 2000 and TA 2006, have inadvertently eroded it. This situation is particularly poignant for Muslim communities, which continue to grapple with the persistent cloud of state suspicion, as noted by Nickels et al. (2012). Whether by design or consequence, measures like profiling, stop-and-search policies, and heightened surveillance possess the potential to stigmatise entire communities. This parallel between the current treatment of the Muslim communities and the historical experiences of the Irish communities during the Northern Ireland conflict has not gone unnoticed (Awan, 2012). Pantazis and Pemberton (2009) shed light on the complex dynamics at play. Despite the discursive portrayal of the Muslim majority as law-abiding and peace-loving, this position has at times been contradicted by statements from public figures. For instance, John Denham MP, who held the position of Home Office minister at the time, made a statement following the July 2005 attacks, which suggested a departure from this narrative. He stated that,

> few terrorist movements have lasted for long without a supportive community. A supportive community does not necessarily condone violence, but they see terrorists are sharing their worldview, part of the struggle to which they belong.
>
> (Denham, 2005, cited in Pantazis & Pemberton, 2009, p. 658)

It is reasonable to assume that Denham's notion of a 'supportive community' may have inadvertently contributed to the stigmatisation of the entire Muslim community. This construction of a 'supportive community' could inadvertently lead to the portrayal of individuals from the Muslim communities as suspects in the eyes of the broader society.

In contrast to Pantazis and Pemberton's (2009) assertion that Muslim communities have become suspects, Greer (2010) offers a dissenting viewpoint. Greer contends that Pantazis and Pemberton paint a 'distasteful' picture of a powerful state oppressing a religious minority through a series of anti-terrorism laws, all underpinned by a hostile and prejudiced official political discourse. He goes on to characterise this perspective as crude, misleading, and one-dimensional, relying more on speculation than on a solid empirical foundation. It is worth noting that Greer's (2010) argument primarily focuses on criticising this portrayal and does not delve deeply into the specific impacts of the TAs on both Irish and Muslim communities. Instead, he opts to discuss other effects, such as the culture of 'official suspicion' that has developed as a result of counterterrorism legislation.

Nevertheless, the concept of a 'suspect' community has been recently employed to encapsulate the outcome of various social, political, and ideological discourses converging to portray Muslims as extremists and the 'enemy within' (Breen-Smyth, 2014; Sentas, 2014). Warsi (2017) asserts that in the United Kingdom, Muslims are the most recent addition to a historical lineage of 'others' labelled as 'the enemy within'. Awan (2018) observes that Muslim communities perceive unfair categorisation as extremists, which significantly affects their sense of identity and belonging. Breen-Smyth (2014) contends that a suspect community is not merely targeted through measures like counterterrorism legislation but is also 'imagined' in the minds of fearful individuals, shaped by broader discourses surrounding the 'war on terror'. As Breen-Smyth (2014, p. 231) explains, 'a suspect community can be understood as constructed through mechanisms deployed by the state to ensure national or state security and reinforced by societal reactions and social practices'. Furthermore, Breen-Smyth (2014) argues that this notion of a 'suspect' community not only solidifies the perception of Muslims as 'suspect' within the general society but also affects how Muslims perceive themselves as 'suspect'. While Breen-Smyth (2014) provides a redefinition of the concept of a suspect community, offering intriguing insights, there remains a challenge in establishing empirical evidence regarding what people actually think.

Critics of the concept of a 'suspect' community, including Greer (2010, 2014) and Hargreaves (2016), raise questions about the existence of concrete evidence supporting claims that Muslims as a whole are labelled as 'suspect' or subjected to intrusive forms of counterterrorism policing. Greer (2014, p. 469) argues that proponents of the suspect community thesis, including Breen-Smyth and Hillyard, have failed to provide credible evidence that 'the UK's anti-terrorism laws have turned the Irish or Muslims in Britain into communities under official suspicion'. He contends that 'since parts of the "suspect Muslim community" are officially trusted, the entire "community" cannot plausibly be regarded as "officially" suspect' (Greer, 2010, p. 1179). However, Greer's argument lacks a clear distinction between being under 'official suspicion' and being otherwise suspect. He suggests that if a police officer suspects someone, that person is under 'official suspicion', whereas if the general public suspects that person, they are not. Breen-Smyth (2014) reports that in 2009, 60,000 civilians were recruited throughout the United Kingdom to participate in counterterrorism activities, participating in the Prevent programme, the government's 'early warning' framework. She questions whether being suspected by one of these quasi-security players should constitute being under 'official suspicion'. In a context where the lines between security forces and citizens blur, the distinction between being officially suspected and being suspected by the general public becomes increasingly unclear (Breen-Smyth, 2014). In response to Breen-Smyth's argument, Greer (2014, p. 468) asserts that the official recruitment of individuals in the Prevent programme 'counts more against the "suspect" community thesis itself than it does against the distinction between official and unofficial suspect'. He further maintains that there is ample evidence of anti-Irish racism and Islamophobia in the United Kingdom. However, there is no conclusive evidence linking these issues to 'official state suspicion' or to the various counterterrorism legislations.

Research from various authors (e.g. Breen-Smyth, 2014; Blackwood, Hopkins, & Reicher, 2013; Mythen, Walklate, & Khan, 2013; Sentas,

2014) consistently demonstrates that the legislative, institutional, ideological, and discursive aspects of the 'war on terror' have a profound impact on the perceptions held by Muslims. These perceptions encompass how they view themselves, their confidence levels, their sense of community, and their attitudes towards the police. These perceptions play a pivotal role in shaping their reactions to being characterised as a suspect group and influence their corresponding evaluations. Moreover, these perceptions mediate their support for efforts to combat terrorism and radicalisation (Breen-Smyth, 2014; Blackwood et al., 2013). Studies (Awan, 2012; 2018; Breen-Smyth, 2014; Cherney & Murphy, 2016; Hickman et al., 2012; Mythen et al., 2013; Pantazis & Pemberton, 2009; Poole, 2018) have consistently indicated the presence of a police bias against Muslims, which directly stems from state suspicion and various counterterrorism legislations. Consequently, these studies argue that Muslim communities have become a new suspect community in contemporary UK society.

New legislation and its effects on the new suspect community

The government's strategy to combat extremism and terrorism, known as the CONTEST strategy, was initially introduced in 2003. Its development began in the aftermath of the 9/11 attacks in 2001, with a primary focus on law enforcement strategies aimed at pursuing and prosecuting those responsible. However, in the wake of the 7 July 2005 London bombings, the government's approach to preventing extremism and terrorism underwent a significant shift. The revised CONTEST strategy was unveiled in 2009, presenting a multidimensional framework divided into four key strands: 'Prevent', 'Pursue', 'Protect', and 'Prepare' (HM Government, 2011). The 'Protection' and 'Preparation' strands emphasised the importance of safeguarding the public by implementing strategies to fortify security against terrorist threats. The objective of 'Pursue' remained unchanged, focusing on the detection and apprehension of individuals suspected of involvement in terrorism. However, the 'Prevent' strand emerged as the most contentious aspect of the CONTEST strategy. Unlike the other strands, 'Prevent' does not primarily aim to prevent actual terrorist plots; instead, its focus is on averting the 'radicalisation' of individuals to prevent them from becoming terrorists.

In the context of Muslims being perceived as a suspect community, Awan (2012) corroborates the findings of Pantazis and Pemberton (2009) by highlighting that the Prevent strand continues to reinforce the labelling of the Muslim community as the 'new' suspect community. Awan argues that within the primary objectives of the Prevent Strategy outlined by the HM Government (2011), the original goal of challenging extremist ideology and those who promote violence has become muddled due to counterterrorism policies. He contends that this shift appears to be more about intelligence gathering than prevention. Furthermore, Awan (2012) suggests that the Prevent Strategy may not effectively prevent extremism or radicalisation but could instead risk stigmatising the Muslim communities. In a recent study conducted by Zempi and Tripli (2023), it was discovered that Prevent hampers freedom of speech, poses a threat to student activism, and compels Muslim students to conceal their Muslim identity to avoid being stigmatised as 'radical'.

Bartlett and Birdwell (2010) support this viewpoint, asserting that the Prevent Strategy has exceeded its intended scope, leading to the alienation of Muslims and the targeting of the wrong individuals. This, in turn, has hindered initiatives that could have promoted community cohesion and exacerbated intercommunity tensions. One example of this approach is the installation of covert and overt CCTV cameras in predominantly Muslim areas in Birmingham, United Kingdom, funded by the Terrorism Allied Fund. These actions have generated feelings of unease, anger, and a loss of trust within the Muslim community. The EHRC (2010) conducted a review that demonstrates how counterterrorism practices have adversely affected Muslims, deepening their sense of being a 'suspect' community and intensifying feelings of estrangement, segregation, anxiety, and vulnerability. It can be argued that community-based efforts that prioritise intelligence gathering over involving Muslim communities in counterterrorism endeavours may have contributed to the construction and perpetuation of the perception of the Muslim communities as suspects.

The Prevent Strategy has faced criticism from multiple perspectives. For instance, Choudhury and Fenwick (2011) and Spalek (2011) argue that British Muslims' reactions to the Prevent Strategy and intervention projects are rooted in a sense of suspicion. This perception leads them to view both the police and the British criminal justice system with resentment. The lack of transparency regarding the purpose of these projects has resulted in significant community anger and a loss of trust (Awan, 2018; Pilkington, & Acik, 2020). After the introduction of the Prevent Strategy in 2009, several British mosques became targets of vandalism, including graffiti and arson. These incidents were seen in the context of the ongoing debate surrounding counterterrorism approaches and the increasing association of terms like 'terrorism' and 'jihad' with Islam and Muslims (Githens-Mazer & Lambert, 2010). Awan (2012) argues that the frequent use of words like 'jihad' and 'terrorism' in a similar narrative has been employed to portray Muslims as a 'problem group'. The media's role in perpetuating this association is deemed potentially harmful, contributing to Islamophobic reactions against Muslim communities (Allen, 2012; Awan, 2012; Awan & Rahman, 2016).

Following the events of September 11, 2001, the United Kingdom witnessed a substantial increase in the number of Asian individuals subjected to stop-and-search procedures under anti-terrorism laws. Mythen, Walklate, and Khan (2009) reported a staggering 400 per cent rise, from 744 incidents in 2001–2002 to 2089 in 2002–2003. The EHRC (2010) conducted an investigation revealing that the use of stop-and-search powers under Section 44 of the TA 2000 had detrimental effects on community relations, eroded trust in the police, and diminished the confidence of Muslim communities. The EHRC report (2010) acknowledges the difficulty in precisely quantifying the number of Muslims subjected to stop-and-search and their likelihood of being stopped compared to individuals from different religious groups. This is because religion, unlike ethnicity, is not recorded during stop-and-search encounters. Nevertheless, the EHRC report underscores that stop-and-search practices undeniably eroded trust within Muslim communities towards the police.

A review by Human Rights Watch (HRW, 2010) found that approximately 450,000 stop-and-searches were carried out under Section 44 of the TA 2000 in the United Kingdom between April 2007 and April 2009. However, no successful prosecutions for terrorism offences resulted from these searches. The independent reviewer of terrorism legislation noted that little, if any, valuable intelligence regarding terrorist plots was obtained. HRW's report (2010) concluded that the government had failed to demonstrate the effectiveness of Section 44 for its stated purpose. The report also raised concerns about the discriminatory and inconsistent use of stop-and-search powers. For example, it pointed out that individuals from Black and Asian backgrounds were subjected to these searches more frequently than White individuals. Furthermore, the data showed disparities in different locations. In London, minorities were disproportionately represented in stop-and-search statistics, while in other locations like Birmingham, Manchester, and Glasgow, where terrorist incidents had occurred or been foiled, the representation was less pronounced.

The findings of the ECHR (2010) and HRW (2010) align with those of Cherney and Murphy (2016), who conducted focus group interviews to explore the 'experiential consequences' of stigmatisation and the labelling of Muslims as 'suspects' in contemporary Australia. They discovered that neglecting the negative experiences and concerns of the Muslim communities could lead to a shift in focus among Muslims towards resistance, drawing attention to perceived intimidation and grievances rather than enabling cooperation with authorities to address terrorism and radicalisation. Cherney and Murphy also propose recognising the adverse impacts of the 'war on terror' on specific communities, with the suspect community thesis highlighting these detrimental outcomes (Cherney & Murphy, 2016). However, it is important to note that Cherney and Murphy's findings may not fully represent the entire Muslim communities in Australia or other Western jurisdictions. Muslims are a diverse group, encompassing various ethnicities and affiliations, such as Shia, Salafi, and Sunni. Additionally, because their study gathered data through focus groups, participants' perspectives may be influenced by respondent bias and social desirability concerns.

The 'war on terror' and 'the enemy within'

Since the 'war on terror' in 2001, the position of the Muslim communities in the United Kingdom has undergone significant transformation. Assumptions about Muslims in Europe, such as 'the enemy within', have become more widespread (Lynch, 2013). The aftermath of terrorist activities in the United States and Europe has led to a noticeable rise in hostility towards Islam and Muslims, commonly referred to as 'Islamophobia'. Numerous researchers (Awan, 2012; Giani, & Merlino, 2021; Hickman et al., 2012; Nickels et al., 2012; Pantazis & Pemberton, 2009) have identified the consequences of 'Islamophobia', including exclusion, violence, discrimination, and prejudice directed towards members of the Muslim communities. Recent terrorist attacks in Western Europe, such as the Brussels suicide bombings, the Bastille Day attack in Nice, the Breitscheidplatz attack in Berlin, and the Palace of Westminster attack in London, exacerbated these tensions.

In the wake of the July 2005 London terrorist attacks, there was a sharp increase in religiously motivated crimes reported against the Muslim communities, with 269 incidents compared to 40 in the same period in 2004 (BBC, 4 August 2005). Several observers (e.g. Poynting & Mason, 2008; Sabir, 2017) argue that the 'radicalised Muslim Other' has become a prominent 'folk devil' in the global West following the 'war on terror'. Despite heightened surveillance of Muslim communities in the post-9/11 era (Awan, 2012), it can be argued that a stereotypical approach towards an entire community may not be the most effective strategy for the state, especially considering historical precedents like those in the Irish context. As Clements (2008, p. 215) notes, 'when the state's response to terrorism becomes increasingly draconian, it inevitably has a detrimental impact on the very society it aims to protect'.

While counterterrorism policies in general foster an environment of low trust, leading to fear and suspicion within Muslim communities, the dispositions of the Prevent Strategy have the potential to problematise Islamic religious identities (Spalek, 2011). This, in turn, can give rise to feelings of racial and religious segregation, as well as ethnic profiling experienced by some Muslims in their daily lives (Awan, 2018). This evidence underscores how, in practice, Muslims in the United Kingdom are often perceived as suspects (Awan, 2012; Breen-Smyth, 2014; Hickman et al., 2012; Mythen et al., 2013; Pantazis & Pemberton, 2009).

Influence of the negative portrayal of a community as suspect

Poynting and Mason (2008) observed that when counterterrorism measures specifically target certain groups, it can inadvertently give society 'permission to hate' these groups. Consequently, this may provide a moral licence for the occurrence of anti-Muslim hate crimes. Awan and Rahman (2016) note that there is evidence indicating a surge in anti-Muslim hate crimes in contemporary UK society. This trend became especially apparent in the aftermath of the murder of Lee Rigby in Woolwich, London, in 2013. Awan and Rahman (2016) conducted a review of 1,022 articles from UK newspapers in the three weeks following Lee Rigby's murder. They discovered that the news coverage tended to generalise about Muslims in an overtly prejudicial manner. These authors assert that this negative portrayal of Muslims in public discourse increases the risk of further fuelling anti-Muslim prejudice in society.

When members of a minority group are consistently portrayed in negative social contexts, such as terrorism, dependency, or crime, classical and evaluative conditioning processes can foster prejudiced mental associations with that minority group (Giani & Merlino, 2021; Walther, Nagengast, & Trasselli, 2005). Once a community is stigmatised as a suspect in public discourse, it can influence the criminal investigative process when police officers reflect the attitudes of the general public from which they are drawn (Smith & Alpert, 2007). Historically, these biased mental associations have contributed to severe human rights violations and tragic miscarriages of justice. For instance, during interviews with Irish suspects, such as the Birmingham Six and the Guildford Four, these individuals confessed to serious crimes under police pressure, crimes they were later found to be innocent of. Police officers displayed bias against these Irish men merely because they belonged to the Irish community (Pantazis & Pemberton, 2009). In the Guildford Four case, Roach and Trotter (2004) argue that the jury was influenced by fear and negative stereotypes. These authors further contend that such cases illustrate how the compartmentalised nature of modern terrorism, coupled with unreliable investigations and forensic evidence, can lead to multiple and interconnected miscarriages of justice (Roach & Trotter, 2004).

In June 2006, during a counterterrorist operation, the Metropolitan Police conducted a raid on a house in Forest Gate, London, leading to the arrest of two Muslim brothers. In the course of the arrest, one of them was shot and wounded. Despite intelligence suggesting the house was being used to manufacture a chemical terrorist weapon, a week-long search yielded nothing incriminating. Subsequently, both brothers were released without any charges. Moreover, Rizwaan Sabir, a postgraduate student specialising in counterterrorism studies, faced arrest under the TA for downloading extremist material but was later released without charges. In the case of Rizwaan Sabir, documents from the Professional Standards Unit revealed that officers had 'fabricated' crucial aspects of the case against him (Awan, 2012, 2018; Miller, Mills, & Harkins, 2011).

In the context of Irish terrorism, Roach and Trotter (2004) previously argued that the horrors associated with terrorism can lead law enforcement to justify the use of 'harsh' means in investigating terrorism-related offences, under the ostensibly 'noble' goal of punishing the perpetrators and preventing harm to innocent civilians. They pointed out that police misconduct in such cases resulted in false confessions and false statements that implicated associates of the Guildford Four detainees. Moreover, they noted that in investigations involving serious crimes like terrorism, the use of aggressive interrogation techniques increases the likelihood of suspects making false admissions and providing false incriminating statements about their associates. For instance, the investigation into the Guildford Four led to information that prompted charges against the 'Maguire Seven' (Roach & Trotter, 2004). Additionally, when the police are convinced they have apprehended the right person, possibly based on what they consider reliable intelligence but lacking sufficient admissible evidence to prove guilt, there may be a strong temptation to coerce individuals into confessing (Gudjonsson, 2018).

The literature discussed above suggests that negative stereotypes have historically played a role in grave violations of human rights, as witnessed in the Irish context in the past. These issues may persist in the current era, particularly in the context of Muslim communities. When such injustices occur, they result in a range of social harms (Hillyard et al., 2004). These social harms encompass but are not limited to, harm to (i) the victims of the original crime and their families, (ii) the criminal justice system and public confidence in it, and (iii) the wider society. Surprisingly, little attention has been given to the impact of such prejudicial stereotypes on the investigative interviewing of suspects. Milne and Bull (1999) emphasise that at the core of police investigations lies the process of interviewing suspects. However, as far as it is known, no research has been conducted in England and Wales to examine the influence of police officers' display of prejudicial stereotyping when conducting investigative interviews with suspects from stigmatised communities. This book aims to investigate whether such prejudicial stereotyping affects police officers' attitudes towards Muslim suspects during the interview process.

Book aims and objectives

From the above literature review, both the suspect community and prejudicial stereotyping emerge as topics in criminal investigation research that have garnered limited interest and some controversy. In the literature, both suspect community stereotyping and prejudicial stereotyping have been found to (i) adversely affect police officers' search for the truth and (ii) influence the outcome(s) of criminal investigations. Therefore, the overarching aim of this book is to explore the perceptions of Muslim suspects and their legal representatives regarding real-life investigative processes, particularly interviews, in England and Wales. Additionally, this book aims to investigate whether prejudicial stereotypes held by police officers towards suspects from the 'suspect' community could impact police officers' investigative decision-making and the outcome(s) of criminal investigations.

To achieve these aims, this book examines the influence of prejudicial stereotyping within the context of investigative and interviewing processes through the course of five studies. Each of these studies has been designed to gather novel information regarding the impact of 'suspect' community stereotyping on criminal investigations, specifically: (i) how such prejudicial stereotyping, if present, could influence police officers' attitudes and investigative decision-making, and (ii) how investigative and interviewing processes may be enhanced.

Overview and structure of the book

The book consists of eight chapters. These are briefly described below to offer a guide to the structure of the book and an overview of what is contained in each chapter.

Chapter 2, which follows next, provides an overview of the literature on police interviewing practices in the United Kingdom. It traces the historical development of these practices, highlighting key milestones, changes, and their impact on the justice system. This chapter has two primary objectives. First, it examines the evolution of police interviewing practices in the United Kingdom, acknowledging that this evolution has not been without problems, including miscarriages of justice. Second, it investigates the role of racial prejudice in contemporary police interview procedures.

Study One, outlined in Chapter 3 of this book, focuses on whether police officers use stereotypes to inform their suspicions when conducting stop-and-searches, rather than engaging in wider debates about policing Black, Asian, and Minority Ethnic (BAME) communities in the United Kingdom. Drawing upon strands of literature from cognitive social psychology, Study One examines how officers: (i) may develop suspicions of individuals and (ii) decide whether or not to conduct a stop-and-search. The findings are then presented based on an analysis of more than 2,100 stop-and-search records held by a police force in England, as well as 20 semi-structured interviews conducted with serving police officers.

When examining prejudicial stereotyping, one should not underestimate the significance of the investigative interview process as a focal point of concern. This significance extends to officers' investigative decision-making, policing practices, and the broader social implications of these processes. Previous research on miscarriages of justice has highlighted that prejudicial stereotypes have played a role in grave violations of human rights with appalling consequences, primarily within the context of investigative interviews.

In Chapters 4, 5, and 6, this book examines the influence of prejudicial stereotyping within the context of investigative interviewing, focusing on 'suspect' community stereotyping. To investigate how such prejudicial stereotyping may impact investigative interviewing, the second study (outlined in Chapter 4) employs a novel approach. For this purpose, the Minhas Investigative Interviewing Prejudicial Stereotyping Scale (MIIPSS) was developed and used to assess the apparent level of interviewers' prejudicial stereotyping towards suspects from certain stigmatised groups.

Subsequently, using this instrument, this book focuses on the role of prejudicial stereotyping within the context of suspect community and investigative interviewing practices in Chapters 5 and 6. To the best of our knowledge, the study presented in Chapter 5 is the first to obtain views from real-life Asian Muslim suspects and explore their perceptions, in order to examine whether prejudicial stereotypes could influence investigative interviews. This part of the book makes an original contribution to the existing body of knowledge and sheds light on the aspect of investigative interviewing of real-life suspects, an area that has not received as much academic attention as other aspects of investigative interviewing.

The fourth study, outlined in Chapter 6 of this book, broke new ground by examining the perceptions of 15 highly experienced legal representatives who had represented suspects in police interviews. The purpose of interviewing lawyers was to gain a holistic view of the interview room and to explore their perceptions of the interactions between police officers and suspects from the Muslim community.

The final study, contained in Chapter 7 of this book, is novel and groundbreaking as it analyses the influence of prejudicial stereotyping on real-life police interviewers' investigative decision-making within the context of suspect community stereotyping. As far as it is known, this fifth study is the first to explore whether suspect community stereotyping could influence police officers' investigative decision-making. This study gathered information through semi-structured interviews conducted individually with 20 serving police officers from a single police organisation in England.

Finally, in Chapter 8, this book makes a significant contribution to original knowledge by synthesising the findings from these five empirical studies. It delves into the potential implications these findings hold for the training of investigative interviewers, the outcomes of cases, and the practices within policing communities considered as suspects.

References

Abbas, M. S. (2019). Producing 'internal suspect bodies': divisive effects of UK counter terrorism measures on Muslim communities in Leeds and Bradford. *British Journal of Sociology*, *70*(1), 261–282.

Allen, C. (2012). A review of the evidence relating to the representation of Muslims and Islam in the British media. *Birmingham, AL: Institute of Applied Social Studies*. Retrieved April 20, 2016. www.birmingham.ac.uk/Documents/college-social-sciences/social-policy/IASS/news-events/MEDIA-ChrisAllen-APPGEvidence-Oct2012.pdf

Awan, I. (2012). 'I Am a Muslim Not an Extremist': How the Prevent Strategy Has Constructed a 'Suspect' Community. *Politics & Policy*, *40*, 1158–1185. Doi:10.1111/j.1747-1346.2012.00397.x

Awan, I. (2018). 'I never did anything wrong'–Trojan Horse: a qualitative study uncovering the impact in Birmingham. *British Journal of Sociology of Education*, *39*, 197–211.

Awan, I., & Rahman, M. (2016). Portrayal of Muslims Following the Murders of Lee Rigby in Woolwich and Mohammed Saleem in Birmingham: A Content Analysis of UK Newspapers. *Journal of Muslim Minority Affairs*, *36*, 16–31.

Baker, P., Gabrielatos, C., & McEnery, T. (2013). *Discourse analysis and media attitudes: The representation of Islam in the British press*. Cambridge: Cambridge University Press.

Bartlett, J. & Birdwell, J. (2010) *From Suspects to Citizens: Preventing Violent Extremism in a Big Society*, London: Demos

BBC News. (2005). Muslim students' police 'distrust'. BBC News. Retrieved from http://news.bbc.co.uk/1/hi/education/4268466.stm

Blackwood, L., Hopkins, N., & Reicher, S. (2013). I know who I am, but who do they think I am? Muslim perspectives on encounters with airport authorities. *Ethnic and Racial Studies*, *36*, 1090–1108.

Blair, T., (2010) Tony Blair, 'Clash about civilizations', speech given in London, 21 March 2006, www.numbeno.gov. uk/output/Page9224.asp, accessed 27 December 2018.

Breen-Smyth, M. (2014). Theorising the 'suspect community': counterterrorism, security practices and the public imagination. *Critical Studies on Terrorism*, 7(2), 223–240

Bull, R. (2018, October). PEACE-full Interviewing/Interrogation: What Research Can Tell Us. In *Diversity in Harmony–Insights from Psychology: Proceedings of the 31st International Congress of Psychology* (pp. 189–210). Chichester, UK: John Wiley & Sons, Ltd.

Cherney, A., & Murphy, K. (2016). Being a 'suspect community' in a post 9/11 world. The impact of the war on terror on Muslim communities in Australia. *Australian & New Zealand Journal of Criminology*, *49*, 480–496.

Choudhury, T., & Fenwick, H. (2011). The impact of counter-terrorism measures on Muslim communities. *International Review of Law, Computers & Technology*, *25*, 151–181.

Clements, P. (2008). *Policing a diverse society*. Oxford: Oxford University Press.

Croft, S., & Moore, C. (2010). The evolution of threat narratives in the age of terror: understanding terrorist threats in Britain. *International Affairs*, *86*(4), 821–835.

Downing, J. D., & Husband, C. (2005). *Representing race: Racisms, ethnicity and the media*. London: Sage.

EHRC. (2010). *Stop and think:* A critical review of the use of stop and search powers in England and Wales. London: Equality and Human Rights Commission.

Fenwick, T. C. H. (2013). The impact of counter-terrorism measures on Muslim communities. In *Developments in Counter-Terrorist Measures and Uses of Technology* (pp. 51–82). London: Routledge.

Fraser, N. (2018). Recognition without ethics? In *The culture of toleration in diverse societies*. Manchester: Manchester University Press.

Githens-Mazer, J., & Lambert, R. (2010). Why conventional wisdom on radicalization fails: the persistence of a failed discourse. *International Affairs*, *86*(4), 889–901.

Giani, M., & Merlino, L. P. (2021). Terrorist attacks and minority perceived discrimination. *British Journal of Sociology*, 72(2), 286–299.

Greer, S. (2010). Anti-terrorist laws and the United Kingdom's 'suspect Muslim community': a reply to Pantazis and Pemberton. *British Journal of Criminology*, *50*, 1171–1190. Doi:10.1080/17539153.2013.867714

Greer, S. (1994), 'Review of Hillyard, P. (1993), Suspect Community: People's Experience of the Prevention of Terrorism Acts in Britain, London: Pluto Press, with Liberty, 1993', *British Journal of Criminology*, 34: 510–11.

Greer, S. (2008). Human rights and the struggle against terrorism in the United Kingdom. *European Human Rights Law Review*, 2, 163.

Greer, S. (2014). Reply to Marie Breen-Smyth, 'Theorising the 'suspect community': counterterrorism, security practices and the public imagination'. *Critical Studies on Terrorism*, 7, 468–471.

Gregory, F., & Wilkinson, P. (2005). Riding pillion for tackling terrorism is a high-risk policy. *Security, Terrorism and the UK*, 2–4.

Gudjonsson, G. H. (2018). *The Psychology of False Confessions: Forty Years of Science and Practice*. Chichester, UK: John Wiley & Sons.

Hargreaves, J. (2016). Risk and resilience in British Muslim communities. *Ethnic and Racial Studies*, *39*, 2601–2620.

Hickman, M. J., & Walter, B. (1997) Discrimination and Irish Communities in Britain. A Report of Research Undrtaken for the Commission for Racial Equality. London: Commission for Racial Equality.

Hickman, M. J., Thomas, L., Nickels, H. C., & Silvestri, S. (2012). Social cohesion and the notion of 'suspect communities': a study of the experiences and impacts of being 'suspect' for Irish communities and Muslim communities in Britain. *Critical Studies on Terrorism*, *5*(1), 89–106.

Hillyard, P. (1993). *Suspect Community: People's Experiences of the Prevention of Terrorism Acts in Britain*. London: Pluto Press.

Hillyard, P., Sim, J., Tombs, S., & Whyte, D. (2004). Leaving a 'Stain upon the Silence' Contemporary Criminology and the Politics of Dissent. *British Journal of Criminology*, 44(3), 369–390.

HM Government. (2011). 'Prevent Strategy'. *Home Office*. Accessed on May 2016. Available online at www.homeoffice.gov.uk/publications/counterterrorism/prevent/preventstrategy/prevent-strategy-review?view=Binary

Human Rights Watch (HRW). (2010). *Without suspicion: stop and search under the Terrorism Act 2000*. www.westmidlands.police.uk/latestnews/docs/Champion_Review_FINAL_30_09_10.pdf

Independent Police Complaints Commission. (2007). Stockwell One: Investigation into the shooting of Jean Charles de Menezes at Stockwell underground station on 22 July 2005. Independent Police Complaints Commission.

Legrand, T., & Lister, M. (2018). From Precaution to Prejudice: Mistakes in Counter terrorism. In *Political Mistakes and Policy Failures in International Relations* (pp.33–53). Cham: Palgrave Macmillan.

Lynch, O. (2013). British Muslim youth: radicalisation, terrorism and the construction of the 'other'. *Critical Studies on Terrorism*, 6, 241–261. Doi:10.1080/17539153.2013.788863

Miller, D., Mills, T., & Harkins, S. (2011). Teaching about terrorism in the United Kingdom: How it is done and what problems it causes. *Critical Studies on Terrorism*, *4*(3), 405–420.

Milne, R, & Bull, R. (1999) *Investigative interviewing: Psychology and Practice*. Chichester: John Wiley & Sons.

Morgan, M. J. (2004). The garrison state revisited: civil–military implications of terrorism and security. *Contemporary Politics*, *10*(1), 5–19.

Mythen, G., Walklate, S., & Khan, F. (2009). 'I'ma Muslim, but I'm not a Terrorist': Victimization, Risky Identities and the Performance of Safety. *British Journal of Criminology*, *49*, 736–754.

Mythen, G., Walklate, S., & Khan, F. (2013). 'Why should we have to prove we're alright?': Counter-terrorism, risk and partial securities. *Sociology*, *47*, 383–398.

Nickels, H. C., Thomas, L., Hickman, M. J., & Silvestri, S. (2012). Deconstructing 'suspect' communities: A critical discourse analysis of British newspaper coverage of Irish and Muslim communities, 1974–2007. *Journalism Studies*, *13*(3), 340–355.

Pantazis, C. & Pemberton, S. (2009). From the 'old' to the 'new' suspect community examining the impacts of recent UK counter-terrorist legislation. *British Journal of Criminology*, *49*, 646–666. DOI: 10.1093/bjc/azp031

Pilkington, H., & Acik, N. (2020). Not entitled to talk:(Mis) recognition, inequality and social activism of young Muslims. *Sociology*, *54*(1), 181–198.
Poole, E. (2006). The effects of September 11 and the war in Iraq on British newspaper coverage. *Muslims and the News Media*, 89–102.
Poole, E. (2018). Constructing 'British Values' within a Radicalisation Narrative: The reporting of the Trojan Horse affair. *Journalism Studies*, *19*, 376–391.
Poole, E., & Richardson, J. E. (Eds.). (2010). *Muslims and the news media*. London: IB Tauris.
Poynting, S., & Mason, V. (2008). The new integrationism, the state and Islamophobia: retreat from multiculturalism in Australia. *International Journal of Law, Crime and Justice*, *36*, 230–246.
Roach, K., & Trotter, G. (2004). Miscarriages of Justice in the War against Terror. *Pennsylvania State Law Review*, *109*, 967.
Roy, O. (2011). 'Al-Qaeda: A True Global Movement', in Jihadi Terrorism and the Radicalisation Challenge: European and American Experiences, 2nd ed., edited by Rik Coolsaet, (pp. 19–25). Surrey: Ashgate.
Sabir, R. (2017). Blurred lines and false dichotomies: Integrating counterinsurgency into the UK's domestic 'war on terror'. *Critical Social Policy*, *37*, 202–224.
Sentas, V. (2014). *Traces of terror: Counter-terrorism law, policing, and race*. Oxford: Oxford University Press.
Smith, M. R., & Alpert, G. P. (2007). Explaining police bias: A theory of social conditioning and illusory correlation. *Criminal Justice and Behavior*, *34*, 1262–1283. 10.1177/0093854807304484
Spalek, B. (2011). New terrorism and crime prevention initiatives involving Muslim young people in the UK: Research and policy contexts. *Religion, State and Society*, *39*, 191–207
Walther, E., Nagengast, B., & Trasselli, C. (2005). Evaluative conditioning in social psychology: Facts and speculations. *Cognition & Emotion*, *19*, 175–196. http://dx.doi.org/10.1080/02699930441000274
Warsi, S. (2017). *The enemy within: A tale of Muslim Britain*. London: Penguin UK.
Zempi, I., & Tripli, A. (2023). Listening to Muslim students' voices on the Prevent Duty in British universities: A qualitative study. *Education, Citizenship and Social Justice*, *18*(2), 230–245

Chapter 2

Police investigative and interviewing practices

Addressing suspect community stereotyping

Police interviewing of suspects in England and Wales

Concerns regarding miscarriages of justice and the developments in the police investigative and interviewing processes

It is widely acknowledged that information serves as the lifeblood of criminal investigations. Consequently, investigators bear the key responsibility of acquiring valuable and dependable information (Milne & Bull, 2016). In many countries, including England and Wales, one of the most prevalent methods employed to extract information is through the process of interviewing suspects, witnesses, or victims. Interviews offer individuals the opportunity to elucidate the extent of their involvement in a given event. This becomes particularly pivotal when alternative forms of evidence against a suspect are scarce or non-existent (Hill, Memon, & McGeorge, 2008).

During the 1970s, English courts witnessed several high-profile convictions that were later discovered to involve significant instances of police malpractice (Baldwin, 1993). Subsequently, in the mid-1980s, a significant wave of academic research commenced, focusing on police interviews of suspects. In the inaugural published study of police interviews with suspects, Irving (1980) examined 60 interviews and identified a range of persuasive and manipulative tactics in use. These tactics included: (i) manipulating the suspect's self-esteem; (ii) feigning possession of more evidence than actually available; and (iii) advising suspects that confessing was in their best interest.

This approach not only yielded confessions likely to be true but also led to false confessions, particularly among vulnerable and suggestible suspects (Williamson, 1993). During that era, police officers had scant guidance on conducting effective interviews, relying primarily on 'on-the-job' training from more experienced colleagues (Milne & Bull, 2016).

DOI: 10.4324/9781003366836-2

However, contemporary interviewing practices with suspects in England and Wales have shifted away from confrontation and towards transparency, thanks to legislative changes such as the PACE Act. Notably, these changes include the mandatory recording of all interviews with suspects (Williamson, 2006).

Introduction of PACE Act 1984

Building on the problematic interviewing practices and the miscarriages of justice (e.g. Guildford Four and the Birmingham Six), the Royal Commission on Criminal Procedure (1981) was established to scrutinise these practices. This, in turn, led to the enactment of the Police and Criminal Evidence Act (PACE) in 1984, which laid down regulations governing the interviewing of suspects in England and Wales (Maguire, 2003). The PACE legislation unequivocally safeguarded the rights of suspects, including the right to legal representation before questioning about their involvement in a crime. Subsequent developments saw the implementation of audio-recording, and later video-recording, of these interviews with suspects.

Several Codes of Practice have been issued under the PACE legislation, outlining the day-to-day procedural requirements for police operations. For the procedure of interviewing suspects, the relevant Codes are Code C and Code E. Furthermore, there are certain other PACE provisions that, while not exclusively aimed at interviewing suspects, wield significant influence in this context. Sections 76 and 78 are notable among them. Section 76 of PACE pertains to challenges regarding the admissibility of confessions. It directs the court to exclude confession evidence obtained through oppressive means, as such circumstances are likely to render the confession unreliable. Meanwhile, Section 78 of PACE offers an additional safeguard against police malpractice. It grants the courts the authority to exclude any evidence that, despite being admissible, would be deemed unfair to introduce against a defendant. Importantly, the combined effect of these provisions places a significant responsibility on the police not only to act fairly but also to be perceived as always acting fairly. As an illustrative example, in the case of *R. v. Heron*, the judge acquitted the defendant, citing, among other reasons, the misleading actions of police officers during the interview regarding identification evidence in a homicide case (Poyser & Milne, 2015).

The effectiveness of PACE legislation in the context of police interviews with suspects has been a subject of debate. In an early assessment of PACE legislation, McConville, Sanders, and Leng (1993) suggested that little had changed in police interviews, particularly concerning 'interrogative suggestibility'. They also asserted that the practice of tape-recording interviews had not significantly altered the power dynamics during interviews, notably the fact that 'interrogation takes place in an environment which increases the vulnerability of the suspect and maximises the authority and control of the police' (McConville et al., 1993, p. 78). Baldwin (1992) observed that the persuasive interviewing styles identified in studies conducted before the introduction of PACE (e.g. Irving, 1980) had been replaced by a more tentative approach after its implementation. Baldwin noted that this less assertive approach occasionally led to suspects being appropriately challenged, but only on rare occasions.

Moston, Stephenson, and Williamson (1992) discovered that police officers allocated little time to obtaining accounts from suspects. Instead, they often adopted an accusatory approach during suspect interviews. Moreover, Moston and Engelberg (1993) analysed 118 real-life police interviews and identified that the predominant interviewing style was confrontational and focused on eliciting confessions. They also observed that a common initial procedure employed by police interviewers was to inform suspects that confessing was in their best interest due to the overwhelming evidence against them.

After the implementation of PACE and the regulation of police practices within the interview room, police interviewing procedures became significantly more transparent (Milne, Shaw, & Bull, 2007). However, wrongful convictions with causes similar to those observed before the introduction of PACE persisted, as exemplified by cases like Christy Walsh (Gudjonsson, 2003). The enduring repercussions of such cases continue to reverberate through the criminal justice system even today (Shipton, 2015), underscoring that inadequate police questioning remains a significant challenge (Poyser & Milne, 2015).

Introduction of the PEACE interviewing model in England and Wales

The revelation of inadequate police investigative and interviewing practices in the early 1990s had a profound effect, leading to a significant erosion of public trust in the criminal justice system and a growing chorus of voices advocating for reform (Milne & Poyser, 2017). Notably, in 1991, the release of six suspects convicted of terrorist bombings (the Birmingham Six) occurred when the confession evidence that had secured their convictions in 1974 was discredited (Gudjonsson, 2003). Subsequent research underscored that the police investigative process continued to heavily rely on confession evidence (Poyser & Milne, 2015). Clearly, despite the introduction of PACE legislation, fundamental changes in police investigative practices were still needed (Milne & Poyser, 2017).

In response to research studies and judicial criticism of police interviewing, particularly in high-profile cases where convictions were subsequently overturned (e.g. *R. v. Heron*), the police service in England and Wales adopted a more ethical approach to police interviewing in 1993. This shift in approach was informed by research into effective communication skills, human memory, and conversation management (Clarke, Milne, & Bull, 2011). At the heart of these changes was the development of an ethical interviewing model known by the mnemonic 'PEACE'. This stands for: Planning and Preparation, Engage and Explain, Account, Closure, and Evaluation, being the five phases of the model (see Milne & Bull, 1999, for a full description of the model).

The PEACE model encompassed two distinct interview types: (i) 'conversation management', designed for dealing with resistant suspects (Shepherd, 1993); and (ii) the 'cognitive interview', tailored for more cooperative interviewees (Fisher & Geiselman, 1992). A fundamental principle underlying this new approach was the recognition that all interviews should serve the purpose of seeking the truth and obtaining accurate, reliable information through non-coercive techniques. The PEACE model promotes a planned, fair, and ethical approach to interviewing, emphasising the importance of interviewer open-mindedness throughout (Williamson, 2006). This model is employed in the training of police officers across England and Wales and has also been adapted for use in various other parts of the world, including Australia, New Zealand, and Norway.

An essential component of this revamped interviewing approach involved the creation of various courses aimed at training police officers. The training specifically focused on enhancing interviewers' proficiency in utilising a range of specific skills, which included: (i) effectively engaging in conversation with a suspect; (ii) articulating the purpose and structure of the interview; (iii) employing appropriate questioning techniques, such as favouring open questions over closed ones; and (iv) steering clear of leading and misleading questions (Powell & Barnett, 2015). Initial assessments regarding the effectiveness of the training in the PEACE model yielded promising results. For instance, McGurk, Carr, and McGurk (1993) observed improvements in officers' skills and knowledge immediately following the training. However, Bull and Cherryman (1996) uncovered evidence suggesting that questioning during police interviews still predominantly consisted of closed questions, accompanied by a continued use of leading questions. They also noted a lack of emphasis on rapport-building, pauses, and silence, as well as shortfalls in both empathy and flexibility. It's worth noting that these evaluations (e.g. McGurk et al., 1993; Bull & Cherryman, 1996) were conducted shortly after the introduction of the PEACE training. Arguably, the newly acquired skills may not have had sufficient time to become fully integrated into regular police practices.

A national evaluation of PEACE revealed that interviews with suspects had indeed improved since its inception, but further development remained necessary (Clarke & Milne, 2001). Clarke and Milne noted the positive use of open questioning techniques and of allowing suspects to provide their accounts of events. They also observed that ethical standards seemed to have become ingrained in police interviewing practices. Later research by Walsh and Milne (2007) supported similar findings, extending to non-police agencies. Following Clarke and Milne's (2001) national evaluation of PEACE, a five-tier structure of interviewing skills was devised to enhance the professionalism of all investigators. Subsequent research has indicated that this evolution in investigative interviewing has led to improvements in interviewing skills (Clarke et al., 2011).

It is argued that ethical interviewing techniques have the potential to yield better outcomes, both in terms of obtaining comprehensive accounts from interviewees (Walsh & Bull, 2012) and possibly in terms of securing admissions from suspects (Holmberg & Christianson, 2002). Holmberg and Christianson conducted a study exploring the perceptions of Swedish prisoners convicted of murder or sexual offences. They found that interviews in which the police were perceived as dominant, displaying fretful, forceful, and abrupt behaviour, were associated with denials. Conversely, interviews marked by a more humane approach, characterised by being inviting, conscious, obliging, and understanding towards the suspect, were associated with admissions. However, it's important to note that Holmberg and Christianson's (2002) study relied on self-reporting by the prisoners and, for some, recollections of interviews that had occurred several years before the study. Consequently, factors such as distorted memories, social desirability bias, and the potential for misunderstandings in self-report studies might have influenced the study's findings.

According to Milne, Poyser, Williamson, and Savage (2010), the investigative process as a whole in the United Kingdom has witnessed improvement and professionalisation over the last 25 years or so. These improvements have been accompanied by changes in legislation, such as the introduction of PACE legislation and the adoption of the PEACE model, within the broader criminal justice context. However, even with these advancements, it remains a formidable challenge for researchers and professionals to identify areas where police interviewing of suspects can be further enhanced.

One of the persistent challenges in police interviewing is finding ways to overcome the resistance of suspects without compromising on ethical principles such as fairness or increasing the likelihood of false confessions (e.g. Gudjonsson, 2018). Gudjonsson (2018, p. 55) argues that in high-profile cases, where the police are under pressure to achieve a particular outcome, such as in murder or terrorism cases, they often resort to their full arsenal of tactics, regardless of their training in investigative interviewing. Under such circumstances, some innocent individuals may erroneously confess to guilt (Sanders, Young, & Burton, 2010). While the introduction of the PEACE model has promoted a more ethical approach to interviews, Bearchell (2010) discovered that a significant number of police officers still hold the view that the ideal outcome of an interview is a confession of guilt.

Prejudicial stereotyping and investigative interviewing

Police officers typically interview individuals whom they suspect of committing an offence. For individuals under investigation, this initial impression of being considered a suspect holds significant weight, as it sets the tone for how police interviewers approach the suspects. This initial impression can lead to interviewers proceeding with a presumption of guilt, which, in turn, can influence the types of questions asked—often leaning towards guilt-presumptive and confirmatory questions—and the use of persuasive tactics aimed at obtaining confessions (Hill et al., 2008; Kassin, Goldstein, & Savitsky, 2003). One consistent finding from earlier research on police interviewing suspects is that police interviewers often presume the suspect to be guilty even before the interview begins (Baldwin, 1992; Bearchell, 2010).

Research on police interviewing sheds light on the impact of holding a presumption of guilt on suspect interviews (Kassin et al., 2003). When police interviewers assume suspects to be guilty before the interview even begins, they may conduct interviews by seeking or interpreting evidence in ways that align with their pre-existing beliefs or hypotheses. Consequently, a presumption of guilt may provide an explanation for why some suspect interviews are still conducted in a less than satisfactory manner.

Kassin et al. (2003) conducted an experimental study using student participants, wherein one group of students was involved in a mock crime, while the other group engaged in an innocent yet similar act. Prior to conducting the interviews, mock interviewers were led to believe that some suspects were guilty, while others were innocent. In their study, Kassin and associates (2003) discovered that interviewers, when presuming suspects to be guilty, exhibited several behaviours: (i) they asked more guilt-presumptive questions; (ii) they employed persistent and coercive questioning tactics; and (iii) they exerted increased pressure on suspects to confess. These findings, as discussed in the literature, raise concerns about the potential for these factors to contribute to false confessions.

Hill et al. (2008), also employing student participants, conducted three studies aimed at examining the impact of presuming guilt on interviewers' questioning styles, confession rates, denial rates, and suspects' verbal behaviour during interviews with mock suspects. Their research revealed that assuming guilt could indeed influence the questioning styles employed by interviewers and could result in a self-fulfilling prophecy. Moreover, suspects subjected to guilt-presumptive questions were observed to be more anxious, defensive, and less plausible in their responses compared to when they faced neutral questions.

It is important to note that both the studies by Hill et al. (2008) and Kassin et al. (2003) used student participants who lacked the same training and expertise as police officers. In real-life interviews, police officers may approach suspects with a more neutral mindset rather than a presumption of guilt. Therefore, it's conceivable that the outcomes could differ in actual investigative situations.

Research studies have identified investigator bias, wherein trained and experienced officers tend to exhibit a bias towards determining individuals as deceitful. For instance, Meissner and Kassin (2002) found that greater prior experience and training were significantly correlated with a tendency to judge suspects as deceitful rather than truthful. However, it was not correlated with the accuracy of their judgements. Consequently, police officers with more experience and training may be particularly susceptible to confirmation biases. Confirmation bias, as described by Nickerson (1998, p. 175), is the 'seeking or interpreting of evidence in ways that are partial to existing beliefs, expectations, or a hypothesis in hand'. This bias can include both looking for information that affirms current beliefs while actively avoiding information that disconfirms such beliefs, as was found in the study conducted by Hill et al. (2008).

In the context of police interviews, Mortimer and Shepherd (1999) observed that an investigative bias towards suspects' wrongdoings could lead to an accusatorial style of interviewing. This approach often involved the use of a confirmatory strategy by police officers to elicit confessions. Such accusatorial methods have been argued to increase the likelihood of false confessions (Gudjonsson, 2018). Additionally, Loftus and Palmer (1974) in their classic study demonstrated that memory can be significantly influenced by externally provided suggestions from interviewers. Their study highlighted how easily events could be remembered incorrectly when misleading or inaccurate cues were introduced. In a related vein, Williamson (2007) argued that subtle changes in wording during interviews could encourage people to report non-existent details of events they never actually experienced. Consequently, it appears that suggestive information has the potential not only to alter the details of events but also to implant entirely false beliefs in people's minds (Ost, 2006).

While research suggests that developments in investigative interviewing have resulted in improvements in interviewing skills (Milne & Poyser, 2017), cases of miscarriages of justice continue to emerge. Notable examples include Frank Johnson, Robert Brown, Patrick Irvine, and Thomas Green (Belfast) in 2002; Anthony Steele in 2003; Paul Blackburn in 2005; Patrick Nolan in 2006; Sam Hallam in 2012; and Victor Nealon in 2013, where a disputed confession lies at the heart of convictions being quashed (Milne et al., 2010; Poyser & Milne, 2015). These cases illustrate that there is no room for complacency, and the need for continuous empirical research to further enhance the police investigative process remains as crucial as ever. Poyser and Milne (2015) propose that the risk of miscarriages of justice can be minimised through (i) developing high-calibre investigation and interview processes to reduce reliance on admission evidence; (ii) conducting good-quality, thorough, and cautious questioning of victims and witnesses, thereby allowing them to provide their best evidence; and (iii) fostering greater awareness and comprehension regarding the interviewing of vulnerable individuals.

While previous research within the context of investigative interviewing has predominantly focused on interviewing skills (e.g. Baldwin, 1993; Bull, 2013; Bull & Cherryman, 1996; Clarke & Milne, 2001; Clarke et al., 2011; Holmberg & Christianson, 2002; McGurk et al., 1993; Moston & Engelberg, 1993; Walsh & Milne, 2007; Walsh & Bull, 2012) and questioning techniques (e.g. Baldwin, 1993; Daviesl, Westcott, & Horan, 2000; Griffiths & Milne, 2006; Myklebust & Bjoklund, 2006; Phillips, Oxburgh, & Myklebust, 2012), there has been a noticeable gap in research. Despite the growth in the depth of research and the introduction of both PACE legislation and the PEACE model in England and Wales, very little research has been conducted to examine the influence of prejudicial stereotyping of suspects within the context of police interviewing practices. Prejudicial stereotyping has been argued to negatively impact police officers' pursuit of truth, which is the stated aim of investigative interviewing in England and Wales (Williamson, 2006). Consequently, there is a pressing need to investigate whether prejudicial stereotyping affects police investigations. Without conducting such research, our understanding of the root causes of miscarriages of justice and criminal investigation failures will remain incomplete. Therefore, one of the primary objectives of the current research is to explore the impact of prejudicial stereotyping on criminal investigations.

Prejudicial stereotyping and the criminal justice system

In recent years, racially biased policing has become a focal point of inquiry not only in the United Kingdom but also in the United States and Canada, drawing attention from both the media and researchers. A multitude of research studies have reported findings that reveal disparities in the treatment of ethnic minority citizens compared to White citizens by law enforcement (e.g. Bowling, 2018; Bowling & Phillips, 2007; Graham & Lowery, 2004; Hall, Hall, & Perry, 2016). Furthermore, research has also demonstrated that negative outcomes within the criminal justice system, ranging from arrests to sentencing, disproportionately affect Black individuals compared to White individuals (Blaine, 2012). In the United Kingdom, the issue of racial profiling gained unprecedented prominence following the publication of the Macpherson inquiry report into the murder of Black teenager Stephen Lawrence. The report conclusively identified racial stereotyping as a factor, citing the over-representation of racial minorities in national stop-and-search data (Macpherson of Cluny, 1999).

One of the perilous forms of bias in the criminal justice system and fair trial is argued to be racial bias, often manifesting as prejudicial stereotyping of particular groups. While this bias may focus on race or ethnicity, it can also encompass negative stereotyping based on group membership (Graham & Lowery, 2004). Racial stereotyping is widely acknowledged as a significant source of partiality in criminal trials (Huggon, 2012). Research on racial stereotyping has indicated that White juries are more likely to convict defendants of a different race than themselves and tend to be more lenient towards defendants of their own race when the victim is of a different race (Huggon, 2012). Moreover, earlier studies (e.g. Cohn, Bucolo, Pride, & Sommers, 2009; Thomas & Balmer, 2007) have consistently suggested that Black defendants are more frequently found guilty and receive harsher sentences compared to their White counterparts.

In the context of prejudicial stereotyping, Bowling, Parmar, and Phillips (2013) argue that British society still grapples with pervasive racist beliefs, xenophobic attitudes, and racial prejudice. They note that while overt forms of racial prejudice (e.g. activism within extreme right political parties) are rare, underlying racist beliefs, anti-immigrant sentiments, xenophobia, and racial prejudice continue to exert a deep and influential influence. Particularly concerning the perspective of the criminal justice system, if police officers reflect a cross section of society, it becomes plausible that some may hold racially prejudiced views (Bowling et al., 2013).

Additionally, an inspection conducted by His Majesty's Chief Inspector of Constabulary (HMIC, 2005) concerning community and race relations policies and practices within the police service concluded that racial discrimination and harassment are pervasive within our society, with the police service being no exception. Reiner (1991) asserted that stereotypes of Black individuals within the police service have shown remarkable consistency. These stereotypes portray Black individuals as more prone to violence and drug abuse, as more suspicious, aggressive, and lacking in cognitive ability, and as more troublesome. Importantly, Reiner's findings have not been limited to constables but have been observed throughout various ranks within the police service.

Research in the field of policing ethnic minority communities has revealed a significant disparity in police stop-and-search practices, with individuals from Asian[1] and Black communities being far more likely to be stopped and searched compared to White individuals (Bowling & Phillips, 2007; Fekete, 2018). Some have attempted to explain this disproportionality by arguing that Asians are involved in gangs and that Blacks are, by nature, more aggressive and prone to violence than Whites, which could lead to higher crime rates and increased rates of police searches among these groups (Bowling et al., 2013). However, it's important to note that Blaine (2012) asserts that there is no substantial evidence to suggest that Black or Asian people are inherently more aggressive than Whites. Blaine further emphasises that research has indicated that aggressive behaviour is more a result of situational factors rather than one's race.

Furthermore, Bowling et al. (2013) have observed a noteworthy shift in the pliability of stereotypes associated with Asians and particularly Muslims, as documented in recent research. This transformation implies that these stereotypes, which were once considered conformist, are now seen as less applicable. Previously, stereotypes assumed that Asian and Muslim communities were law-abiding due to their tight-knit nature and high level of social control. However, contemporary research, such as that by Hudson and Bramhall (2005), suggests that these stereotypes are now thought to promote criminal and deviant activities among Asian and Muslim youth. This shift in perception is argued to have its roots in both local and global notions of Asian Muslim youth becoming increasingly involved in gangs, violence, and riots. Moreover, Bowling et al. (2013) point out that the ethnic background of individuals subjected to stop-and-searches under S.44 (1) (2) of the TA 2000 indicates a significant disparity. Asian people were more likely to be stopped and searched using these powers than Black people.

Mythen, Walklate, and Khan (2013) argue that the increased number of Asians in stop-and-search figures since the 'war on terror' may be connected to the growing anti-Muslim sentiments in England and Wales. Webster (2004) points out that without studies and statistics that disaggregate 'Asian', it is challenging to determine whether there is disproportionate treatment, particularly targeting Muslims, or if it applies to all Asians. Consequently, further research is essential to establish whether the surge in the number of Asians in stop-and-search statistics following the 'war on terror' is indeed linked to anti-Muslim sentiments.

Understanding prejudice and stereotyping

Prejudice, defined as an unjustified negative judgement towards an individual based on their social group identity (Allport, 1954), encompasses a complex interplay of attitudes, beliefs, and behaviours, as delineated by Allport (1954) in his seminal work. According to Allport (1954), attitudes are mental and neural states of readiness shaped by experiences, exerting a directive and dynamic influence on an individual's responses to various stimuli and situations related to them. Beliefs, on the other hand, often stem from overgeneralisation or misinformation. Allport's perspective suggests that prejudice arises as an almost inevitable consequence of the typical categorisation process, commonly known as stereotyping. Stereotypes can be defined as 'shared beliefs about personal attributes, typically personality traits, but also behaviours, associated with a particular group of people' (Leyens, Yzerbyt, & Schadron, 1994, p. 3).

Devine (1989) observed that stereotypes are heuristically or automatically applied to members of social groups. She further contended that as long as stereotypes exist, prejudice will inevitably follow. However, the notion of the inevitability of prejudicial attitudes overlooks a crucial distinction between awareness of negative stereotypes and their endorsement. This implies that while individuals may possess knowledge of stereotypes associated with particular groups, their personal beliefs may or may not align with these stereotypes. There is no strong evidence to suggest that knowledge of stereotypes necessarily translates into prejudice against the groups in question (O'Connor, 2017). For instance, in a study involving war veterans, Bettleheim and Janowitz (1964) discovered no significant relationship between veterans' reported stereotypes about Black and Jewish individuals and the degree of prejudice they displayed towards these groups. Although knowledge of stereotypes does not inherently result in prejudice towards a group, it remains essential to understand how prejudicial stereotyping emerges. Therefore, the origins and development of prejudicial stereotyping will be discussed next.

Emergence of prejudicial stereotyping

Prejudice involves harbouring negative emotions towards individuals based on their group membership, while stereotyping entails holding negative beliefs and thoughts about these groups (Blaine, 2012; Passini, 2018). The process of prejudicial stereotyping of individuals and groups typically unfolds in three sequential steps, as described by various researchers (e.g. Casper, Rothermund, & Wentura, 2010; Cloutier, Mason, & Macrae, 2005). Firstly, individuals or groups are categorised, often based on characteristics such as race, criminal background, age, sex, or sexuality. Next, automatic activation of stereotypes occurs, leading to the formation of stereotypical expectations. Finally, subsequent to the activation of these stereotypes, the behaviour of others is interpreted through the lens of these stereotypes. Furthermore, stereotypes have the potential to evoke specific emotional and behavioural responses in observers (Cuddy, Fiske, & Glick, 2007). As a result, prejudicial stereotyping can be rooted in any group label, encompassing commonly recognised categories such as ethnicity, social class, religion, nationality, or cultural identity (Blaine, 2012). Blaine (2012) contends that prejudicial stereotyping remains prevalent and persists in various settings, including schools, workplaces, and communities. There are four prominent types of prejudice identified by Blaine: (i) racism; (ii) sexism; (iii) weights-based prejudice; and (iv) prejudice that is rooted in religious beliefs and ideology.

To explore the emergence of prejudicial stereotyping, Bond, Di Candia, and McKinnon (1988) conducted a study comparing the treatment of patients in a psychiatric hospital operated by an all-White professional staff. The researchers focused on the two primary methods employed by staff members to manage patients' violent behaviour:

i. Secluding the individual in a timeout room.
ii. Restraining the individual using a straitjacket and administering tranquillising drugs.

Examining hospital records spanning 85 days, they discovered that the more severe approach involving physical and chemical restraint was utilised on Black patients nearly four times as frequently as on White patients. Interestingly, this pattern persisted despite a notable absence of differences in the number of violent incidents involving Black and White patients. Furthermore, this discriminatory treatment persisted even though Black patients, upon admission, had been diagnosed as slightly less prone to violence compared to their White counterparts.

The manifestation of discriminatory behaviour and the expression of negative feelings and responses towards 'others' based on their social group identity depend on the interplay of automatic negative impulses, thoughtful and fair-minded social beliefs, and principles embraced by the majority of society's members (Blaine, 2012; Hogg, Abrams, & Brewer, 2017). As outlined by Bargh (1994), automatic mental associations and processes exhibit some or all of the following characteristics:

i. Spontaneity: They occur in the absence of any intention.
ii. Efficiency: They do not require significant intentional resources for execution.
iii. Uncontrollability: They operate in a ballistic fashion and are challenging to halt once initiated.
iv. Unconsciousness: They can operate without awareness.

Such automatic mental associations tend to activate whenever a member of the stereotyped group is encountered (Devine, 1989). These automatic mental associations and evaluations can be activated unintentionally and with minimal cognitive effort. The activation of these associations can lead to perceptions and responses that are biased in alignment with these associations. For instance, if there is an automatic association like 'Muslims are bad', encountering a Muslim person may trigger this association, causing any ambiguous information about the individual to be interpreted negatively. This interpretation is often driven by a confirmatory mechanism that biases attention, memory, and interpretation (Todd et al., 2011). Furthermore, Todd et al. (2011) argue that automatic associations can not only influence perceptions and judgements but also overt behaviours, especially spontaneous actions such as nonverbal reactions.

This might explain the surge in hate crimes targeting Muslims following a terrorist incident involving a suspected Muslim offender. Research has indicated a connection between such corrosive forms of social hostility and intergroup bias (Wilder & Simon, 2001). Intergroup bias, in general, refers to the systematic tendency to favourably evaluate one's own membership group (the in-group) or its members in comparison to a non-membership group (the out-group) (Rhodes et al., 2018). Understanding the precise mechanisms behind the emergence of intergroup biases is crucial. Therefore, let's delve into the origins of intergroup biases.

Intergroup biases

Stereotypes elicit specific emotional and behavioural responses in observers (Hogg et al., 2017). They can be viewed as simplifying perceptions, judgements, and actions, although researchers emphasise the distinction between stereotype activation (unconscious) and application (conscious) (Monteith, Sherman, & Devine, 1998). Unconscious and conscious stereotypes represent two distinct forms of intergroup biases. Unconscious stereotypes arise from the automatic activation of mental associations that may not be personally endorsed but are prevalent in contemporary society. In contrast, conscious stereotypes stem from intentional, deliberative mental processes (Devine, 1989). Devine argued that all individuals, regardless of their intentions to be fair-minded and unbiased, possess knowledge of stereotypes associated with different groups. She further asserted that internalising such beliefs can lead to the adoption of negative emotional responses towards those groups.

These well-learned attitudes and responses operate automatically when encountering a member of a stereotyped group due to ongoing social representations of such groups (Todd et al., 2011). Moreover, one of the most significant consequences of unconscious stereotypes has been argued to be their inevitability and almost unavoidable impact. In situations where members of any minority group are consistently depicted in negative social contexts, such as terrorism, dependency, or crime, classical and evaluative conditioning processes might produce prejudiced mental affiliations with them.

Devine (1989) proposed a powerful model of prejudice and stereotyping. Her model focuses on both automatic and controlled components of prejudice. It assumes that individuals with high levels of bias, as well as those with low bias, are equally familiar with cultural stereotypes. These socially shared stereotypes are likely to be accessible and automatically activated in the presence of a minority group member. However, what distinguishes biased from unbiased individuals is not the automatic component, but the controlled component. Unbiased individuals are presumed to hold personal beliefs that motivate them to suppress the effects of automatically activated cultural stereotypes. Therefore, Devine's model suggests that personal beliefs must be consciously attended to through controlled procedures in order to have any influence.

Devine's (1989) model has not gone unchallenged. Lepore and Brown (1997) argued that many of the primes she employed to activate stereotype-related information were negative valence of stereotypic traits. They further contended that the priming procedure did not enable an unbiased spontaneous activation of participants' implicit stereotypic knowledge. In their contrasting studies addressing the methodological issues of Devine's (1989) research, they suggested that there are more variations in the stereotypic process than credited by Devine. Specifically, Lepore and Brown (1997) found that low-prejudiced individuals may not possess automatic stereotypic associations, so when they encounter members of the stereotypic group, there is little that is stereotypic to activate the automatic associations. Other studies (e.g. Macrae, Bodenhausen, Milne, Thorn, & Castelli, 1997) found that stereotype activation is more a function of the perceiver's goals than of the availability of cognitive resources. Macrae and colleagues (1997) argued that low-prejudiced individuals have become exceedingly skilled at promptly suppressing stereotype activation, even though they still have stereotypic associations in their minds.

Whether stereotypes are socially shared, culturally learned, or personal evaluations, the above-discussed research shows that it might be impossible to avoid the influence of these biases. People may not realise the extent of their own prejudicial stereotyping because these biases are so well-learned and operate outside of our awareness.

Impact of intergroup biases on the criminal justice system

Research, as exemplified by studies such as those conducted by Devine, Buddenbaum, Houp, Studebaker, and Stolle (2009) and Levett, Danielsen, Kovera, and Cutler (2005), has indicated that the personal characteristics of defendants, including factors like race, gender, and financial status, can influence the outcomes of criminal investigations. Specifically, there is evidence to suggest that jurors may exhibit a bias favouring individuals they perceive as similar (in-group), leading to a greater likelihood of acquittal, while individuals who are seen as dissimilar (out-group) may be more prone to conviction, as argued by Brewer (2007). Brewer's perspective posits that these in-group biases and intergroup discrimination stem from a preference for one's own group rather than direct hostility towards members of out-groups. Meanwhile, the potential for a 'black sheep effect', as proposed by Marques (1990), could come into play depending on the strength of the evidence against the defendant.

In essence, the black sheep effect suggests that jurors may be more inclined to acquit an in-group defendant when the evidence is weak, but conversely, they might be more inclined to convict when the evidence is strong, as proposed by Marques (1990). Taking a punitive stance towards an in-group defendant who faces compelling evidence of guilt essentially functions as a way for jurors to distance themselves from an in-group member who has violated group norms, as discussed by Devine and colleagues (2009).

Additionally, there is a growing body of research that establishes a link between race and jury decisions in real trials, particularly those involving more serious offences such as murder and rape. This research, which is exemplified by studies conducted by Baldus, Pulaski, and Woodworth (1983); Bjerregaard, Smith, Cochran, and Fogel (2017); Chadee, Ali, Burke, and Young (2017); Devine and colleagues (2009); and Leippe, Bergold, and Eisenstadt (2017), generally supports the presence of an in-group–out-group bias based on the participants' race. However, it's worth noting that two mock jury studies have offered partial support for the black sheep effect, as seen in studies by Chadee (1996) and Kerr, Hymes, Anderson, and Weathers (1995). Nevertheless, two field studies that investigated bias associated with participant race did not yield clear evidence in favour of the black sheep effect, as demonstrated by research conducted by Taylor and Hosch (2004).

Recent research on the presence of unconscious racial stereotypes has raised concerns about individuals' ability to make impartial decisions regarding out-group members, as highlighted in studies by Correll and colleagues (2007) and Fazio, Jackson, Dunton, and Williams (1995). This research suggests that negative stereotypes against individuals from specific minority groups can significantly influence how people interact with members of these groups. These negative stereotypes often operate at an unconscious level, implying that even individuals who outwardly claim to be fair-minded may exhibit biases in their decisions on a subconscious level (Lammers & Staple, 2011). Studies have indicated that negative stereotypes are automatically activated when individuals encounter out-group members, which could potentially impact one's decisions, even if they consciously strive to avoid being influenced by these stereotypes. This phenomenon is discussed in research conducted by Banaji and Greenwald (1995), Devine (1989), Fazio et al. (1995), and Macrae and Bodenhausen (2000).

Social identity theory provides a compelling explanation for the origins of in-group and out-group biases in society. According to this theory, group membership plays a vital role in boosting an individual's self-esteem, leading people to favour members of their in-group over those in the out-group, as proposed by Tajfel and Turner (1979). This phenomenon has been discussed extensively in the literature, with works by Devine (1989) and Huggon (2012) supporting these findings. Negative stereotypes related to factors such as race or religion, as discussed by Tajfel and Turner (1979), could have detrimental effects on the processes involved in criminal investigations. These stereotypes may exert a more pronounced negative impact when law enforcement is dealing with suspects from out-group communities.

Within the criminal justice system, specific ethnic minorities often face negative stereotypes associating them with traits perceived to increase their likelihood of engaging in criminal behaviour, as noted by Correll and colleagues (2007). For instance, Ware (2007) contends that police culture deeply ingrains the portrayal of young Black men as potentially dangerous criminals. These negative stereotypes have the potential to significantly influence how individuals within the criminal justice system interact with and treat suspects from these ethnic minority groups, as discussed by Lammers and Staple (2011).

Decisions made by individuals within the criminal justice system, such as police officers and judges, carry significant consequences for the individuals involved. Recent research has indicated that even critical decisions can be influenced by racial stereotypes. For instance, studies suggest that a police officer's decision regarding whether to use lethal force against a potentially armed suspect may be impacted by the suspect's ethnicity, as highlighted in research by Correll and colleagues (2007) and Hall et al. (2016). Consequently, unconscious negative stereotyping may play a role in shaping legal decisions, as discussed in the research conducted by Greenwald and Krieger (2006). In the United States, an analysis conducted by ProPublica, using federal data on fatal police shootings between 2010 and 2012, revealed a significant disparity. The analysis found that young Black male civilians were 21 times more likely to be fatally shot by police compared to young White male civilians, as reported by Gabrielson, Jones, and Sagara (2014).

Furthermore, the concept of 'illusory correlation' provides another potential explanation for racial stereotyping among police officers, as discussed by Smith and Alpert (2007). In essence, illusory correlation refers to a perceived connection between two sets of events that are either not as strongly associated or correlated to a lesser extent than what is believed, as initially described by Chapman (1967). The existence of an illusory correlation between specific behaviours and minority communities was initially identified by Hamilton and Gifford (1976). These researchers suggested that individual subjective experiences in forming group stereotypes might reinforce stereotypes that are transmitted through social means.

When police officers encounter negative behaviours exhibited by individuals from minority groups, they may tend to overestimate the prevalence of these behaviours. This tendency can further reinforce existing racial stereotypes. Smith and Alpert (2007) propose that racial profiling might be a consequence of unconscious racial stereotyping, resurfacing either due to differential exposure to group criminality or as a result of the illusory correlation phenomenon. Consequently, this can lead to police officers potentially overestimating the frequency of negative behaviours among minority citizens, as highlighted by Smith and Alpert (2007).

In the context of racial stereotyping, Graham and Lowery (2004) explored the relationship between unconscious racial stereotypes and decision-making in controlled experimental settings. They utilised subliminal racial priming, a technique designed to evoke unconscious racial stereotyping, to examine how negative racial stereotypes held by police officers and juvenile probation officers might affect their assessments of hypothetical adolescent offenders. The findings from their study revealed that participants who had been subjected to racial priming rated the hypothetical delinquents as older in age and attributed to them higher negative traits associated with violence and bad character. Furthermore, these participants deemed these delinquents more culpable and deserving of harsher treatment. This study suggested that unconscious racial stereotypes can be activated in decision-makers within the criminal justice system. Once activated, these stereotypes can significantly influence subsequent judgements and intentions regarding behaviour. These findings provide insight into how unconscious racial stereotyping might contribute to racial disparities observed in many law enforcement agencies, as discussed by Smith and Alpert (2007).

While there is a substantial body of literature focused on the development of racial stereotypes, as evident in studies by Correll et al. (2007), Graham and Lowery (2004), Greenwald and Krieger (2006), Lammers and Staple (2011), Todd et al. (2011), and Ware (2007), there remains a notable gap in our understanding of the connection between prejudicial stereotypes and the decision-making processes of police officers when it comes to suspects from stigmatised communities. In instances where a traffic patrolling officer stops a vehicle, they are presented with various options that can determine the outcome of the stop. When a violation is observed, a police officer may need to decide between imposing a more severe charge, such as speeding, as opposed to a lesser one like reckless driving. In other scenarios, the officer might opt to issue a formal warning or proceed with a custodial arrest. This less-explored area of research concerning the influence of prejudicial stereotypes on the investigative decision-making of law enforcement officers in cases involving individuals from marginalised communities warrants further investigation.

Another possible course of action for a police officer during a traffic stop is to allow the citizen to proceed either with or without a warning. Additionally, police officers have the authority to make decisions related to other aspects of their work, such as checking computer records for evidence or conducting stop-and-search procedures. All of these decisions reflect the discretionary power held by police officers, as discussed in the research by Smith, Makarios, and Alpert (2006). Therefore, it is crucial to investigate whether prejudicial stereotyping influences the decision-making processes in criminal investigations. This examination is necessary to gain a comprehensive understanding of the true underlying factors contributing to racial disparities observed in many law enforcement agencies, instances of miscarriages of justice, and failures in criminal investigations.

Conclusions

A comprehensive review of the literature, as seen in studies by Brewer (2007), Devine (1989), Devine and colleagues (2009), Hall and colleagues (2016), Mackie, Hamilton, Susskind, and Rosselli (1996), and Ware (2007), sheds light on the formation of stereotypes. Stereotypes are cognitive structures residing in the mind of the perceiver, consisting of the perceiver's knowledge, beliefs, and expectations regarding a specific social group. From a criminal justice perspective, at the initial stage of abductive reasoning, negative stereotypes may come into play when officers are making decisions regarding a particular suspect based on their pre-existing mental associations with the group to which the suspect belongs. Abductive reasoning constitutes the first step in any investigative process, during which an investigator attempts to formulate theories that can later be evaluated, as explained by Fahsing and Ask (2016). In essence, 'abduction is the process of forming explanatory hypotheses', as stated by Peirce (1965). This implies that unconscious stereotypes can be activated within the investigative decision-making processes of police officers. Once activated, these stereotypes can potentially influence decisions related to a suspect's profile and perceived culpability. Importantly, such stereotype activation does not necessarily require the perceiver to openly endorse the stereotype, as indicated by research conducted by Correll and colleagues (2007).

In the literature, a crucial distinction is drawn between an individual's privately held beliefs about members of social groups, known as personal stereotypes, and the widely accepted or shared perceptions of those groups, referred to as cultural stereotypes, as emphasised by Graham and Lowery (2004). In the context of the thesis presented in this book, the focus primarily lies on cultural stereotypes. The research discussed previously suggests that in the United Kingdom, cultural stereotypes of Muslims have transformed in the wake of the 'war on terror'. Since the onset of this campaign, studies examining the portrayal of Muslims as 'suspects' have indicated a significant increase in hostility towards Muslims.

In the context of cultural stereotypes, Brewer (2007) argued that societies highly divided along a single primary categorisation, such as ethnicity or religion, may exhibit strong in-group favouritism and out-group antagonism. This effect becomes even more pronounced if the categorisation is binary, dividing the society into two significant subgroups. Such division fosters social comparison, which can lead to negative attitudes towards out-groups and an increased potential for conflict. Research studies have provided evidence of the negative portrayal of Muslims in political and public discourses, which tend to depict Muslims as the 'enemy within'. This portrayal has the potential to contribute to prejudicial stereotyping of Muslims within the broader public, as reflected in studies conducted by Awan (2012, 2018), Awan and Rahman (2016), Brown and Richards (2016), Choudhury and Fenwick (2011), Pantazis and Pemberton (2009), and Hickman and colleagues (2012).

In the realm of criminal investigations, Roach and Trotter (2004) argue that when hostile investigative methods are coupled with negative stereotypes associating a defendant's ethnicity or religion with serious offences, it creates a potent recipe for what is known as investigative tunnel vision. This tunnel vision leads individuals within the criminal justice system to become excessively focused on a suspect, selectively filtering and emphasising evidence that supports the case for conviction while disregarding or suppressing evidence that points away from guilt. As Findley and Scott (2006) pointed out, this phenomenon can result in a situation where investigators concentrate on building a case against a suspect and overlook or intentionally hide evidence that could favour the defendant.

The likelihood of tunnel vision occurring appears to be higher in investigative processes when the suspect is from a stigmatised community. An example from British history involves Irish cases where even expert scientists failed to disclose false-positive test results that could have been considered exculpatory evidence. Consequently, tunnel vision can be seen as a contributing factor that brings together various shortcomings within the criminal justice system, including police negligence and misconduct, biased expert testimony, and the failure to discover or disclose exculpatory evidence, as discussed by Findley and Scott (2006).

Furthermore, the influence of prejudicial stereotyping within the context of investigative interviewing has received negligible attention. As such, no research (as far as it is known) has been conducted in England and Wales to examine the influence of prejudicial stereotyping on investigative interviewing concerning suspects from the suspect community. This book seeks to address this gap by investigating whether prejudicial stereotyping plays a role in legal decisions about Muslim offenders and whether investigative decisions could be affected by such prejudicial stereotyping.

Note

1 Asian—here should be taken as an ethnicity. In stop-and-search records the ethnicity of an individual is recorded (not religion); therefore, here Asian ethnicity should not be taken as Asian Muslims but as the broader Asian community (regardless of religion).

References

Allport, G. W. (1954). *The nature of prejudice.* Cambridge, MA: Addison-Wesley

Awan, I. (2012). 'I Am a Muslim Not an Extremist': How the Prevent Strategy Has Constructed a 'Suspect' Community. *Politics & Policy*, *40*, 1158–1185. Doi:10.1111/j.1747-1346.2012.00397.x

Awan, I. (2018). 'I never did anything wrong'–Trojan Horse: a qualitative study uncovering the impact in Birmingham. *British Journal of Sociology of Education*, *39*, 197–211.

Awan, I., & Rahman, M. (2016). Portrayal of Muslims Following the Murders of Lee Rigby in Woolwich and Mohammed Saleem in Birmingham: A Content Analysis of UK Newspapers. *Journal of Muslim Minority Affairs*, *36*, 16–31.

Baldus, D. C., Pulaski, C., & Woodworth, G. (1983). Comparative review of death sentences: An empirical study of the Georgia experience. *Journal of Criminal Law and Criminology*, *74*, 661–753.

Baldwin, J. (1992). Videotaping police interviews with suspects – an evaluation. The Home Office. London Police Research Series Paper 1.

Baldwin, J. (1993). Police interview techniques: Establishing truth or proof?. *British Journal of Criminology*, *33*, 325–352.

Banaji, M. R., & Greenwald, A. G. (1995). Implicit gender stereotyping in judgments of fame. *Journal of Personality and Social Psychology*, *68*, 181–192.

Bargh, J. A. (1994). The four horsemen of automaticity: Awareness, intention, efficiency, and control in social cognition. In: R. S. Wyer, Jr. & T. K. Srull, eds. Handbook of social cognition, 2nd ed., (pp. 1–40), Erlbaum

Bearchell, J. (2010). UK police interviews with suspects: a short modern history. In: J. Adler and J. Gray, eds. Forensic psychology: concepts, debates and practice (pp. 90–105), Cullompton: Willan

Bettleheim, B., & Janowitz, M. (1964). *Social change and prejudice*. New York: Free Press of Glencoe

Bjerregaard, B. E., Smith, M. D., Cochran, J. K., & Fogel, S. J. (2017). A further examination of the liberation hypothesis in capital murder trials. *Crime & Delinquency*, *63*, 1017–1038.

Blaine, B. E. (2012). *Understanding the psychology of diversity*. London: Sage

Bond, C., Di Candia, C., & McKinnon, J.R. (1988). Response to violence in psychiatric settings. *Personality and Social Psychology*, 14, 448–458.

Bowling, B. & Phillips, C. (2007). Disproportionate and discriminatory: reviewing the evidence on police stop and search. *Modern Law Review*, 70, pp. 936–961.

Bowling, B. (2018). Pulled over: how police stops define race and citizenship. *Policing and Society*, 1–4.

Bowling, B., Parmar, A., & Phillips, C. (2013). Policing ethnic minority communities. In T. Newburn (Ed.) *The Handbook of Policing* (pp. 611–641), 2nd edn, Cullompton: Willan.

Brewer, M. B. (2007). The importance of being we: Human nature and intergroup relations. *American Psychologist*, *62*, 728.

Brown, L., & Richards, B. (2016). Media Representations of Islam in Britain: A Sojourner Perspective. *Journal of Muslim Minority Affairs*, *36*, 350–363.

Bull, R. (2013). What is 'believed' or actually 'known' about characteristics that may contribute to being a good/effective interviewer? *Investigative Interviewing: Research and Practice (II—RP)*, *5* (2), 128–143

Bull, R., & Cherryman, J. (1996). *Helping to identify skills gaps in specialist investigative interviewing: Enhancement of professional skills*. Great Britain, Home Office, Research, Development and Statistics Directorate.

Casper, C., Rothermund, K. & Wentura, D. (2010). Automatic stereotype activation is context dependent. *Social Psychology*, *41*, 131–36. DOI:http://dx.doi.org/10.1027/1864-9335/a000019

Chadee, D. (1996). Race, trial evidence and jury decision making. *Caribbean Journal of Criminology and Social Psychology*, 1, 49–86

Chadee, D., Ali, S., Burke, A., & Young, J. (2017). Fear of crime and community concerns: Mediating effect of risk and pragmatic fear. *Journal of Community & Applied Social Psychology*, *27*, 450–462.

Chapman, L. J. (1967). Illusory correlation in observational report. *Journal of Verbal Learning and Verbal Behavior*, *6*, 151–155. DOI:10.1016/S00225371(67)80066-5

Choudhury, T., & Fenwick, H. (2011). The impact of counter-terrorism measures on Muslim communities. *International Review of Law, Computers & Technology*, *25*, 151–181.

Clarke, C., & Milne, R. (2001). *National evaluation of the PEACE investigative interviewing course*. Police Research Award Scheme Report No. PRAS/149. London: Home Office.

Clarke, C., Milne, R., & Bull, R. (2011). Interviewing suspects of crime: The impact of PEACE training, supervision and the presence of a legal advisor. *Journal of Investigative Psychology and Offender Profiling*, *8*, 149–162. DOI: 10.1002/jip.144

Cloutier, J., Mason, M. F. & Macrae, C. N. (2005). The perceptual determinants of person construal: Reopening the social-cognitive toolbox. *Journal of Personality and Social Psychology*, *88*, 885–94. http://dx.doi.org/10.1037/0022-3514.88.6.885

Cohn, E.S., Bucolo, D., Pride, M., & Sommers, S. R. (2009). Racial salience and racial bias in the courts: Do racial attitudes make a difference? *Journal of Applied Social Psychology, 39*, 1953–1973.

Correll, J., Park, B., Judd, C. M., Wittenbrink, B., Sadler, M. S., & Keesee, T. (2007). Across the thin blue line: Police officers and racial bias in the decision to shoot. *Journal of Personality and Social Psychology, 92*, 1006–1023. http://dx.doi.org/10.1037

Cuddy, A. J. C., Fiske, S. T. & Glick, P. (2007). The BIAS map: Behaviors from intergroup affect and stereotypes. *Journal of Personality and Social Psychology*, 92, 631–648. http://dx.doi.org/10.1037/0022-3514.92.4.631

Daviesl, G. M., Westcott, H. L., & Horan, N. (2000). The impact of questioning style on the content of investigative interviews with suspected child sexual abuse victims. *Psychology, Crime and Law*, *6*(2), 81–97.

Devine, D. J., Buddenbaum, J., Houp, S., Studebaker, N., & Stolle, D. P. (2009). Strength of evidence, extraevidentiary influence, and the liberation hypothesis: Data from the field. *Law and Human Behavior*, *33*, 136–148.

Devine, P. G. (1989). Stereotypes and prejudice: their automatic and controlled components. *Journal of Personality and Social Psychology*, *56*, 5. Doi:10.1037/0022-3514.56.1.5

Fahsing, I., & Ask, K. (2016). The making of an expert detective: The role of experience in English and Norwegian police officers' investigative decision making. *Psychology, Crime & Law*, 22, 203–223. http://dx.doi.org/10.1080/1068316X.2015.1077249

Fazio, R. H., Jackson, J. R., Dunton, B. C.,&Williams, C. J. (1995).Variability in automatic activation as an unobtrusive measure of racial attitudes: a bona fide pipeline? *Journal of Personality and Social Psychology, 69,* 1013–1027.

Fekete, L. (2018). Lammy Review: without racial justice, can there be trust? *Race & Class, 59*, 75–79.

Findley, K. A. & Scott, M. S. (2006). The Multiple Dimensions of Tunnel Vision in *Criminal Cases. Wisconsin Law Review,* Vol. 2, 2006; Univ. of Wisconsin Legal Studies Research Paper No. 1023. Available at SSRN: https://ssrn.com/abstract=911240

Fisher, R. P., & Geiselman, R. E. (1992). *Memory enhancing techniques for investigative interviewing: The cognitive interview.* Charles C Thomas Publisher.

Gabrielson, R., Jones, R. G., & Sagara, E. (2014). Deadly force, in black and white. *ProPublica.*

Graham, S., & Lowery, B. S. (2004). Priming unconscious racial stereotypes about adolescent offenders. *Law and Human Behavior, 28*, 483.

Greenwald, A. G., & Krieger, L. H. (2006). Implicit bias: Scientific foundations. *California Law Review, 94*, 945–967.

Griffiths, A., & Milne, R. (2006). Will it all end in tiers? Police interviews with suspects in Britain. In T. Williamson (Ed.) *Investigative Interviewing*, pp. 167–189. London.

Gudjonsson, G. (2003). *The psychology of interrogations and confessions.* Chichester: John Wiley & Sons, Ltd.

Gudjonsson, G. H. (2018). *The Psychology of False Confessions: Forty Years of Science and Practice.* John Wiley & Sons.

Hall, A. V., Hall, E. V., & Perry, J. L. (2016). Black and blue: Exploring racial bias and law enforcement in the killings of unarmed black male civilians. *American Psychologist, 71*, 175.

Hamilton, D. L., & Gifford, R. K. (1976). Illusory correlation in interpersonal perception: A cognitive basis of stereotypic judgments. *Journal of Experimental Social Psychology, 12*, 392–407.

Hickman, M. J., Thomas, L., Nickels, H. C., & Silvestri, S. (2012). Social cohesion and the notion of 'suspect communities': a study of the experiences and impacts of being 'suspect' for Irish communities and Muslim communities in Britain. *Critical Studies on Terrorism, 5*(1), 89–106.

Hill, C., Memon, A., & McGeorge, P. (2008). The role of confirmation bias in suspect interviews: A systematic evaluation. *Legal and Criminological Psychology, 13*, 357–371. doi:10.1348/135532507X238682

HMIC (2005) *Community and race relations: Policies and practices within the police service.* London: Home Office.

Hogg, M. A., Abrams, D., & Brewer, M. B. (2017). Social identity: The role of self in group processes and intergroup relations. *Group Processes & Intergroup Relations, 20*, 570–581.

Holmberg, U., & Christianson, S. Å. (2002). Murderers' and sexual offenders' experiences of police interviews and their inclination to admit or deny crimes. *Behavioral Sciences & The Law, 20*, 31–45. doi: 10.1002/bsl.470

Hudson, B. & Bramhall, G. (2005) Assessing the 'Other': constructions of 'Asianness' in risk assessments by probation officers. *British Journal of Criminology, 45,* 721–740.
Huggon, W. G. (2012). *Subtle Bias in Legal Decision Making: How Attitudes and Social Norms Affect Primary and Peripheral Targets.* Unpublished doctoral dissertation: University of Toronto
Irving, B. (1980). *Police interrogation: a case study of current practice:* Research Study No.2. Royal Commission on Criminal Procedure. London: HMSO.
Kassin, S. M., Goldstein, C. C., & Savitsky, K. (2003). Behavioral confirmation in the interrogation room: On the dangers of presuming guilt. *Law and Human Behavior, 27,*187–203. Doi.org/10.1023/A:1022599230598
Kerr, N. L., Hymes, R. W., Anderson, A. B., & Weathers, J. E. (1995). Defendant-juror similarity and mock juror judgments. *Law and Human Behavior, 19,* 545–567.
Lammers, J., & Stapel, D. A. (2011). Retracted: Racist biases in legal decisions are reduced by a justice focus. *European Journal of Social Psychology, 41,* 375–387. DOI:10.1002/ejsp.783
Leippe, M. R., Bergold, A. N., & Eisenstadt, D. (2017). Prejudice and terror management at trial: Effects of defendant race/ethnicity and mortality salience on mock-jurors' verdict judgments. *Journal of Social Psychology, 157,* 279–294.
Lepore, L., & Brown, R. (1997). Category and stereotype activation: Is prejudice inevitable?. *Journal of Personality and Social Psychology, 72,* 275.
Levett, L. M., Danielsen, E. M., Kovera, M. B., & Cutler, B. L. (2005). The psychology of jury and juror decision making. *Psychology and law: An Empirical Perspective,* 365–406.
Leyens, J. P., Yzerbyt, V., & Schadron, G. (1994). *Stereotypes and social cognition.* London: Sage.
Loftus, E. F., & Palmer, J. C. (1974). Reconstruction of automobile destruction: An example of the interaction between language and memory. *Journal of verbal learning and verbal behavior, 13,* 585–589.
Mackie, D. M., Hamilton, D. L., Susskind, J., & Rosselli, F. (1996). Social psychological foundations of stereotype formation. In C. N. Macrae, C. Stangor, & M. Hewstone (Eds.), *Stereotypes and stereotyping* (pp. 41–78). New York: Guilford.
Macpherson of Cluny. (1999). The Stephen Lawrence Inquiry, Report of an inquiry by Sir William Macpherson of Cluny. *London: Stationery Office, Parliamentary papers, Cm, 4262,* 3–10.
Macrae, C. N., & Bodenhausen, G. V. (2000). Social cognition: Thinking categorically about others. *Annual review of psychology, 51,* 93–120.
Macrae, C. N., Bodenhausen, G. V., Milne, A. B., Thorn, T. M., & Castelli, L. (1997). On the activation of social stereotypes: The moderating role of processing objectives. *Journalof Experimental Social Psychology, 33,* 471–489.
Maguire, M. (2003). Criminal investigation and crime control. *Handbook of policing,* 363–393.
Marques, J. M. (1990). The black-sheep effect: Out-group homogeneity in social comparison settings. In D. Abrams & M. A. Hogg (Eds.), Social identity

theory: Constructive and critical advances: (pp. 131–151). London: Harvester Wheatsheaf.

McConville, M., Sanders, A., & Leng, R. (1993). *The case for the prosecution: Police suspects and the construction of criminality*. London: Routledge.

McGurk, B. J., Carr, M. J., & McGurk D. (1993). *Investigative interviewing courses for police officers: An evaluation. Police Research Group* Paper No. 4, London: Home Office.

Meissner, C. A., & Kassin, S. M. (2002). 'He's guilty!': Investigator bias in judgments of truth and deception. *Law and human behavior*, 26, 469–480.

Milne, B., & Poyser, S. (2017). The role of police investigative processes in causing miscarriages of justice. In *Forensic Science Reform: Protecting the Innocent. Vol 2: Psychological and Sociological Issues*. Elsevier.

Milne, B., Shaw, G., & Bull, R. (2007). Investigative interviewing: The role of research. *Applying psychology to criminal justice*, 65–80.

Milne, R, & Bull, R. (1999) *Investigative interviewing: Psychology and Practice*. Chichester: John Wiley & Sons Ltd.

Milne, R. J., & Bull, R. (2016). Investigative interviewing: investigation and probative value. *The Journal of Forensic Practice.*, *18*(2). DOI: 10.1108/JFP-01-2016-0006

Milne, R., Poyser, S., Williamson, T., & Savage, S. P. (2010). Miscarriages of justice: what can we learn?. In *Forensic Psychology* (pp. 49–69). Willan.

Monteith, M. J., Sherman, J. W. & Devine, P. G. (1998). Suppression as a stereotype control strategy. *Personality and Social Psychology Review*, 2, 63–82. http://dx.doi.org/10.1207%2Fs15327957pspr0201_4

Mortimer, A., & Shepherd, E. (1999). Frames of mind: Schemata guiding cognition and conduct in the interviewing of suspected offenders. In A. Memon & R. Bull (Eds.), *Handbook of the psychology of interviewing* (pp. 293–315). Chichester: Wiley.

Moston, S., & Engelberg, T. (1993). Police questioning techniques in tape recorded interviews with criminal suspects. *Policing and Society: An International Journal*, *3*, 223–237. DOI: 10.1080/10439463.1993.9964670

Moston, S., Stephenson, G. M., & Williamson, T. M. (1992). The effects of case characteristics on suspect behaviour during police questioning. *British Journal of Criminology*, *32*, 23–40.

Myklebust, T., & Bjørklund, R. A. (2006). The effect of long-term training on police officers' use of open and closed questions in field investigative interviews of children (FIIC). *Journal of Investigative Psychology and Offender Profiling*, *3*(3), 165–181.

Mythen, G., Walklate, S., & Khan, F. (2013). 'Why should we have to prove we're alright?': Counter-terrorism, risk and partial securities. *Sociology*, *47*, 383–398.

Nickerson, R. S. (1998). Confirmation bias: A ubiquitous phenomenon in many guises. *Review of General Psychology*, 2, 175–220. Doi: 10.1037/1089-2680.2.2.175

O'Connor, A. (2017). *An Analysis of Gordon W. Allport's The Nature of Prejudice*. London, UK: CRC Press.

Ost, J. (2006). 'Recovered memories', in T. M. Williamson (ed). *Investigative interviewing: Developments in Rights, Research and Regulation*. Cullompton: William Publishing.

Pantazis, C. & Pemberton, S. (2009). From the 'old' to the 'new' suspect community examining the impacts of recent UK counter-terrorist legislation. *British Journal of Criminology*, *49*, 646–666. DOI: 10.1093/bjc/azp031

Passini, S. (2018). The indifference that makes a difference: Why unconcern for minorities disguises prejudicial attitudes. *Journal of Moral Education*, 1–12.

Peirce, C. S. (1965). *Pragmatism and pragmaticism* (Vol. 5): Harvard University: Belknap Press of Harvard University Press.

Phillips, E., Oxburgh, G., Gavin, A., & Myklebust, T. (2012). Investigative interviews with victims of child sexual abuse: The relationship between question type and investigation relevant information. *Journal of Police and Criminal Psychology, 27*, 45–54.

Powell, M. B., & Barnett, M. (2015). Elements underpinning successful implementation of a national best-practice child investigative interviewing framework. *Psychiatry, Psychology and Law*, *22*, 368–377.

Poyser, S., & Milne, R. (2015). No grounds for complacency and plenty for continued vigilance: miscarriages of justice as drivers for research on reforming the investigative interviewing process. *The Police Journal*, *88*, 265–280.

Reiner, R. (1991). *Chief constables*. Oxford: Oxford University Press. Oxford, UK.

Rhodes, M., Leslie, S. J., Saunders, K., Dunham, Y., & Cimpian, A. (2018). How does social essentialism affect the development of inter-group relations? *Developmental Science*, *21*, e12509

Roach, K., & Trotter, G. (2004). Miscarriages of Justice in the War against Terror. *Pennsylvania State Law Review*, *109*, 967.

Sanders, A., Young, R., & Burton, M. (2010). *Criminal justice*. USA: Oxford University Press.

Shepherd, E. (1993). Resistance in interviews; The contribution of police perception and behaviour. *Issues in Criminal and Legal Psychology, 18,* 5–12.

Shipton, M. (2015) Lynette White: Home Secretary 'to order new inquiry' into the collapse of country's biggest ever police corruption trial. Wales Online. 9 February. Available from: www.walesonline.co.uk/news/wales-news/home-secretary-toorder-new 8611418 [Accessed 20 March 2015].

Smith, M. R., & Alpert, G. P. (2007). Explaining police bias: A theory of social conditioning and illusory correlation. *Criminal Justice and Behavior, 34*, 1262–1283. 10.1177/0093854807304484

Smith, M. R., Makarios, M., & Alpert, G. P. (2006). Differential suspicion: Theory specification and gender effects in the traffic stop context. *Justice Quarterly, 23*, 271–295. http://dx.doi.org/10.1080/07418820600688883

Tajfel, H., & Turner, J. C. (1979). An integrative theory of intergroup conflict. In W. G. Austin & S. Worchel (Eds.), *The social psychology of intergroup relations* (pp. 33–47). Monterey, CA: Brooks/Cole.

Taylor, T. S., & Hosch, H. M. (2004). An examination of jury verdicts for evidence of a similarity–leniency effect, an out-group punitiveness effect or a black sheep effect. *Law and Human Behavior*, 28, 587–598. doi:10.1023/B:LAHU.0000046436.36228.71

Thomas, C., & Balmer, N. (2007). Diversity and fairness in the jury system. *Ministry of Justice Research Series*. Retrieved April 24, 2015, from www.justice.gov.uk/docs/PagesfromJuries-report2-07C1.pdf

Todd, A. R., Bodenhausen, G. V., Richeson, J. A., & Galinsky, A. D. (2011). Perspective taking combats automatic expressions of racial bias. *Journal of Personality and Social Psychology*, *100*, 1027–1042.

Walsh, D., & Bull, R. (2012). Examining rapport in investigative interviews with suspects: Does its building and maintenance work? *Journal of Police and Criminal Psychology* 27, 73–84. Doi:10.1007/s11896-011-9087-x

Walsh, D., & Milne, R. (2007). Perceptions of benefit fraud staff in the UK: Giving PEACE a chance? *Public Administration*, *85*, 525–540.

Webster, C. (2004) 'Policing British Asian Communities' in J. Hopkins-Burke (ed.), Hard Cop, Soft Cop: Dilemmas and Debates in Contemporary Policing, (pp. 78–93) Devon: Willan.

Wilder, D. A., & Simon, A. F. (2001). Affect as a Cause of Intergroup Bias. S. 153–172 in: Brown, R./Gaertner, SL (Hrsg.), Intergroup Processes.

Williamson, T. (1993). Review and prospect. In Eric Shepherd (Ed) *Aspects of police interviewing*. Issues in Criminological and Legal Psychology, pp. 57–59.

Williamson, T. (2006) *Investigative interviewing: Rights, research, regulation*. Devon: Willan Publishing.

Williamson, T. (2007). Psychology and criminal investigations. *Handbook of criminal investigation*. Devon: William Publishing.

Chapter 3

Police stop-and-search practices

Reasonable suspicion or stereotypical suspicion?

Background

In the United Kingdom, a number of research studies have reported findings showing disparities in police treatment between ethnic minority citizens and White citizens (Bowling & Weber, 2011; Graham & Lowery, 2004; Parmar, 2011). Following the publication of the Macpherson inquiry report (Macpherson of Cluny, 1999) into the murder of Black teenager Stephen Lawrence in 1993, the issue of 'racial profiling' reached new heights of intensity. The report established that the over-representation of racial minorities in the national stop-and-search data led to the clear core conclusion of racial stereotyping (Macpherson of Cluny, 1999). Studies of stop-and-search found that the required reasonable grounds for suspicion were often not adhered to (Bowling & Phillips, 2007; Jefferson & Walker, 1993; Quinton, 2011), with stereotypes potentially playing a role in informing suspicions (Smith & Gray 1985; Quinton, 2011). Research studies (e.g. Bowling & Phillips, 2007; Cain, 2015; Graef, 1989; Jefferson & Walker, 1993; Quinton, 2011; Young, 1994) have found that certain stereotypes are commonly used by police officers to classify people based on their ethnic origin.

The use of stop-and-search powers by the police has been the most controversial issue in debates about policing ethnic minority communities (Bowling & Weber 2011; Bradford, 2017; McCandless et al., 2016; Phillips & Bowling, 2012; Quinton, 2011). This may always have been the situation since stop-and-search powers emerged in 1824 via Section 4 and Section 6 of the Vagrancy Act (Qureshi & Farrell, 2006). Under the 1824 Vagrancy Act, people could be stopped for frequenting or loitering in public places with intent to commit an arrestable offence. Since its inception, the Act has been criticised for its apparent disproportionate use against young Black men (DeMuth, 1978). Following the work of the Scrap Sus Campaign in 1979 and the conclusions of the Royal Commission on Criminal Procedure in 1981, the Police and Criminal Evidence Act (PACE)

DOI: 10.4324/9781003366836-3

1984 was introduced to regulate police powers, which came into force in January 1986. The PACE sought to introduce safeguards against discriminatory policing and structure the use of police discretion (Brown, 1997).

Police officers are empowered with many legislative instruments to stop and search people, and the most frequently used powers are those under Section 1 of the PACE, Section 23 of the Misuse of Drugs Act 1971, Section 47 of the Firearms Act 1968, Section 60 of the Criminal Justice and Public Order Act 1994, Section 44 (1) (2) of the Terrorism Act 2000, and Section 163 of the Road Traffic Act 1988 (Bowling & Phillips, 2007). The requirement in addition to these legislative instruments is that the police officer must have reasonable suspicion 'for suspecting that they will find stolen or prohibited articles' (Section 1 (3) PACE Act 1984). According to the PACE Code of Practice A (p. 8), the primary purpose of the stop-and-search power is 'to enable officers to allay or confirm suspicions about individuals without exercising their powers of arrest'. The critical element of the PACE (1984) was the concept of 'reasonable suspicion', which was intended as a safeguard both against discriminatory policing and to reduce the possibility that individuals were subject to indiscriminate stop-and-search (Qureshi & Farrell, 2006). Reasonable grounds for suspicion depend upon the circumstances of each case, according to the PACE Code of Practice A:

> There must be an objective basis for that suspicion based on facts, information, and/or intelligence which are relevant to the likelihood of finding an article of a certain kind.

It adds that:

> reasonable suspicion can never be supported on the basis of personal factors alone without reliable or supporting intelligence or information or some specific behaviour by the person concerned.
>
> (PACE, 1984, p. 8)

The original PACE reforms relied primarily on legal challenges to regulate police behaviour (i.e. to establish a balance between the powers of the police and the rights and freedoms of the public)—an approach that has been met with scepticism by a number of authors (e.g. Baldwin & Kinsey, 1982; Dixon et al., 1989; Dixon 1997; McConville, Sanders, & Leng, 1991; Smith & Gray, 1985). For example, Dixon et al. (1989) highlighted that those legal definitions of 'reasonable grounds of search' lacked clarity and relevance. Fitzgerald (1999) identified three key areas where discretion might lead to abuses of stop-and-search powers. First, police officers have to interpret legal rules for which no amount of guidance can cover every eventuality. Second, the concept of reasonable suspicion is vague, and officers differ widely in their understanding of it. Finally, individuals who consent to stop-and-search are not provided with sufficient safeguards under the PACE Act (1984). This may well be very problematic since the concept of 'consent' is elastic because individuals subject to stop-and-search may be ignorant of their rights to refuse to be searched (Dixon et al., 1990; Quinton, 2011).

Stop-and-search is primarily an investigative power used for the purposes of crime detection or prevention concerning a specific individual at a specific time (Lustgarten, 2002). However, police officers frequently use stop-and-search powers to 'gain intelligence' on people 'known' to police, to break up groups of young people, and for 'social control' more generally (Bowling, 2018; Bowling & Phillips, 2007). The legal regulation of stop-and-search powers does not prevent the abuse of discretion (Young, 1994). Kleining (1996, p. 83) observed that police discretion was deemed to be 'permission, privilege or prerogative to use one's own judgment about how to make a practical determination'. Bowling and Phillips (2007) argue that the PACE gives powers to police officers to stop and search individuals but does not criminalise actions taken without those powers (i.e. a stop without reasonable suspicion). Therefore, while an individual who refuses to submit to a police search commits a criminal offence, the legislation does not penalise police who act without a lawful basis. If the searches do not satisfy the precondition of 'reasonable suspicion', does this mean that the police are acting illegally in such circumstances?

If a police officer steps outside the provisions of the Act while searching, this may lead to a charge of assault (Stone, 2014). However, 'the absence of a clear statutory penalty for unlawful stops and searches allows the police discretion to act without adequate accountability' (Bowling & Phillips, 2007, p. 939). As such, discretionary practices within stop-and-search could provide the opportunity for police officers to exercise their discretionary powers based on their prejudices (Kleining, 1996). Studies of stop-and-search after the introduction of the PACE Act (1984) indicate that reasonable grounds for suspicion were often not adhered to (Quinton et al. 2000; Quinton, 2011), with negative stereotypes potentially playing a role in informing suspicions (Brown, 1997; Dixon et al., 1989; Smith & Gray, 1985; Quinton, 2011; Young, 1994).

Additionally, negative stereotypes can result from wrongdoing among specific groups coming more frequently to the attention of the authorities, which in turn can reinforce police and public stereotypes about such groups' involvement in particular types of crimes (Bowling & Weber, 2011; Murray et al., 2021). Consequently, a considerable portion of these groups end up being perceived and treated as 'suspects' (Phillips & Bowling, 2012). The impact of this on the law-abiding citizens within such groups creates a perception of unfairness and injustice (Parmar, 2011). The 'subjective experience of feeling profiled might be equally as damaging to trust in the police as the objective one of being profiled' (Tyler & Wakslak, 2004, p. 254). The disproportionate use of stop-and-search powers has corrosively affected social solidarity and led to feelings of exclusion, resentment, police distrust, alienation, and social as well as political disenfranchisement (Bowling & Weber, 2011). The experience of being unjustifiably targeted by the police undermines the legitimacy of policing, which has material effects on voluntary compliance with the law, and additionally with respect to victims and witnesses coming forward (Tyler, 1990).

Stereotypes may be vital to decision-making in stop-and-search practices which could result in the police concentrating on the socially marginal (Quinton, 2011). As Dixon et al. (1989) noted, a man who fits a stereotype just ends up noticeably suspicious in a stop-and-search context. Quinton (2011, p. 364) quoted a statement by an officer in which the officer revealed the connotation that young people wearing tracksuits and hooded tops are not respectable: 'you develop the stereotypes through experience, the people you see are involved in crime. In this area, its people in sports gear'. Quinton further quoted a statement from another officer, who said, 'whenever a robbery comes in, 90% you will be thinking it's a Black male because of the description and because you know who does a robbery in the past' (Quinton, 2011, p. 364).

Moreover, in the UK criminal justice system, stereotypes about Black people posit them as criminally disposed, drug-abusing, and violent (*The Lammy Review*, 2017). Such views can be traced back to the classificatory systems of the Enlightenment thinkers (de Gobineau, 1853). Asian men have increasingly come to be perceived as disorderly, militant, culturally separatist, and inclined towards Islamic terrorism (Bowling & Phillips, 2007; Shaw, 2016). Quinton (2011) found that Black people were commonly associated with robbery and drugs, but White individuals with a wide range of other crimes (e.g. criminal damage, theft, and vehicle crimes). Such stereotypes often continue unwittingly but can be directives of action since they work at the level of discernment and desire (Graham & Lowery, 2004). Consequently, it may be inescapable that such focus on particular groups of a community would result in youngsters from deprived backgrounds and ethnic minorities being targeted.

The impact of stereotypes, as such, is to mark out the limits between 'them' and 'us' (Tajfel, 2010). Stereotypes operate unwittingly and can be directives of actions since they work at the level of discernment and desire.

These authors also found that stereotypes were remarkably stable over time, being transmitted and maintained through informal work routines (Hall, McLaughlin, & Lewis, 1998). Concerning stop-and-search practices, the PACE (1984) states that reasonable grounds of suspicion cannot be based on stereotypes or individual qualities (including previous criminal record). However, the formation of reasonable suspicion is viewed as a rational process which includes officers looking over the material facts around them and weighing up the probability of finding a prohibited item. Therefore, it (i.e. the formation of reasonable suspicion) neglects the extent to which practical rules of thumb are central to investigative decision-making (Dixon et al., 1989).

According to a report by the Equality and Human Rights Commission (EHRC) (2010), stop-and-search powers have been used in a discriminatory manner. More importantly, this report emphasises that various explanations have been put forward as to why the police use stop-and-search powers disproportionately against certain ethnic groups. For example: (i) perhaps Black people are generally more often involved in crime; (ii) stop-and-search plays a role in preventing and detecting crime; and (iii) certain ethnic minorities' have a greater presence on the streets. Even taken together, these explanations provide very little justification for the extent and persistence of the problem (Weber & Bowling, 2011). The evidence points to racial discrimination being a significant factor as to why Black and Asian people are more likely to be stopped and searched than White people (EHRC, 2010). The EHRC (2010) report maintained that stop-and-search powers might well be used in a discriminatory and unlawful way. Even the *Macpherson Report* (1999, para. 45.10) acknowledged that 'the majority of police officers who testified before us accepted that an element of the disparity was the result of discrimination'.

In the United States, much like in the United Kingdom, significant concerns have arisen regarding racial disparities in stop-and-search practices. Numerous studies and data have consistently shown that Black and Hispanic individuals are disproportionately targeted for stop-and-search encounters compared to their White counterparts. For instance, in a study conducted by Stelter, Essien, Sander, and Degner (2022), they examined the connections between racial disparities in police traffic stops and regional-level racial bias. They found that most counties exhibited a disproportionate rate of traffic stops involving Black drivers. Furthermore, they observed that counties with higher levels of racial prejudice among White residents (ranging from rs = .07 to .36) tended to have a greater disparity in the rates of stops involving Black drivers. Similarly, Ekstrom et al. (2022) found that counties with higher average levels of racial bias tended to display larger racial disparities in traffic stops. Notably, both

Stelter et al. (2022) and Ekstrom et al. (2022) found that this association held true for both explicitly measured and implicitly measured racial bias. Furthermore, in a comprehensive analysis of traffic stop data from 20 states spanning the years 2011 to 2015, Pierson et al. (2020) found that racial disparities in police stops extended beyond isolated areas. This nationwide study revealed that Black drivers were stopped by police officers at a higher frequency compared to White drivers, even when considering their respective proportions within the driving-age population (Pierson et al., 2020).

Following the Home Office Action Plan (Home Office, 1999) in response to the Stephen Lawrence inquiry report, a number of studies were conducted in order to examine police use of stop-and-search powers (e.g. Bland, Miller, & Quinton, 2000; Bowling & Phillips, 2007; HMIC, 2013; HMIC, 2015; Home Office, 2003; Home Office, 2006; Miller, 2010; Stone & Pettigrew, 2000). Each successive study indicates that aggregate disparities in stop-and-search figures show no improvement following reforms (HMIC, 2013). In addition to these studies, a recent review published by the UK Ministry of Justice found that BAME communities make up 14 per cent of the population of England and Wales, but 25 per cent of adult prisoners and 41 per cent of under age 18 in custody (*The Lammy Review*, 2017). Such long-observed ethnic disproportionality can be partially attributed to racialisation and discrimination by individual police officers on the streets (Phillips, 2011). When the decisions to conduct stop-and-searches are carried out guided by stereotypes for little reason, are perceived to be unfair, or are poorly handled, this can have a profoundly negative effect on the public's perception (Stone & Pettigrew, 2000). It is, therefore, essential to improve our understanding of the processes by which police officers inform suspicion or anticipate wrongdoing and decide to conduct a stop-and-search (Quinton, 2011). As such, the present study is focused on the examination of whether police officers use negative stereotypes in day-to-day policing to inform suspicion. This study also examines what other factors may influence police officers' decisions to initiate a stop-and-search encounter.

Methods

The present study used a mixed-methods approach. It consists of two phases. The first phase involves an examination of 2,118 individual search records, which were provided by an English police force. The second phase entailed a thematic analysis of 20 semi-structured interviews, which were conducted with serving patrol officers of the same force. This sequential method was devised to initially identify potential factors that could prompt an officer to initiate a stop-and-search encounter. Subsequently, the findings obtained from the analysis of search records were further explored and explained by conducting interviews with serving police officers. All study protocols and instruments were reviewed and approved by the University of Derby's Institutional Ethics Committee.

Phase 1

Phase 1 of the analysis examines the following questions:

- What factors make officers decide whom to stop and search? What are the grounds for searches reported by police officers to inform suspicion?
- Does a relationship exist between those belonging to Black, Asian, and Mixed Ethnicity groups and the greater rate of their being searched?

Data collection and procedures

Following the completion of the author's Non-Police Personnel (NPP) Level One[1] vetting procedure (the police constabulary carried out checks on National Police Computer systems, and local systems and requested checks from Forces that cover any addresses provided in the author's application), and ethical approval by the police force and the author's then-home university, a data set was sent to the author via a secure email within an Excel spreadsheet containing a record of 2,118 searches. This data set included information regarding who was searched, when, what powers were used to search, and on what grounds the search was conducted. The data set also contained information including the gender, ethnicity, the age of the individual when s/he was searched, whether arrested or not, and reasons for arrest (if the arrest was made following the search). The database was compiled using documentary records of searches conducted throughout the entire area of the police force, spanning from 1 July 2014 to 31 December 2014.

Results

During the first stage, these data were meticulously examined to identify the factors that could potentially trigger officers' suspicions concerning an individual. Thematic analysis (Braun & Clarke, 2006; see Phase 2 for further details on the thematic analysis) was employed by the author to examine the 'grounds of search' for each recorded search. Consequently, the analysis led to the identification of eight common factors utilised by officers to inform their suspicions about individuals and determine whether a formal stop-and-search is warranted (see Table 3.1). Following this, the

Table 3.1 Grounds for searches reported by the police officers to inform suspicion

Grounds for searches	*Number of searches*	*Percentage of total searches*
Being previously known to the police	198	9.35
Being located in a known crime hotspot	169	7.9
Fitting a reported suspect's description	126	5.9
Suspicious activity	310	14.64
Drugs-related suspicion	897	42.35
Reported or suspected of being in possession of an offensive weapon	88	4.1
Suspected of carrying stolen goods or going equipped	234	11.05
Responding to a reported incident	96	4.5

data set was coded based on (i) grounds of search; (ii) what powers were exercised by police officers; (iii) gender; (iv) age; (v) ethnicity; (vi) whether arrest was made following a search; and (vii) reasons for arrest. As such, the 'grounds of search' were examined for each recorded search, which provided information about the officers' origins of suspicion. The coded data were then imported into SPSS software to conduct statistical analyses.

As a result of the 2,118 searches, 288 (13.6 per cent) arrests were made. Where arrests took place, the data set did not provide any subsequent details of the outcomes of these arrests (such as the number resulting in charges, cautions, or no further action).

It was found that nearly half (49.6 per cent) of the searches were conducted with individuals aged between 18 to 30 years old—for individuals aged between 12 to 17 (20.3 per cent), 31 to 40 (22.5 per cent), and 41 to 70 (7.5 per cent). As a result of the 2,118 searches, 288 (13.6 per cent) arrests were made. Where arrests took place, the data set did not provide any subsequent details of the outcomes of these arrests (such as the number resulting in charges, cautions, or no further action).

To ascertain whether a correlation exists between individuals belonging to the Black, Asian, and Mixed ethnicity groups and a higher search rate, the coefficient of the confidence level (both the lower- and upper-bound value) and the f-test (Wald test) were examined. The results are presented in Table 3.2. The confidence interval (CI) coefficient and the ethnicity values (0.48:3.04) indicated that ethnicity significantly impacts the frequency of stop-and-search encounters. Overall, using the Wald F-test, as shown in Table 3.2, determines whether gender, age, grounds of search, and ethnicity jointly predict whether an individual can be stopped and searched. The analyses revealed a significant combined impact of these

Table 3.2 Influence of ethnicity on the likelihood of an individual being stopped and searched

	B	*S.E.*	*Wald*	*df*	*Sig.*	*Exp(B)*	*95% C.I. for EXP(B)*	
							Lower	*Upper*
PPower	.027	.667	.002	1	.967	1.028	.278	3.801
Grouds	−.028	.071	.153	1	.696	.972	.846	1.118
Gen	.616	1.157	.284	1	.594	1.852	.192	17.879
Age	−.463	.265	3.051	1	.081	.629	.374	1.058
Ethnicity	.189	.471	.161	1	.688	1.208	.480	3.040
Reasons	.091	.247	.135	1	.713	1.095	.674	1.779
Constant	−4.105	1.417	8.391	1	.004	.016		

Table 3.3 Chi-square tests

	Value	*df*	*Asymp. Sig. (2-sided)*	*Exact Sig. (2-sided)*	*Exact Sig. (1-sided)*
Pearson Chi-square	137.654[a]	1	.000		
Continuity Correction[b]	136.607	1	.000		
Likelihood Ratio	108.982	1	.000		
Fisher's Exact Test				.000	.000
Linear-by-Linear Association	137.654	1	.000		
N of Valid Cases	1018438				

variables on the occurrence of stop-and-search encounters, suggesting that individuals from Black, Asian, and Mixed ethnicity groups are more prone to being stopped and searched compared to White individuals.

Additionally, a chi-square test of independence was conducted to examine whether ethnicity influences the probability of an individual being subjected to stop-and-search encounters. This test aimed to obtain whether there is a statistically significant association between being (i) a member of Black, Asian, and Mixed communities and (ii) being searched by police. Where the degree of freedom was one with $\alpha = 0.01$, the null hypothesis is that search rates are independent of race, and the alternative hypothesis is that search rates are not independent of race. It was revealed that $p < 0.005$ indicates there is a relationship between belonging to the Black, Asian, and Mixed communities and the likelihood of being searched. Table 3.3 shows the results of the chi-square tests.

Furthermore, the search rates were compared with population statistics (obtained via the Office for National Statistics, 2011). Table 3.4 shows that those individuals belonging to Black, Asian, and Mixed communities

Table 3.4 Risk estimate of being searched and belonging to the BAME group

	Value	*95% Confidence Interval*	
		Lower	*Upper*
Odds Ratio for Ethnicity (BAME / REST POP)	.470	.414	.535
For cohort Search = NO	.998	.997	.998
For cohort Search = Yes	2.121	1.865	2.412
N of Valid Cases	1018438		

were found to have a 2.12 times higher likelihood of being searched compared to the rest of the population in the area covered by the constabulary.

Phase 2

The purpose of phase 2 was to explore the officers' views, in order to answer the following questions:

- What constitutes an effective stop-and-search encounter?
- What is the basis for suspicion and what factors make officers decide whom to stop and search?
- To what extent do officers use stereotypes to develop suspicion in stop-and-searches decision-making?

Participants and procedures

Interviews can yield rich insights into peoples' experiences, opinions, attitudes, and feelings. In the present study, the author employed semi-structured interviews, providing the officers with the opportunity to develop and elaborate on their experiences and ideas qualitatively. The open-ended nature of the questions allowed officers to freely discuss topics related to the questions asked and, in many cases, these diversions provided valuable insights and fostered a strong rapport between the author and the officers. The author interviewed a range of police officers from each division of the police force, concentrating mainly on patrol officers. These interviews include a wide variety of ages, backgrounds, and lengths of service, in order to cover a variety of police tasks and experience. While the data collected may not present a complete picture, it does offer a valid insight into the decision-making process of police officers as they conduct stop-and-search encounters, along with the various contexts that influence these decisions.

During September–December 2015, the author undertook interviews with 20 officers (17 of whom were males). The police organisation designated the responsibility of providing officers for interviews to one of the on-duty sergeants. The sergeant had preselected police officers from all the divisions across the police force and provided a timetable for them to be interviewed. All the participants were frontline patrolling officers and had experience in conducting stop-and-searches. Their experience ranged from one to 22 years (M = 8.88 years, SD = 4.96 years) and ages ranged from 23 to 56 years (M = 36.47, SD = 8.68). The interviews were conducted in the most private available space in the police station. Each interview had an approximate duration of 40 minutes. The researcher began all interviews by asking for demographic information such as age, sex, self-defined ethnicity, rank, and length of time in the force. Each officer was asked the same standardised set of questions during the interviews. However, when required, the author offered elaboration and clarification to ensure a comprehensive understanding of the responses.

To ensure the anonymity of all participants, each interview was assigned a numerical code, and the responses were kept confidential throughout the entire process. The officers' names and badge numbers were not taken to maintain anonymity. Additionally, the author offered the option for officers to receive a letter containing this information to take away if they desired to do so. All the officers provided consent to record interviews. Furthermore, to protect the anonymity of participants, audacity software was used to alter their voices during the interviews. After each interview, the author immediately transferred the voice recording to the password-protected laptop computer before leaving the police station. Subsequently, the recording was wiped from the digital voice recorder (DVR) to ensure the data's security and confidentiality. Transcripts were prepared for each interview, and these formed the basis for the examination and analysis of the data.

Qualitative data analysis

In order to examine the semi-structured interviews, the present research employed a thematic analysis of interview transcriptions. One of the benefits of thematic analysis is its theoretical freedom, and it can be either inductive (data-driven) (Boyatzis, 1998) or deductive (theory-driven) (Crabtree & Miller, 1999). The thematic analysis sets itself apart from other qualitative analytical methods by focusing on identifying and interpreting themes within the data rather than merely searching for patterns (Braun & Clarke, 2006). For example, thematic analysis differs from thematic discourse analysis (Potter & Wetherell, 1987), grounded theory

(GT) (Glaser & Strauss, 1967; Strauss & Corbin, 1997), and interpretative phenomenological analysis (IPA) (Smith & Osborn, 2007). Both IPA and GT seek patterns in the data. According to Braun and Clarke (2006), IPA as proposed by Smith and Osborn (2007) is primarily focused on the analysis of participants' experiences. This method is theoretically bound to phenomenology, meaning it aims to explore and interpret the lived experiences of participants from their own perspectives. On the other hand, GT, introduced by Strauss and Corbin (1997), is used to analyse participants' experiences as well, but it differs in its theoretical approach. GT does not adhere to a specific theoretical framework from the outset; instead, it aims to generate or develop a plausible theory of the phenomena based on patterns and concepts that emerge from the data itself (i.e. grounded in the data). In contrast to GT and IPA, 'thematic analysis is a method which is not wedded to any prior theoretical framework, as such it can be utilised within different theoretical frameworks, and to do different things within them' (Braun & Clarke, 2006, p. 82). Given that the thematic analysis does not require detailed theoretical knowledge of approaches such as IPA and GT, it can offer a more open form of analysis (Braun & Clarke, 2006).

The thematic analysis also gives a platform for the clear and straightforward definition of the theoretical position a study adopts in its approach to analysing its data (Braun & Clarke, 2006). The method of analysis chosen for the present study was inductive thematic analysis, also known as data-driven thematic analysis, as proposed by Boyatzis (1998). An inductive approach includes identifying themes that are strongly connected to the data itself. Therefore, inductive analysis is a procedure for coding the data without trying to fit it into a pre-existing coding frame (Boyatizis, 1998). In the present study, the codes were accordingly inductive, originating from the participants' theoretical and practical understandings concerning stop-and-search practices (Miles & Huberman, 1994). By employing inductive thematic analysis, the author not only identified the components of effective stop-and-search encounters but also examined the factors that influence officers' decisions to conduct such searches. Accordingly, in the present research, the inductive analysis took a semantic or explicit approach (Boyatzis, 1998). That is, the themes were identified from the 'explicit or surface meaning of data' (Braun & Clarke, 2006, p. 84).

The first step of the analysis included an initial reading of the interview transcriptions. This step was important to gain familiarity with the content and understand the context of the interviews before delving deeper into the thematic analysis. In the second reading, a line-by-line coding was undertaken to ascribe each sentence a code that described the main essence of the sentence. This coding process helped in organising the data and identifying meaningful units of information, laying the foundation for further thematic analysis. In the current research, the data were coded following the guidelines for conducting thematic analysis developed by Braun and Clarke (2006). Firstly, all the data were coded, and codes were merged into larger units organising those that seemed similar in meaning content. This process allowed for the organisation and grouping of related codes, which formed the basis for identifying potential themes and patterns in the data. This was followed by sorting the different codes into potential themes and collating all the relevant coded data extracts within the identified themes and subthemes for each interview transcription. In the current study, a theme was defined as the smallest meaningful unit that could effectively express and encapsulate the codes included within it. From the individual summary sheets, an overall list of themes was constructed. Themes were refined and grouped into clusters to form the following superordinate themes: (i) what constitutes an effective stop-and-search encounter; (ii) the basis for suspicion; (iii) the use of stereotypes in stop-and-searches decision making; and (iv) possible factors playing a role in disproportionality.

Inter-rater reliability

Following the coding process of interview transcripts, a PhD researcher (with an established knowledge of thematic analysis) coded a randomly selected half of the interview transcripts. This rater worked with clean copies of transcripts independently, having no knowledge of the author's coding results. An examination of the inter-rater reliability for identifying all themes revealed a Cohen's kappa of .90 between the two sets of scores, signifying a robust level of agreement (Fleiss, 1981).

Results

Thematic analysis of the interview transcripts was conducted to identify themes emerging from the answers to questions and subsequent contributions made by officers. The findings are discussed and presented under these main themes:

I. What constitutes an effective stop-and-search encounter.
II. The basis for suspicion.
III. The use of stereotypes (generalisations) in stop-and-searches decision-making.
IV. The possible factors playing any role in disproportionality.

An analytical narrative was constructed, and extracts from the transcripts are now presented to illustrate each of the above four themes.

What constitutes an effective stop-and-search encounter?

All police officers who participated in the current study were asked about their understanding of an effective stop-and-search encounter based on their experience. According to their views, a stop-and-search encounter is effective when it meets the following criteria:

a) *Definable suspicious behaviour.* Ninety per cent of participants (n = 18) reported that their decision to conduct a stop-and-search is more effective when it is grounded in identifiable suspicious behaviour, as outlined in the PACE Act (1984) Code A.
b) *Guided by up-to-date operational intelligence* (e.g. focused on active and more serious offenders, local crime trends, and specific crime hotspots). Ninety per cent of the participants (n = 18) stated that their decision to conduct a search is more effective when the grounds for a stop-and-search encounter are based on current operational intelligence.
c) *Carried out in a respectable manner.* All 20 participants reported that a stop-and-search encounter which is carried out respectably with a clear explanation of the reason for a stop-and-search would significantly enhance public confidence.
d) *Carried out in the context of police–community relations and cooperation.* Eighty-five per cent of participants (n = 17) reported that an effective stop-and-search encounter is one which is carried out in the context of police–community relations and cooperation.

Bases for suspicion—factors that make officers decide whom to stop and search

Officers stated they generally stop and search someone whom they suspect of committing or being likely to commit a crime. In this regard, the police officers identified three factors that could trigger their suspicion and potentially result in a stop-and-search encounter. These factors are (i) appearance; (ii) behaviour; and (iii) time and place. Each of these factors will now be examined.

APPEARANCE

During the interviews, 15 of the participants (75 per cent) stated that their suspicion might be prompted if a person appears young. For example, participant (20) stated,

> I would say its White males from 17 to 30-ish. I would say 99 per cent are in that age group because they're the ones that are committing, from where I work, the drug offences, the shoplifting offences. I mean, yes, you are going to go slightly above that age bracket, but there aren't [...] it's very far and few between that are above that. So, if it is above that age range, then I'd say it's probably more shop theft than drug offences.

Also, 13 (65 per cent) of these participants mentioned that individuals wearing a baseball cap or going 'hooded-up' or wearing two sets of dark clothes at night might also attract their attention. There was a sense among these participants that young people wearing dark clothes during the night could be trying to make themselves harder to see. For example, participant (09) described the following:

> I have had instances before where you have got youths, about 16, 17-year-olds that are wearing two sets of clothing, one over the other, dark clothes, dead at night, the only reason why they are doing that is so they can discard that top clothing and having different clothing underneath.

Another participant stated,

> Probably young White males, late [...] well, I say mid-teens to early twenties probably, yes, probably from 14, 15 upwards to around, yes, early twenties are predominately the main ones.

Twelve of the participants (60 per cent) stated that they would stop and search an individual who is previously known to the police if they located him in a crime hotspot. For example, participant (17) stated,

> I probably would stop him, very likely to stop him. If it's a drug hot-spot, then it gives me more grounds to actually go and speak to the person and also carry out a search to see whether that person is actually carrying [...] because if he's known to me to carry drugs previously, then that gives me reasonable grounds to actually stop and search him to see whether he is actually carrying any substance or drugs.

Another participant (04) stated,

> I'd stop and speak to them at the very least, yes, and want to know why they are where they are and then again take it from there really and see how they are with it. If they give you a story as to why they are there, but at the same time appear nervous, or they cannot keep eye contact

> with you, you know, just sometimes you think this doesn't seem quite right, you know, what is he doing here? He does not live around here. There is no purpose for him being here, then, yes, I probably would search him.

However, in contrast, for the remaining eight participants (40 per cent), simply being known to the police was not a good enough reason for them to stop and search an individual. These participants indicated that they would need reasonable suspicion to act at that moment, such as observed offending or fresh and up-to-date intelligence. For example, participant (15) described this by saying,

> Previously known to me or police would not make any difference to me, just because they are known, and they are on a crime hotspot, that would not be enough for me to have reasonable grounds to suspect. I would need more information than that.

BEHAVIOUR

During the interviews, 14 of the participants (70 per cent) stated that the behaviour of an individual is the primary reason for their decision to stop and search someone. For instance, one participant (1) stated,

> I would have to look, if it's a high crime area looking at the intelligence we have had, if there's been a lot of burglaries, what sort of clothing they are wearing at that time of night, if it's black, they have got gloves on and its summer. I would be looking for stuff that's out of character to what you would class as, I would say normal, but it's not I suppose the correct word, but the average person would be doing at that time of night at that time at that place.

These participants stated that they might stop and search people who are seen 'loitering', 'looking into cars', 'looking into gardens', or 'checking locks'. For example, participant (11) stated,

> Well, if they are like going up and down people's driveways at that time in the morning or they are looking in people's cars, they are looking in car windows, or they are going along trying car door handles and that sort of thing, to me that's suspicious. There's no other reason why they are doing that rather than to find an opportunity to either try and steal something from within or look.

Participants also referred to 'suspicious behaviour' as 'furtive' or 'elusive' behaviour and described it in a number of ways, such as (i) avoiding being seen (hiding face, looking away, driving off); (ii) running away on seeing officers; and (iii) attempting to hide objects in the surrounding area or throwing away something. For instance, participant (19) stated,

> If I was to see somebody loitering, looking like they were doing something, and they were hiding something as they see me approach, you know, then that could arouse my suspicions. Turning their back towards me could arouse my suspicions.

Another, participant (04), stated,

> It bears nothing on who gets stopped. If somebody is looking suspicious it makes no difference whether they are Black, White, Asian, Chinese, or whatever, you know. It's merely the person, the circumstances rather than what ethnicity they are or sex or whatever. If anybody that will be acting in a suspicious manner is equally [...] could arouse my suspicions.

However, six of the participants (30 per cent) stated that 'suspicious behaviour' such as 'furtive' or 'elusive' behaviour is irrelevant to their decision to stop and search someone. For instance, participant (07) stated,

> If you looked away, why would I consider that to be suspicious, because you may not like police, you know, you may be looking round to catch the bus. If I am walking towards you in uniform, for example, you could be looking around for a bus; I would not say that's suspicious. I would not stop someone on such basis.

Half of the participants expressed that the 'stop-and-search form' is too small and does not allow them to provide a comprehensive account of the 'suspicious behaviour' or fully explain the background of the stop-and-search encounter. For instance, participant (05) described this in the following way:

> Part of our issue is we have a very small form to write the details on. We have a very small thing to write that on, and we send that off to our supervisor who signs it, who then sends it off to an administrator who puts the details onto the computer system. How it used to happen was, we would put the details on the computer system, but you have only got a box really small to fill it out, so when we put it on the computer

> system we really ought to explain all the background behind it, you know, what have we seen. But, when you have got two lines, you can literally write seen acting suspiciously.

TIME AND PLACE

Fifteen of the participants (75 per cent) stated that the time and place in their decision-making process concerning stop-and-search encounters was either of medium or high priority. These participants relied on their knowledge of a particular location and what activities should or should not be expected after a particular time to form a suspicion. For instance, participant (13) stated,

> It's a, like you say, notorious place in the city that it's just known for drug use or drug possession, somebody's there, three o'clock in the morning on their own, to me, yes, I have got reasonable suspicion that you may have something on you, and to me, I would search you.

Another participant (15) stated,

> I think if it was somebody that was known and they were not near to their home address at three o'clock in the morning, I think they would be at the very least asked to account for why they were where they were, because you and I would not be found a mile and a half from our home address at three in the morning walking the streets, why are you here? At the very least whether or not, they'll be searched or not, they'll be asked to say what you are doing here, you know.

However, for the remaining 25 per cent of participants, time and place were irrelevant in their decision-making to stop and search someone and whether they informed suspicion. For instance, participant (10) stated,

> No, not because of a particular time or location, because he is not doing anything, you know, unfortunately, people do walk around [...] you know, in my area where I work that's a little stranger because you don't find people walking around at three o'clock in the morning, on those circumstances I would not feel comfortable to search him. It's quite difficult because I tend to find reasonable suspicion to be quite a high threshold test.

Use of stereotypes in stop-and-search decision-making

According to the PACE Code of Practice (1984), the decision to stop and search must be based on objective information relating to a specific individual suspected of involvement in a specific offence at a specific time. In other words, that decision cannot be based on a generalised belief that a particular group of people are more likely to be involved in crime. Thirteen of the participants (65 per cent) stated a number of stereotypes they use when making a decision about whom to stop and search. These stereotypes include factors like dress, age, employment status, and being present in crime hotspots. For example, as participant (19) described this,

> They are usually the ones that really [...] because they are the ones that will come in, or they are the ones that will try and float it a bit because they have got this sort of mentality that they can get away with anything. The older you get, the more, sort of, cautious you are being and stuff like that. So, yes, I would say 16 to 20.

Another participant (02) described this in the following way:

> So, for me, the main people that I would be looking and doing stop searching out at night are going to probably be White, the early twenties, early thirties, unemployed, usually people of substance abuse that are out stealing for a reason, to fund their other problems in life.

Furthermore, another participant (12) stated,

> In relation to unemployed, if you are looking at people that are, sort of, career criminals, the ones that are known to us, the ones that may potentially be stopped more often because they are out there, let's say a known burglar, chances are they will be unemployed because burglarising is their job. So, you may say potentially that you are stopping more unemployed people.

Possible factors playing a role in disproportionality

Suspect descriptions usually come from information from the general public, witnesses, or victims, and are either passed directly to patrolling officers or more widely through police command and control systems. During the interviews, 60 per cent of the participants (n = 12) indicated that a description of a suspected offender should not be treated as a straightforward form of information. More importantly, four participants stated that poor or vaguely described information about an offender's description could be attributed to the possible causes of disproportionality, as suspected offenders' descriptions mainly focused on ethnicity and clothing. For instance, participant (11) stated,

> Well, I think from my own experience I could probably count the number of Black people I have searched on one hand, from my own experience. I act on the information that I am given, and I do not care whether Black, White, Asian, or whatever, if that person matches the description that's passed to me on the radio of a crime that's just happened, then I will search if I have got the grounds, you know. If I have seen the person acting suspiciously and by grounds, then, yes, I don't care what colour they are. I don't know why you know.

Another participant (07) stated,

> Yes, it's a very, very, very White area and so, for example, if I have a report where they say a Black male has burgled a property or a Black male has drugs on him and I, for example, two minutes later find a Black person around the corner, I am going to search that Black person and I'll tell him why he's being searched and what have you. Whereas, obviously, if it's a White person and that's all I have got, it's more difficult for me to pinpoint the White person, and it's almost like a [...] whether it's right or wrong, it's almost like scale, the scale of the population if you know what I mean in the area, so ....

Furthermore, another participant (18) described this in the following way:

> If it was they reported it was a large White male and I drive past three large White males, I am less likely to stop those three large White males before I get to the home address. If I see a large Black male, they have reported a large Black male, and it's the only one I see, I am likely to stop him purely just to stop encounter we used to call it, to talk to while someone goes and gets the details at the address. That might be why they are disproportionately stopped, particularly if they are in sort of predominantly White areas.

Twelve participants (60 per cent) stated that they would not target people from ethnic minorities. However, one participant (20) stated that Black ethnic minorities are perceived to be involved in drug use and drug dealing, suggesting, however, such a notion did inform his judgement and decision-making. He described his thinking in this way:

> I would suggest that predominantly drug use and drug dealing is part of the Black minority. It's just how [...] it's how it's perceived in society, I think, that's my honest opinion as for how it's perceived in society, and that's me, that's what I think. I would say so, yes, because like I say, it's predominantly Black ethnic minorities that will be drug dealers. That's

my opinion because that's how it's perceived and that's how it's shown to you. I think that just gets into your mind. It gets into other people's minds as well.

Discussion

The present study sought to examine whether police officers rely on stereotypes to inform their suspicions while carrying out stop-and-searches. The analyses of recorded stop-and-search data sets revealed that stop-and-search powers are disproportionality weighted against Black, Asian, and Mixed communities. Further, it was revealed in the data set of stop-and-search records that officers rely on stereotypes to inform their suspicions (e.g. the individual being previously known to the police, or their being in a known crime hotspot). The analyses of research interviews indicated that people's age, appearance, their being known to the police, their location, and social class play a role when officers make decisions about whom to stop and search. The stereotypes identified in the analyses of the interview transcripts were triangulated with the grounds for searches reported in the data set by officers. These findings suggest a relationship between specific stereotypes (i.e. young people on the street in deprived areas as potential criminals) and the formation of suspicion (being seen in a particular location at a particular time). These findings are aligned with the previous research (e.g. Quinton, 2011), which indicated that such stereotypes play a critical role in decision-making processes, leading to a focus by the police on socially marginalised groups.

The analyses of interview transcripts revealed that a quarter of the participants expressed their preference for requiring reasonable suspicion before acting. They emphasised that they would need reasonable suspicions before stopping anyone (such as either observed offending or possessing up-to-date intelligence on the individual, rather than relying on stereotypes based, say, on someone's age, employment status, or location). This finding suggests that among these officers, reasonable suspicion is subject to a high threshold test (which is also in line with the PACE legislation in England and Wales, concerning when to conduct stop-and-searches). However, in cases where officers were observed heavily relying on stereotypes to inform their suspicions, they appeared to be using their powers under this legislation in ways that could be deemed unlawful and discriminatory. That is, according to the PACE (1984), individual officers and their supervisors are legally obliged to base their decision to stop and search on reasonable suspicion that the concerned individual has committed or is about to commit, a particular offence. Therefore, it is considered unlawful to target individuals solely based on officers' generalised beliefs. In the data set of documented records 367 searches appeared to be conducted on the grounds of 'an individual being previously known to the police' (n = 198) or 'being in a known crime hotspot' (n = 169). This finding aligns with the views expressed by officers during the interviews conducted by the author. The officers acknowledged that such generalisations are vital to their decision-making process when it comes to determining whom to stop and search. Although stereotypes that associate crime with age, location, time, and appearance may occasionally provide useful leads to stop someone, there is a potential risk that individuals who do not warrant police attention may also be identified as suspicious. This can be a major cause of public resentment towards the police (Quinton, 2011).

By contrast, one-quarter of police officers stated that suspicious behaviour or elusive behaviour is irrelevant in their decision to stop and search someone. Conversely, three-quarters of the police officers the author interviewed said that they relied on people's suspicious behaviour as the primary grounds to conduct stop-and-searches. Over two-thirds of these officers described suspicious behaviour in various ways, indicating that they had diverse criteria or indicators for determining what they considered as suspicious concerning the decision-making process during stop-and-searches (e.g. individuals running away or hiding their face after seeing officers). These findings are also triangulated with the data set of documented records of stop-and-search. In this context, 310 searches were stated to have been conducted when 'suspicious activity' appeared to have been observed. Similarly, once an officer forms cues of suspicion based on generalised beliefs, schemas, or preconceived notions about actions or individuals that they perceive as not fitting the environment or situation, they may proceed to act upon those cues and stop the individual in question. Although in many circumstances, such cues may indeed be reasonable, they have often been found to be linked to issues of ethnicity. This connection raises concerns about the potential for racial or ethnic profiling during stop-and-search practices (Alpert et al., 2005). As such, suspicions developed from a cognitive schema may be more ones of supposition, but not necessarily ones concerning the actual behaviours or actions of people. Such perceptions may lead to officers undertaking racial profiling, which has the effect of creating a cycle of profiling of suspected offenders (irrespective of the accuracy of these negative perceptions) (Delsol, 2015).

Furthermore, the present study revealed that the recorded grounds for stop-and-search in the documentary records examined by the author lacked sufficient detail, particularly concerning information that would have been known to police officers. This lack of comprehensive information may raise questions about the transparency and accuracy of stop-and-search procedures. For instance, more than 75 per cent of police officers reported the place of stop (being known as a crime hotspot), the time of day or night it occurred, or the age of the person stopped as their justification for grounds of search, but these criteria were only found cited in 9 per cent of the documentary data set. Similarly, 75 per cent of police officers advised that people's suspicious behaviour would prompt a stop-and-search, yet these reasons were cited by just 15 per cent as grounds for searches in the documented data set.

Indeed, this latter finding suggests that officers might be unconsciously relying on stereotypes to a greater extent than they realise. The discrepancies between their reported justifications for stop-and-search and the actual documented grounds raise the possibility that implicit biases and stereotypes may be influencing their decision-making processes. Such a situation may well mean that the searches that have been conducted by the police were based either on insufficient grounds (where grounds are limited and questionable in legal terms), or there is a tendency to record fewer details concerning the grounds for their stop-and-search than were present at the time (which indicates that an inadequate explanation of the reasons for a search is being recorded). Either explanation reflects a most unsatisfactory situation. During Phase 2 of the present study, when the author asked for clarity regarding the lack of details in the documentary data concerning stop-and-search grounds, over half of the officers pointed out that the stop-and-search form, which needs to be manually completed at the time of the stop-and-search, is too small. They emphasised that the limited space on the form does not allow them adequate room to fully explain the grounds for the search. As a result, crucial information that could provide context and transparency may be omitted due to this constraint. Nevertheless, officers did not offer (what is thought as) rather simple solutions to this problem, such as turning the form over to record full details on its other (blank) side (or entering such information in their pocketbooks). This might reflect a malaise concerning the lack of necessary attention to maintaining comprehensive records. Regardless, failure to record specific details and refer to all the available direct and indirect evidence poses significant risks to the legality (PACE, 1984) and the effectiveness of searches. It also undermines public confidence in policing (Quinton et al., 2000). Furthermore, these findings suggest that reasonable grounds for suspicion were frequently not followed, indicating an over-reliance on the use of stereotypes, which has been previously documented in the literature (i.e. Quinton et al., 2000; Quinton, 2011).

The analyses of both the documentary data sets and the transcriptions of the interviews revealed that officers also relied heavily on their knowledge of specific locations to form their suspicions. They considered what activities should or should not be expected at a particular time of day in those locations. This suggests that officers' familiarity with the areas they patrol plays a significant role in shaping their perceptions and decision-making processes to inform suspicions concerning stop-and-searches.

Officers' perceptions concerning crime hotspots may lead them to believe that people in that particular area are engaged in criminal activity, which may pose a threat to police–community relations (Weisburd et al., 2011). Indeed, deploying police resources in hotspot areas can be an effective strategy to disrupt criminal activity to a certain extent. However, such deployments may affect how police officers interact with the residents of that area, threatening police–community relations and thus the effectiveness of community policing strategies (Quinton, 2011). Chainey and Macdonald (2012) found that stop-and-searches conducted in crime hotspots had a significant impact on police officers' perceptions and actions. It made the officers more suspicious of people in that area in general, and this suspicion led to an increase in police-initiated actions, such as conducting more stop-and-searches. At the same time, a benefit that emerges from the policing of crime hotspots is that it can provide the police with important contextual information that might help them develop enhanced justifications for a search. Furthermore, continuous reminders during daily briefings that hotspot policing must not influence how officers behave and interact with the members of the particular area can be an essential step in reducing negative stop-and-searches. By emphasising the importance of fairness, professionalism, and respect in all interactions with the public, regardless of the location, law enforcement agencies can mitigate the potential for biased or discriminatory practices. Consistent reinforcement of these principles can help foster a culture of accountability and ensure that officers are mindful of the impact their actions may have on community trust and confidence.

One of the interesting findings of the present study was police officers' perceptions of the correlation between disproportionality and the descriptions of reported offenders. Officers emphasised that the issue of disproportionality might be related to inadequate and inaccurate information concerning such descriptions as these details primarily centred around ethnicity and clothing. Most of the officers expressed the need to define the essential components of a 'suspected offender' description for operational purposes. A description fitting that of a reported offender can inform direct evidence (Quinton, 2011). If the description of the suspected offender is vague, inaccurate, or originates from an unreliable source, suspicions may be based on tenuous grounds (which may result in the stop-and-search of innocent people) (Bowling & Phillips, 2007). For instance, when there is insufficient and inaccurate information regarding the description of a reported offender, with a primary focus on ethnicity and clothing (when combined with an officer's pre-existing cues of suspicion based on generalised beliefs), this may arguably lead to individuals being subjected to stop-and-searches based on their social class and ethnicity. During the interviews, officers stated that in cases where they receive inadequate information about a reported offender, they tend to blend such details with their pre-existing assumptions related to their generalised beliefs and the suspect's ethnicity. These generalised beliefs, specifically those based on ethnicity, may become activated during the decision-making process. Once activated, these stereotypes influence relevant decisions concerning suspects' perceived culpability. This implies that the combination of focusing on ethnicity, along with pre-existing generalised beliefs, may inevitably lead to young individuals from disadvantaged backgrounds and ethnic minority communities being disproportionately targeted by the police for stop-and-search. Indeed, acknowledging the significance of accurate and reliable information regarding the description of a reported offender, it is important for future studies to investigate whether vague or inaccurate descriptions of suspects contribute to disproportionality in stop-and-search statistics.

These negative stereotypes were found to be present in both the stop-and-search data set and in the interviews when officers carry out searches. Previous research studies (e.g. Hall et al., 1998; Loftus, 2009) have identified that stereotypes (e.g. suspicion based on age, location, and social class) are perpetuated and upheld through informal police work routines, which can be problematic as they reinforce the perception that certain groups are more likely to be involved in specific crimes. Interestingly, only those stereotypes which are associated with a suspect's race, however, have been consistently mentioned in all prior studies within the context of stop-and-search (e.g. Bowling & Phillips, 2007; Bradford, 2017; Quinton, 2011; Shiner & Delsol, 2015; Young, 1994). If these stereotypes are recognised as consistent indicators of disproportionality in stop-and-search statistics, it suggests that racial stereotypes alone may be sufficient to influence an officer's decision-making process.

Limitations

In this convenience sample of police officers, the police served as gatekeepers, facilitating access to the participants for the study. Nevertheless, the interviews were carried out with police officers from various units within this police force, offering a valuable snapshot of their decision-making processes when conducting searches (and also of the contexts in which these decisions take place). The findings from both the force's data set and the interviews may also be affected by the author's unconscious biases. However, a strong level of inter-rater agreement was found, which suggests that such biases were not evident (James, Demaree, & Wolf, 1984). Police officers' responses during the interviews may have been affected by their training and their awareness regarding the highly sensitive issue of disproportionality in stop-and-search figures. As a result, their responses might well be a case of their either attempting 'impression management' (Schoderbek & Deshpande, 1996) or providing socially desirable answers (Zerbe & Paulhus, 1987).

Conclusions

The current research revealed that officers use stereotypes to inform their suspicions. These stereotypes encompass various factors such as age, appearance, being someone known to the police, location, and social class. This suggests a potential link between prejudicial stereotypes and the formation of suspicion. The use of prejudicial stereotypes is, undoubtedly, of concern, as it can lead officers to develop the belief that people from a particular area, or a certain ethnicity are engaged in a particular criminal activity. This perception could potentially pose a threat to police–community relations (Weisburd et al., 2011). The impact of stereotypes, as such, is to mark out the limits between 'them' and 'us' (Tajfel, 2010). The disproportional use of stop-and-search powers reflects a collective pattern of police culture and practice (Reiner, 2010). The present study highlights that the use of prejudicial stereotypes to inform suspicion could be seen in various aspects of the police culture, including processes, attitudes, and beliefs. As such, these stereotypes operate unconsciously but persist consistently over time, being transmitted and upheld through informal work routines (Hall et al., 1998). Research studies (e.g. Graham & Lowery, 2004; Minhas & Walsh, 2018) have revealed that negative stereotypes, particularly those related to a suspect's race, can influence officers' decision-making processes during investigations. This influence might lead to varying outcomes in criminal investigations when the suspects involved belong to different ethnic groups, highlighting the potential for bias in criminal investigations. The findings from both the current study and previous research (e.g. Bowling & Phillips, 2007; Bradford, 2017; Quinton, 2011; Shiner & Delsol, 2015; Young, 1994) indicate that negative stereotypes could play a significant role as a potential contributing factor to the disproportionate number of Black, Asian, and Mixed communities in stop-and-search statistics. This suggests a concerning connection between negative stereotypes and the over-representation of certain ethnic groups in law enforcement practices such as stop-and-search. The findings of the current study underscore the need for significant efforts to ensure fairness and reduce disproportionality in stop-and-search practices. It indicates that there are still considerable challenges ahead in addressing bias and creating more equitable law enforcement procedures. Recognising the influence of prejudicial stereotypes within the context of disproportionality in stop-and-searches might well be a starting point for a more transparent and effective policing This awareness can pave the way for meaningful reforms and improved police–community relations.

The following chapter will build upon these findings by exploring their implications within the context of criminal investigations. It aims to investigate how these prejudicial stereotypes might impact the way investigative interviews are conducted with suspects from stigmatised communities. By examining this aspect, the chapter seeks to shed light on the potential biases that could arise during interviews and their potential consequences for the overall investigative process. This investigation is essential for identifying areas of improvement in police practices and fostering more equitable treatment of suspects, regardless of their background or community affiliation.

Note

1 Non-Police Personnel (NPP) Level 1 Vetting: Confidential security vetting checks are carried out on all applicants for posts working for or with Constabulary. The checks comply with the standards laid out by Association of Chief Police Officers National Vetting Policy and Home Office guidelines to determine whether the candidate represents a risk to the assets of the Force or the Police Service as a whole.

References

Alpert, G.P., MacDonald, J.M. & Dunham, R.G. (2005). Police suspicion and discretionary decision making during citizen stops. *Criminology,* 43(2), pp. 407–434.

Baldwin, R. & Kinsey, R. (1982). *Police powers and politics.* UK: Quartet Books.

Bland, N., Miller, J. & Quinton, P. (2000). *Upping the PACE?: An Evaluation of the Recommendations of the Stephen Lawrence Inquiry on Stops and Searches.* London: Home Office, Policing and Reducing Crime Unit, Research, Development and Statistics Directorate.

Bowling, B. (2018). Pulled over: how police stops define race and citizenship. *Policing and Society*, 28(5), 626–629.

Bowling, B. & Phillips, C. (2007). Disproportionate and discriminatory: reviewing the evidence on police stop and search. *Modern Law Review,* 70(6), pp.936–961.

Bowling, B., & Weber, L. (2011). Stop and search in global context: an overview. *Policing and Society*, 21, 480–488.

Boyatzis, R.E. (1998). *Transforming qualitative information: Thematic analysis and code development.* California: Sage Publications

Bradford, B. (2017). *Stop and Search and Police Legitimacy* (Vol. 42). London, UK: Taylor & Francis.

Braun, V. & Clarke, V. (2006). Using thematic analysis in psychology. *Qualitative Research in Psychology*, 3(2), pp.77–101.

Brown, D. (1997). *PACE Ten Years On: A Review of the Research.* London: HMSO.

Cain, M.E. (2015). *Society and the Policeman's Role.* London: Routledge.
Chainey, S., & Macdonald, I. (2012). *Stop and search, the use of intelligence and geographic targeting: Findings from case study research.* London: National Policing Improvement Agency.
Crabtree, B.F. & Miller, W.L. eds. (1999). *Doing qualitative research.* California: Sage publications.
De Gobineau, A. (1853). *Essay on the Inequality of the Human Races. The Idea of Race.* Hackett, Indianapolis.
Delsol, R. (2015). Racial profiling. *Criminal Justice Matters*, 101, 34–35.
DeMuth, C. (1978). *'Sus' a Report on the Vagrancy Act 1824.* London: Runnymede Trust.
Dixon, D. (1997). *Law in policing: legal regulation and police practices.* Oxford: Clarendon.
Dixon, D., Bottomley, A.K., Coleman, C.A., Gill, M. & Wall, D. (1989). Reality and rules in the construction and regulation of police suspicion. *International Journal of the Sociology of Law*, 17: pp. 185–206.
Dixon, D., Bottomley, K., Coleman, C., Gill, M. & Wall, D. (1990). Safeguarding the rights of suspects in police custody. *Policing and Society: An International Journal,* 1(2), pp.115–140.
Equality and Human Rights Commission, EHRC (2010). *Stop and think: A critical review of the use of stop and search powers in England and Wales.* London: EHRC.
Ekstrom, P. D., Le Forestier, J. M., & Lai, C. K. (2022). Racial demographics explain the link between racial disparities in traffic stops and county-level racial attitudes. *Psychological Science,* 33(4), 497–509.
FitzGerald, M. (1999). *Final report into stop and search.* London: Home Office.
Fleiss, J.L. (1981). Balanced incomplete block designs for inter-rater reliability studies. *Applied Psychological Measurement,* 5(1), pp.105–112.
Glaser, B., & Strauss, A. (1967). *The discovery of grounded theory.* Chicago: Aldine de Gruyter.
Graef, R. (1989). *Talking blues: the police in their own words.* Collins Harvill.
Graham, S. & Lowery, B.S. (2004). Priming unconscious racial stereotypes about adolescent offenders. *Law and Human Behavior,* 28(5), pp. 483.
Hall, S., McLaughlin, E. & Lewis, G. (1998). *Racial stereotyping in the police: statement on research on racial attitudes and stereotyping*, Report prepared for Deighton Guedalla Solicitors. Milton Keynes: Open University.
HMIC. (2013). Stop and search powers: Are the police using them effectively and fairly? London: HMIC.
HMIC. (2015). Stop and search powers 2: Are the police using them effectively and fairly? London: HMIC.
Home Office. (1999). *Stephen Lawrence Inquiry: Home Secretary's action plan.* London: Home Office
Home Office. (2003). *Statistics on Race and the Criminal Justice System 2002: A Home Office Publication under Section 95 of the Criminal Justice Act 1991.* London: Home Office.

Home Office. (2006). *Statistics on Race and the Criminal Justice System 2005: A Home Office Publication under Section 95 of the Criminal Justice Act 1991.* London: Home Office.

James, L.R., Demaree, R.G. & Wolf, G. (1984). Estimating within-group interrater reliability with and without response bias. *Journal of Applied Psychology*, 69(1), p.85.

Jefferson, T. & Walker, M.A. (1993). Attitudes to the police of ethnic minorities in a provincial city. *British Journal of Criminology*, 33(2), pp. 251–266.

Kleinig, J. (1996). *The ethics of policing.* Cambridge: Cambridge University Press.

Loftus, B. (2009). *Police culture in a changing world.* New York: Oxford University Press.

Lustgarten, L. (2002). The future of stop and search. Criminal Law Review. London 603–618.

Macpherson, C. (1999.) *The Stephen Lawrence Inquiry: report of an inquiry.* London: Stationary Office.

McCandless, R., Feist, A., Allan, J. and Morgan, N. (2016*). Do initiatives involving substantial increases in stop and search reduce crime? Assessing the impact of Operation BLUNT 2.* London: Home Office.

McConville, M., Sanders, A. & Leng, R., (1991). *The Case for the Prosecution: Police Suspects and the Construction of Crime.* London: Routledge.

Miles, M. B., & Huberman, A. M. (1994). *Qualitative data analysis: An expanded sourcebook.* Thousand Oaks, CA: SAGE.

Miller, J. (2010). Stop and search in England: A reformed tactic or business as usual? *British Journal of Criminology,* 50(5), pp. 954–974.

Minhas, R., & Walsh, D. (2018). Influence of racial stereotypes on investigative decision-making in criminal investigations: a qualitative comparative analysis. *Cogent Social Sciences*, 4(1), 1538588.

Murray, K., McVie, S., Farren, D., Herlitz, L., Hough, M., & Norris, P. (2021). Procedural justice, compliance with the law and police stop-and-search: a study of young people in England and Scotland. *Policing and Society*, 31(3), 263–282.

Office for National Statistics (2011). 2011 Census. Retrieved 28 June 2018 www.ons.gov.uk/census/2011census

PACE. (1984). Police and Criminal Evidence Act 1984 codes of practices. *Home Office*. GOV.UK. 26 March 2013. Retrieved 1 December 2017 www.gov.uk/guidance/police-and-criminal-evidence-act-1984-pace-codes-of- practice

Parmar, A. (2011). Stop and search in London: counter-terrorist or counter-productive? *Policing and Society,* 21(4), pp.369–382.

Phillips, C. (2011). Institutional racism and ethnic inequalities: an expanded multi-level framework. *Journal of Social Policy,* 40(1), pp. 173–192.

Phillips, C. & Bowling, B., (2012). *Ethnicities, racism, crime and criminal justice* Oxford: Oxford University Press.

Pierson, E., Simoiu, C., Overgoor, J., Corbett-Davies, S., Jenson, D., Shoemaker, A., ... Goel, S. (2020). A large-scale analysis of racial disparities in police stops across the United States. *Nature Human Behaviour*, 4(7), 736–745. www.nature.com/articles/s41562-020-0858-1https://doi.org/10.1038/s41562-020-0858-1

Police and Criminal Evidence Act 1984 (PACE) codes of practice. *Home Office*. GOV.UK. 26 March 2013. Retrieved 1 December 2017 www.gov.uk/guidance/police-and-criminal-evidence-act-1984-pace-codes-of- practice

Potter, J. & Wetherell, M., (1987). *Discourse and social psychology: Beyond attitudes and behaviour*. London: Sage.

Quinton, P. (2011). The formation of suspicions: Police stop and search practices in England and Wales. *Policing and Society,* 21(4), pp. 357–368.

Quinton, P., Bland, N. & Miller, J. (2000). *Police stops, decision-making and practice*. London: Home Office.

Qureshi, F., & Farrell, G. (2006). Stop and search in 2004: a survey of police officer views and experiences. *International Journal of Police Science & Management*, 83–103.

Reiner, R. (2010). *The politics of the police*. OUP Oxford.

Schoderbek, P.P. & Deshpande, S.P. (1996). Impression management, overclaiming, and perceived unethical conduct: The role of male and female managers. *Journal of Business Ethics*, 15(4), pp. 409–414.

Shaw, I.S. (2016). Reporting the Lee Rigby Murder and Anti-Muslim Hostilities in the UK in 2013: The Cultural Clash Communication and Human Wrongs Journalism Nexus. In: Roy, S., & Shaw, I. S. (Eds.). (2016). *Communicating Differences (pp. 29–53)*. UK: Palgrave Macmillan.

Shiner, M., & Delsol, R. (2015). The politics of the powers. In Stop and Search (pp. 31–56). London: Palgrave Macmillan.

Smith, D.J. & Gray, J. (1985). *Police and people in London*: Aldershot: Avebury.

Smith, J.A. & Osborn, M. (2007). Pain as an assault on the self: An interpretative phenomenological analysis of the psychological impact of chronic benign low back pain. *Psychology and Health,* 22(5), pp. 517–534.

Stelter, M., Essien, I., Sander, C., & Degner, J. (2022). Racial bias in police traffic stops: White residents' county-level prejudice and stereotypes are related to disproportionate stopping of Black drivers. *Psychological Science,* 33(4), 483–496.

Stone, R. (2014). *Textbook on civil liberties and human rights*. Oxford: Oxford University Press.

Stone, V. and Pettigrew, N. (2000). *The views of the public on stops and searches*. London: Home Office.

Strauss, A. & Corbin, J.M. (1997). *Grounded theory in practice*. California: Sage Publications.

Tajfel, H. (2010). *Social identity and intergroup relations*. Cambridge: Cambridge University Press.

The Lammy Review. (2017). *An independent review into the treatment of, and outcomes for, Black, Asian and Minority Ethnic individuals in the Criminal Justice System*. www.gov.uk/government/uploads/system/uploads/attachment_data/file/643001 /lammy-review-final-report.pdf

Tyler, T. (1990). *Why people obey the law*. New Haven: Yale University Press.

Tyler, T.R. & Wakslak, C.J. (2004). Profiling and police legitimacy: Procedural justice, attributions of motive, and acceptance of police authority. *Criminology*, 42(2), pp. 253–282.

Weber, L. & Bowling, B. (2011). Stop and search in global context. *Policing and Society,* 21(4), pp. 353–356.

Weisburd, D., Hinkle, J.C., Famega, C. & Ready, J. (2011). The possible 'backfire' effects of hot spots policing: an experimental assessment of impacts on legitimacy, fear and collective efficacy. *Journal of Experimental Criminology,* 7(4), pp. 297–320.

Young, J. (1994). *Policing the streets: stops and search in north London.* London: Islington Council.

Zerbe, W.J. & Paulhus, D.L. (1987). Socially desirable responding in organisational behavior: A reconception. *Academy of Management Review.* 12(2), pp. 250–264.

Chapter 4

Measuring prejudicial stereotyping in investigative and interviewing processes within criminal investigations

Introduction

Following on from the previous chapter's findings, which highlighted police officers' reliance on certain types of stereotypes to inform suspicion about people, the current chapter developed an instrument to measure the presence of any prejudicial stereotypes in police interviews. One of the most notable findings from earlier research on police interviewing of suspects is that police held a presumption of the suspect's guilt even before conducting the interview (Mortimer & Shepherd, 1999; Moston, Stephenson, & Williamson, 1992). Research on confirmation bias offers valuable insights into how preconceived notions of guilt can significantly impact interviews with suspects (Hill, Memon, & McGeorge, 2008; Kassin, Goldstein, & Savitsky, 2003). Research has also explored the impact of confirmation bias on the hypothesis-testing process during social interactions. (e.g. Charman, Kavetski, & Mueller, 2017; Hill et al., 2008; Kassin et al. 2003; Trope, Bassok, & Alon, 1984). For example, Hill et al. (2008) found that the assumption of guilt can indeed influence the questioning styles used by interviewers and may even lead to the emergence of a self-fulfilling prophecy during the interview process. A self-fulfilling prophecy is a belief or expectation that can lead to outcomes aligning with the initial belief, effectively making reality conform to that belief. In other words, when a person believes something will happen, their actions and behaviours may unconsciously cause that belief to come true (Merton, 2016). This psychological phenomenon highlights the powerful role that beliefs and expectations can play in shaping human behaviours and outcomes. In the context of criminal investigations, this can happen when police investigators fail to understand how their personal beliefs have contributed to constructing a false reality (Biggs, 2009).

DOI: 10.4324/9781003366836-4

The present study

In the United Kingdom, there has been a lack of substantial focus on the impact of prejudicial stereotyping in the context of police interviews. As far as it is known, no research has been conducted to examine the influence of prejudicial stereotyping on investigative interviewing practices specifically concerning suspects from stigmatised communities. To fill this gap in the existing literature regarding investigative interviewing, the main aim of the present study is, therefore, to

- Develop an instrument to measure the presence of possible prejudicial stereotyping in investigative interviews.

Additionally, the present study also

- Identifies the factors that may lead an interviewer to display prejudicial stereotyping in investigative interviews towards suspects from certain groups,
- Examines whether the presumption of guilt affects the questioning style and leads to the emergence of a self-fulfilling prophecy.

Measuring attitudes

An overview of observational and self-report methods of attitude assessment, along with the advantages and inherent problems of each type, are presented below.

Observational methods

Research conducted to assess attitudes using observational methods has suggested that techniques employed to assess attitudes rely on the assumption of a strong correlation between physiological responses and affective states (Moser & Kalton, 2017). Earlier studies have indicated that autonomic responses might function as valid indicators of a strong attitude but might be insensitive to lesser attitudinal reactions (Dwyer, 1993; Mueller, 1970; Porier & Lott, 1967; Westie & De Fleur, 1959; Woodmansee, 1970). Nonetheless, researchers have acknowledged that the capacity to ascertain the directionality of a response through the analysis of physiological reactions is extremely limited (Dwyer, 1993).

According to Anderson (1981), the use of observational methods to gather data on attitudes relies on the assumption that it is possible to infer attitudes from the observation of overt behaviours or physiological responses. Observational research methodology reportedly faces three significant issues: (i) incorrectly gathering affective characteristics from overt behaviour; (ii) determining which behaviours to observe and accurately recording the observed behaviours; and (iii misjudging the behaviour noted by the observer (Dwyer, 1993). Anderson (1981) proposed potential solutions for these issues. For the first issue related to making inferences, Anderson recommended that correct inferences are more likely to be made if multiple observations are made of the same behaviour in a variety of settings or over time in the same setting. As to the second issue (i.e. observing relevant behaviours), he recommended that appropriate inferences can be made if the affective characteristics are clearly defined at the start and care is taken to observe only those clearly defined behaviours in an appropriate context. For the third issue, that of misinterpreting behaviours, he proposed utilising more than one carefully trained observer in a similar setting to minimise misinterpretations (errors). By implementing these steps, any concerns related to observational research methodology can be effectively mitigated (Dwyer, 1993; Moser & Kalton, 2017).

Self-report methods

Self-report methods for attitude assessment typically consist of a set of questions, adjectives, or statements related to a particular attitude or object. Participants are required to read and respond to each question, adjective, or statement by indicating their level of agreement or disagreement (Moser & Kalton, 2017). Following the participants' responses, their attitudes towards the attitudinal object are scored based on their level of positiveness. In certain cases, the responses are aggregated, and a total score is calculated to measure the overall attitude (Dwyer, 1993).

The major difficulty related to self-report methods of attitude assessment is that subjects may provide misinformation to the researcher (Denzin, 2017). According to Anderson (1981), individuals may occasionally provide misinformation to the researcher when responding to a question, statement, or adjective. This can happen when they believe that their response aligns with what the researcher finds socially acceptable or when they respond in a manner that is acquiescent rather than expressing their true feelings. Acquiescence, in this occurrence, refers to the tendency of an individual to agree with a question, statement, or adjective when they are unsure of their response (Denzin, 2017). To lessen the issue of misinformation, Thurstone and Chave (1929, p. 10) recommended that researchers should minimise as far as possible the conditions that may be 'preventing people from telling the truth, or else to adjust their interpretation accordingly'.

Major techniques to construct attitude scales

Scaling refers to various procedures of measuring or ordering entities to quantify attributes or traits (Denzin, 2017; Manheim, 1977). Fundamentally, the majority of scaling techniques have been developed since the late 1920s, particularly in association with research related to attitudes (Manheim, 1977). The four major types of attitude scales described in the literature are (i) Thurstone scales (Thurstone & Chave, 1929); (ii) Likert scales (Likert, 1932); (iii) semantic differential scales (Osgood, Suci, & Tannenbaum, 1957); and (iv) Guttman scales (Guttman, 1944). An overview of each of these four attitude measurement types is presented below.

Thurstone scales

Thurstone and Chave (1929) developed the method of equal-appearing intervals for evaluating attitudes. According to Thurstone and Chave (1929, p. 554), 'the essential characteristic of the method of equal-appearing intervals is the series of evenly graduated opinions so arranged that equal steps or intervals on the scale seem to most people to represent equally noticeable shifts in attitude'. Using the technique of equal-appearing intervals created by Thurstone and Chave (1929), perceptions about an attitudinal object can be gathered from nominated samples and the related academic literature. The collected opinion statements about the object of focus can then be edited. The editing procedure attempts to select statements covering the broadest possible range from the most intensely negative to the most intensely positive attitudes towards the object. The carefully chosen items are each printed on a separate slip of paper and participants are given a copy of each item (Denzin, 2017; Dwyer, 1993).

The participants are asked to sort the items into 11 piles representing an equally graduated series of attitudes from extremely negative (pile 1) through extremely positive (pile 11) towards the attitudinal object. Subsequently, the data is tabulated to show how each subject placed every one of the statements. Finally, the average of those selected statements would be calculated to determine the individual's attitude. Issues with creating Thurstone scales include: (i) it can be time-consuming and costly; (ii) examples for the midpoints of the scale for which there is a consensus among the participants (judges) can be challenging to obtain; and (iii) different participants can gain exactly the same score from agreeing with different items (Latham, Fay, & Saari, 1979).

Likert scales

Likert scales are a well-known technique for assessing attitudes (Burns & Grove, 1997; Crano & Brewer, 1973; Joshi, Kale, Chandel, & Pal, 2015; Oppenheim, 1966). The Likert method of scale construction is less laborious than the Thurstone technique (Burns & Grove, 1997). Previous studies have suggested that it is the most efficient and effective method of developing highly reliable scales (e.g. Crano & Brewer, 1973; Dwyer, 1993; Joshi et al., 2015).

The Likert scale was developed by Rensis Likert (1932). The primary concern for such a scale was, to the point that it measures a unidimensional construct, all items should measure the same thing. The Likert scaling technique is often called the 'method of summated ratings' since it involves computing the aggregate score for each participant by summing their responses to each item (Edwards, 1957; Selltiz, Wrightsman, & Cook, 1976). The summated score, therefore, represents the degree of favourable or unfavourable attitude towards the object under consideration.

Likert-type scales use fixed-choice response formats and are intended to assess attitudes or perceptions (Burns & Grove, 1997; Joshi et al., 2015). These ordinal scales measure levels of agreement or disagreement. A Likert-type scale expects that the quality or intensity of the experience is linear (i.e. on a continuum from strongly agree to disagree strongly, and makes the supposition that attitudes can be assessed/measured). Respondents may be offered a choice of five to seven (or even nine) pre-coded responses with the neutral point being 'neither agree nor disagree'. In its final form, the Likert scale is a scale which is used to let the individual express how much they agree or disagree with a specific statement (Dwyer, 1993).

However, Likert scales are limited by the presumption that all items in the given survey (questionnaire) have an equal level of difficulty (Uhlaner, 2005). Consequently, the true attitudes of respondents might not be assessed accurately. It is not unlikely that respondents' answers will be influenced by previous questions or will focus on one response side (agree or disagree). Frequently, respondents abstain from choosing the 'extreme' options on the scale, because of the negative implications involved with 'extremists', regardless of the possibility as to whether an extreme choice would be the most valid. Additionally, the validity of the Likert scale attitude measurement can also be compromised due to social desirability (Fisher, 1993).

Semantic differential scales

The semantic differential (SD) technique was developed by Osgood, Suci, and Tannenbaum (1957) for measuring attitudes. This technique is adjective-based and gathers responses from participants to pairs of bipolar adjectives with implications almost as opposite as possible (Osgood, 1952). For example, good–bad, happy–sad, and so on. The SD scale measures the directionality of the response and also the strength of the reaction (Osgood & Suci, 1955). Heise (1970) reported that ratings on SD scales tend to involve around three fundamental measurements of a response representing the vast majority of the covariance in ratings. These measurements of response include (i) evaluation (E); (ii) potency (P); and (iii) activity (A). SD scales generally contain adjectives from all three dimensions. For example, EPA types might include (i) Evaluation – good or bad; (ii) Potency – hard or soft; and (iii) Activity – fast or slow. Lists of evaluative adjective pairs are included in a text by Osgood et al. (1957).

According to DeVellis (2016), both theory and empiricism provide substantial evidence supporting the adoption of the SD scale, as it offers specific advantages over other measurement techniques. However, to benefit from its potential as an accurate measurement technique, researchers in fields such as information systems, marketing, and behavioural sciences ought to recognise that the SD scale depends intensely upon the adequate use of linguistics in general and of bipolarity specifically (Verhagen, van den Hooff, & Meents, 2015). Furthermore, the SD scale requires respondents who are intelligent and cooperative. It requires respondents with a good knowledge of the language, who are prepared and able to make fine distinctions (Fisher, 1993). This may make it inappropriate for children or vulnerable adults unless introduced in a simplified form (Bradley & Lang, 1994).

Verhagen et al. (2015) proposed to address these issues by synthesising established scale validation and semantic requirements in a framework of suggested action for SD development and usage. This integration aims to fill the gap left by general scale validation guidelines that do not specifically cater to the nuances of the SD technique (MacKenzie, Podsakoff, & Podsakoff, 2011; Straub, Boudreau, & Gefen, 2004).

Guttman scales

An alternative to the Thurstone, Likert, and semantic differential scales is a Guttman (named after Louis Guttman) or 'cumulative' scale. In a Guttman scale, responses to items are dependent on the amount of an underlying construct. The items on such a scale measure only a single dimension.

Consequently, if an individual agrees with a particular item, they should also agree with all other items representing the same dimension, arranged from the least extreme to the most extreme attitude (Guttman, 1950; Manheim, 1977). An important property of a Guttman scale is that a person's entire set of responses to all items can be anticipated from the 'cumulative' score because the model is deterministic (Andrich, 1985; Moser & Kalton, 2017). For instance, if a person scores a '3' on a five-item Guttman scale, it means they agreed with items 1 to 3 and disagreed with items 4 to 5. Guttman scales are distinguished by the 'implicational' or 'scalable' nature of their items, where responses to items imply agreement with lower-level items if higher-level items are agreed upon. That is, the tasks that can be completed when component subtasks are completed in a certain order, are then considered implicational (Gothwal et al., 2009). According to Crano and Brewer (1973), in constructing a Guttman scale, statements appearing to have the following characteristics are written or selected:

a. Statements have common content.
b. Statements are ordered along a continuum from least positive to most positive.
c. Agreement with a given statement implies agreement with every other less positive statement.

Given an instrument with statements about an attitudinal object meeting the criteria described above, participants are then instructed to check each statement with which they agree. When a subject agrees with an attitude statement, the subject receives a score of '1' for the item, and if they disagree with the attitude statement, they receive a score of '0' for the item. The final score obtained from Guttman scaling is equivalent to the highest item the respondent has answered. From this final score, one can summarise all other items that the participant has answered. Under these conditions, the scale is said to be fully implicational (Moser & Kalton, 2017).

Methods

In the current study, the author designed the Minhas Investigative Interviewing Prejudicial Stereotyping Scale (MIIPSS) to assess potential prejudicial stereotyping by police interviewers towards suspects during investigations. For the development of the MIIPSS, Guttman's principle was applied to sequentially identify the factors that allow for the development of the scale, which in turn assesses whether the interviewers possess any negative attitudes towards suspects.

The rationale for using the Guttman analysis to develop the MIIPSS

The Guttman scalogram analysis is considered a suitable technique to assess the unidimensionality of the MIIPSS, which is also seen as an essential part of construct validity (Ekinci & Riley, 1999). In the context of the MIIPSS, unidimensionality (or cumulativeness) pertains to the degree of an interviewer's negative perceptions about a suspect. It measures the strength or intensity of the negative attitudes held by the interviewer towards the individual under investigation.

According to Gerbing and Anderson (1988), the exploratory factor analysis is not suitable for confirming unidimensionality. Fundamentally, factor analysis depends on a linear correlation and is consequently a type of probability modelling. The key assumption is that if there is a linear relationship between the scale items, it is considered to be unidimensional (Moser & Kalton, 2017). Nevertheless, a linear relationship, in some cases, indicates homogeneity instead of unidimensionality (Hattie, 1985). A Guttman scale is a deterministic form of modelling that provides two unique parameters for establishing unidimensionality in contrast to probability modelling. As such, a scale has to be ordinal and cumulative (Yoon & Ekinci, 2003). Because the Guttman scalogram analysis requires an ordinal and cumulative structure, therefore unidimensionality is established by checking the response patterns in the data (Oppenheim, 1966).

The development of the MIIPSS is grounded in the rationale that if a police interviewer harbours negative perceptions about suspects based on their group membership, it can potentially lead to a coercive form of interviewing. The scale aims to assess and address the existence of prejudicial stereotyping among interviewers, as such biased attitudes may influence their approach during interviews and impact the quality and fairness of the investigative process. By identifying and understanding these negative perceptions, measures can be taken to improve the interviewing techniques and reduce the potential for coercion or unfair treatment of suspects based on their group affiliation.

MIIPSS hypothesis

To develop the MIIPSS, it is hypothesised that interviewers' attitudes towards a member of a group are based on perceived positive and negative aspects of that group (Fishbein & Ajzen, 1974). It is further hypothesised that if the interviewer holds negative attitudes towards the suspect, this could lead to judging the suspect by that perceived negative aspect (such as members of a particular ethnic group are drug dealers or involved in knife crimes, or the community in a particular area is troublesome). There is a possibility this may lead the interviewer to presume the suspect guilty even before the interview is conducted. Once the interviewer has presumed the suspect guilty, the interviewer's expectations of guilt may lead the interviewer to a self-fulfilling prophecy. Their expectations of guilt would result in both seeking information that confirms an existing belief, while not seeking, and even avoiding, information that disconfirms the belief (Hill et al., 2008; Kassin et al., 2003). Both Hill et al. (2008) and Kassin et al. (2003) found that stereotyping affected questioning styles, which can lead to a coercive form of interviewing.

Constructs and context articulation

Table 4.1 depicts five essential constructs ordered by increasing negativity in attitudes that inform the MIIPSS. These five constructs include (i) influencing perceptions; (ii) use of schemas; (iii) guilt presumption; (iv) self-fulfilling prophecy; and (v) hostile approach. These constructs have emerged from extensive research of the previous literature on investigative interviewing, being found (or argued) to be the major causes of investigative interviewing failures. These five constructs will now be examined in turn.

Influencing perceptions

Perception involves individuals or groups selecting, organising, and interpreting information, influenced by their socialisation process and personal experiences (Brown & Hewstone, 2005). Stephan and Stephan (1985) found that interactions between members of different groups can sometimes be anxiety-provoking affairs. They suggested that this could be due to the pre-existing conflict between the protagonists or merely through tensions born out of ignorance, embarrassment, or misperception. The encounters between members of different groups become breeding grounds for the growth of stereotypical judgements. Individuals who hold strong negative stereotypes about a particular group are likely to experience higher levels of anxiety in any form of contact with that group (Brown & Hewstone, 2005).

In his classic experiment, Dijker (1987) found that the anticipation of Dutch participants in meetings with ethnic minority groups was associated with feelings of anxiety and irritation. A police interviewer's attitude towards a member of a specific group is, to some extent, influenced by their perception of both the positive and the negative aspects associated with that group. Accordingly, if the interviewer perceives more positive

Table 4.1 Emergence of MIIPSS constructs from previous research studies on investigative interviewing

	Influencing perceptions	*Use of schemas*	*Guilt presumption*	*Self-fulfilling prophecy*	*Hostile approach*
Milne & Bull, 1999	✓	✓	✓	✓	✓
Holmberg & Christianson, 2002	✓			✓	✓
Shepherd & Milne, 1999	✓	✓	✓	✓	
Hill, Memon, & McGeorge, 2008	✓	✓	✓	✓	
Walsh & Bull, 2011	✓		✓		✓
Cherryman, Bull, & Vrij, 2000				✓	✓
Baldwin, 1992			✓		✓
Hurren, Kebbell, & Mazerolle, 2006	✓	✓		✓	✓
Kassin, Goldstein, & Savitsky, 2003	✓	✓	✓	✓	✓
Oxburgh, 2011	✓		✓		✓
Clarke & Milne, 2001				✓	✓
Walsh &Milne, 2007				✓	
Shawyer & Milne, 2009	✓				✓
Mortimer & Shepherd, 1999		✓	✓	✓	
Gudjonsson, 2003	✓	✓			
Irving, 1980			✓	✓	✓
Bull & Cherryman, 1996					✓
Pearse & Gudjonsson, 1996		✓		✓	
Shepherd, 1991; 1993	✓	✓	✓	✓	✓
Williamson,1993; 2006				✓	✓
Cherryman & Bull, 2001	✓				✓
Stockdale, 1993			✓	✓	✓

aspects of the group, the more positive their attitude will be towards a suspect within that group, but if they perceive more negative aspects of the group, the more negative their attitude will be towards a suspect within that group (Fishbein & Ajzen, 1974). Consequently, the attitudes of police interviewers towards suspects may be influenced by their perception of positive or negative aspects associated with the group to which the suspects belong.

According to MIIPSS, an interview will be considered as affected by the interviewer's negative *perceptions* if the research participants identify one or more of the following indicators as present during the interview: (i) the interviewer's perceived attitudes towards him/her were negative; (ii) there was a lack of empathy; and (iii) there was an absence of good relationship (or rapport) between the suspect and the interviewer.

Use of schemas

Schemas may lead individuals to misinterpret situations by holding specific beliefs about particular group members (Bartlett, 1932). Schemas prevent people from seeing the world as it truly is and inhibit them from taking in new information by systematically influencing perceptions, interpretations, and judgements (Hoffman & Hurst, 1990). One of the primary functions of schemas is to act as mental shortcuts (Venema, 2016). The potential misuse of schemas can be conspicuous and evident, for instance, when a particular ethnic group is inaccurately labelled as greedy, lazy, or linked to specific crimes like drug-related offences, knife crimes, or violent extremism (Brown & Hewstone, 2005). Consequently, such schemas can lead individuals to perceive that all individuals belonging to that particular group or community share these negative traits or associations.

According to the MIIPSS, the interviewer will be considered as possibly using *schemas* if the research participants believed that the interviewer's negative attitudes towards him/her were due to one or more of the following: (i) his/her group membership; (ii) his/her race; (iii) his/her religion; (iv) the particular nature of the crime (such as sexual crimes, paedophilia, or drug-related crimes); or (v) his/her previous criminal record (previously known to the police).

Guilt presumption

One of the major findings from earlier research on the investigative interviewing of suspects is that the police interviewer often assumes the suspect's guilt even before the interview takes place (Baldwin, 1992; Cherryman, Bull, & Vrij, 2000; Kassin et al., 2003; Mortimer & Shepherd, 1999).

These assumptions of guilt influenced the kind of questions that police officers asked, with leading questions and repetitive questions being used frequently (McGurk, Carr, & McGurk, 1993). Furthermore, McGurk et al. (1993) found that in several interviews, admissions were made only in response to a series of leading and repetitive questions.

According to the MIIPSS, the interviewer will be deemed to have presumed the suspect guilty if the research participants identify one or more of the following indicators as present during the interview:

(i) the interviewer asked guilt-presumptive questions (i.e. questions displaying the interviewer's confirmation bias, where the interviewer selectively searches for information in support of their belief or expectations (Kassin et al., 2003), e.g. Do you still sell drugs?); or
(ii) the interviewer asked provocative questions (questions described by the participants were asked merely to make them angry, anxious, and heighten their stress, e.g. would you still be selling drugs if you walked free after this interview?); or
(iii) the interviewer demonstrated bluffing tactics (e.g. the police interviewer 'bluffed' the interviewee into thinking evidence was to hand but which did not exist); or
(iv) the interviewer demonstrated inflexibility (e.g. the police interviewer did not allow the interviewee the opportunity to establish their position/account properly, or the interviewer did not adjust their stance in light of new information received from the interviewee); or
(v) the interviewer reacted to the suspect's behaviour with destabilising, disturbing, or confusing (non-verbal) responses (e.g. the police interviewer mentioned that the interviewee's non-verbal behaviour is associated with deception).

Self-fulfilling prophecy effect

A self-fulfilling prophecy is 'the case whereby people (a) have an expectation about what another person is like, which (b) influences how they act towards that person, which (c) causes that person to behave in a way consistent with people's original expectations' (Aronson, Wilson, & Akert, 1999, p. 527). It is arguable that when someone fails to understand how their own beliefs have contributed to the construction of a false reality, such an event becomes equally likely to occur (Biggs, 2009). When a person becomes convinced that members of a specific group behave in certain ways, they are more likely to seek and find evidence supporting that belief rather than considering opposing evidence, often disregarding the actual facts (Merton, 2016). When there is a presumption of a relationship, individuals tend to seek evidence supporting that relationship, even when there is little or none to be found. If evidence is present, they may either overemphasise or downplay it, leading to a conclusion that exceeds what the evidence justifies (Nickerson, 1998).

According to the MIIPSS, the interview will be considered affected by the self-fulfilling prophecy effect if the participants identified one or more of the following indicators as present during the interview:

(i) the interviewer overweighed the evidence (e.g. the police interviewer actively exaggerated the strength of the evidence against the interviewee during the interview); or
(ii) the interviewer ignored evidence that could have gone in the suspect's favour (or at least did not lead to any belief of guilt); or
(iii) the interviewer maximised (e.g. the interviewer mentioned that the participant would feel worse if they did not confess) or minimised (e.g. the interviewer spoke in a way which functioned to lessen the seriousness of the offence and offer a moral justification—for example, by blaming the victim or other circumstances (Kassin et al., 2003)) the nature of the offence; or
(iv) the interviewer repeatedly accused the interviewee of the crime(s); or
(v) the interviewer repetitively asked either leading questions (questions which function to produce a response desired by an interviewer – e.g. you saw the gun, didn't you?) or guilt-presumptive questions (questions displaying interviewer's confirmation bias, where the interviewer selectively searches for information in support of his/her belief or expectations (Kassin et al., 2003), e.g. do you still sell drugs?).

Hostile approach

The use of empathy during police interviews has been found in previous studies as beneficial both to rapport building and to the number of increased admissions from some suspects (Dando & Oxburgh, 2016; Oxburgh, 2011). However, previous research on investigative interviewing has shown that when the police interviewer holds negative feelings towards a suspect and assumes their guilt, there is a reduced presence of empathy, and the interviewer's demeanour may become hostile (although sometimes subtle in its manifestation) (Bull & Cherryman, 1996; Cherryman & Bull, 2001; Gudjonsson, 2018; Holmberg & Christianson, 2002; Milne & Bull, 1999, 2016; Williamson, 1993, 2006).

According to the MIIPSS, the approach of the interviewer will be considered *hostile* if the research participant identified one or both of the following indicators as present during the interview:

(i) interviewer's behaviour was oppressive (e.g. instances of undue pressure, bullying, or continual challenge); or
(ii) questioning during the interview was persistent and coercive (the police interviewer persistently asked confirmation-seeking questions, such as you saw the gun, didn't you?).

MIIPSS constructs a pattern for an ideal Guttman scale

The five constructs of the MIIPSS (mentioned above) are presented in Table 4.2 in the predicted order for a perfect Guttman scale (below). A scale score of '0' means that the research participant would judge the interviewer as someone who treated the suspect fairly and the interview began unaffected by the interviewer's perceptions. A scale score of '1' reflects that the interviewer has perceived negative attitudes towards the suspect. A scale score of '2' suggests that an interviewer was viewed as judging the suspect by perceived negative attitudes. When the interviewer appeared to presume the suspect was guilty, a score of '3' was allocated, while a scale score of '4' refers to the expectation of guilt, which may have led the interviewer to a self-fulfilling prophecy effect. Finally, a scale score of '5' was given when there were apparent effects on the questioning style and possibly coercion (i.e. hostility). Table 4.2 depicts five constructs of the MIIPSS for a perfect Guttman scale.

Materials

Participants

Twenty semi-structured interviews were conducted with male individuals from the Asian Muslim community, who had been interviewed by the English police on at least one occasion as suspects of crime between 2010 and 2014. Individuals were contacted to ask if they wished to participate

Table 4.2 Ideal responses pattern for a perfect Guttman scale on the MIIPSS

Influencing perceptions	*Use of schemas*	*Guilt presumption*	*Self-fulfilling prophecy*	*Hostile approach*	*Scale score*
0	0	0	0	0	0
1	0	0	0	0	1
1	1	0	0	0	2
1	1	1	0	0	3
1	1	1	1	0	4
1	1	1	1	1	5

and those who agreed were requested to participate in face-to-face interviews. The participants were contacted through the author's associates, who were asked if they knew anyone who had been interviewed by police within the last five years as a suspect in a crime. They relayed the author's contact details to the participants. From these contacts, the author was successful in securing 14 interviews. One of the author's associates, who is a criminal lawyer, was requested to ask some of his clients if they would agree to take part in the present study. Six suspects (also Asian Muslims living in the United Kingdom) were sourced via this criminal lawyer.

The police interviewed the suspects who took part in this study as suspects of a range of offences, including possession of drugs with intent to supply, sexual offences, serious physical assault, human trafficking, attempted murder, domestic violence, and terrorism-related offences. The sample involved suspects from major English cities including the West Midlands, London, Greater Manchester, and Bristol. None of the suspects was known to each other.

Additionally, a total of eight semi-structured interviews were conducted with legal representatives (all males) who had represented suspects from diverse ethnic backgrounds across England and Wales. Two of the lawyers were associates of the author, who each, in turn, provided contact details of a total of six further criminal defence lawyers. Subsequently, it was discovered that each participating legal representative in this study had represented over a thousand suspects during police interviews.

Procedures

During the research interviews, the suspects were asked to provide interpretations of their experiences during police interviewing and of interviewers' attitudes towards them. When a participant believed that the interviewers' attitudes were negative towards him and endorsed particular constructs of the MIIPSS, then it was matched to the indicators of the construct's operational definition. If this verified that the suspect had correctly identified a construct, the construct was subjected to a Guttman pattern (see Table 4.2) by asking the suspect further questions to establish whether he believed (through open questions) that the constructs lower on the scale were also present during the interview. Any missing constructs in the banding pattern were identified as errors and indicated as '0*'. Similarly, legal representatives were asked to provide their interpretations regarding police interviewers' attitudes towards suspects from different ethnic groups. Their responses were also evaluated concerning the operational definition of each construct to the MIIPSS.

Instrumentation

Finally, the 28 (audio-recorded) interview transcripts were analysed concerning the operational definition of each construct. All the responses given by the participants to each construct were evaluated. A value of '1' was given if the research participant indicated the presence of that construct during the interview. A value of '0' was given if the participant did not indicate that the construct was present during the interview. If the response from participants mismatched the predicted order, the response is considered an 'error', which is indicated with '0*'. All the responses given to each construct by the suspects and legal representatives are presented in Table 4.3 and Table 4.4.

Table 4.3 Guttman scalogram for the five constructs on the MIIPSS and responses given to each construct (columns) by each participant (rows)

Participants	*Influencing perceptions*	*Use of schemas*	*Guilt presumption*	*Self-fulfilling prophecy*	*Hostile approach*	*scale score*
S1	1	1	1	1	0	4
S2	1	1	0*	0*	1	3
S3	1	1	1	0	0	3
S4	0*	0*	1	1	1	3
S5	1	1	1	0*	1	4
S6	1	1	1	1	0	4
S7	1	1	1	1	1	5
S8	0	0	0	0	0	0
S9	1	0*	1	0	0	2
S10	1	0*	1	0*	1	3
S11	1	1	1	1	1	5
S12	0	0	0	0	0	0
S13	1	0	0	0	0	1
S14	1	1	1	0	0	3
S15	1	1	1	1	1	5
S16	1	1	0	0	0	2
S17	1	1	1	1	1	5
S18	0	0	0	0	0	0
S19	1	1	0*	1	0	3
S20	1	1	0	0	0	2
LR1	1	1	1	1	1	5
LR2	1	1	0	0	0	2
LR3	1	0	0	0	0	1
LR4	1	1	1	1	1	5
LR5	0*	1	1	0	0	2
LR6	1	1	1	1	1	5
LR7	1	0*	1	1	0	3
LR8	1	1	1	1	0	4

S = Suspect LR = Legal Representative

Table 4.4 Responses given to MIIPSS constructs

Construct	*Responses (n = 28)*	
	Yes	*No*
Influencing perceptions	23	5
Use of schemas	19	9
Guilt presumption	18	10
Self-fulfilling prophecy	13	15
Hostile approach	11	17

Data Analysis

The data was analysed according to the following steps: (i) ordering of the constructs from influencing perceptions to extreme hostile approach (i.e. *(1) perceptions, (2) use of schemas, (3) guilt presumption, (4) self-fulfilling prophecy, and (5) hostile approach*); (ii) analysis of the number of constructs endorsed by each participant; (iii) calculation of the total number of errors from the mismatch of the predicted order; and (iv) calculation of statistical values.

In order to determine whether the scale is valid, four statistics are produced: (i) the coefficient of reproducibility (CR); (ii), the minimum marginal reproducibility (MMR); (iii) the percentage improvement (PI); and (iv) the coefficient of scalability (CS) (Cliff, 1977; Gothwal et al., 2009; Guttman, 1944).

Guttman (1950) originally proposed the CR to assess the degree of scalability of empirical data. According to Guttman (1950, p. 77),

> The amount by which a scale deviates from the ideal pattern is measured by a coefficient of reproducibility. This coefficient is simply a measure of the relative degree to which the obtained multivariate distribution corresponds to the expected multivariate distribution of a perfect scale. It is secured by counting up the number of responses which would have been predicted wrongly for each person based on his scale score, dividing these errors by the total number of responses and subtracting a fraction from one.

The CR indicates how often responses fit the ideal pattern. CR varies from 0 to 1. The formula for CR may be expressed as follows:

$$\begin{aligned} CR &= 1.0 - (\#errors)/total\ responses \\ &= 1.0 - (\#errors)/\ ((items) \times (\#respondents)) \end{aligned}$$

CR, calculated according to the requirements of the particular scale construction technique, is a measure of 'goodness of fit' between the observed and the predicted ideal response pattern (McIver & Carmines, 1981). Guttman (1950) established the standard that a set of items should be considered scalable if the observed error in reproduction equals 10 per cent or less of the total responses. The CR value to conform to the MIIPSS is calculated below:

$$CR = 1 - \left(\frac{total\, number\, of\, errors}{total\, number\, possible\, errors} \right)$$

$$CR = 1 - 11/140$$

$$CR = 1 - 0.078$$

$$CR = 0.92$$

A CR value of more than 0.90 is considered acceptable and suggests that it is a valid cumulative and unidimensional scale (Guttman, 1944). The high CR value signifies that the pattern of constructs is cumulative and validates the MIIPSS instrument (Cliff, 1977; Guttman, 1944).

Edwards (1957) noted that a CR of 0.90 is not a sufficient condition for the scalability of a set of statements. According to Edwards (1957, p. 184), 'Guttman's CR measurement was inconsistent with the proposed cumulative interpretation of the scalogram theory. As a result, CR value fails to reproduce the originally observed pattern within the stated limits of accuracy.' Since the CR is affected by the proportion of responses in the modal category (the category with the most responses), an artificially high but relatively meaningless CR can be achieved for even an unsatisfactory scale. That is, a high CR with an uneven distribution of responses may be misleading. To interpret the coefficient of reproducibility properly, one needs some idea of how low the CR value could go, given the particular distribution of responses received (Bailey, 2008). This can be determined by computing the minimum marginal reproducibility (MMR). The calculation of MMR depends on the fact that an item's reproducibility can be no less than the proportion of responses in its modal category. Therefore, total reproducibility cannot be less than the sum of the proportion of responses in the modal category for each item in the scale, divided by the number of items (McIver & Carmines, 1981). The MMR value reflects the reproducibility of a series of items based only on knowledge of the item's marginal distribution.

$$MMR = \sum_{i=1}^{n} (\%\ responses\ in\ model\ category\ /\ N)$$

Where N = *total number of constructs.*

The MMR value to test the validity of the MIIPSS is calculated as follows:

$$MMR = \left(\frac{23}{28}+\frac{19}{28}+\frac{18}{28}+\frac{15}{28}+\frac{17}{28}\right)/5$$

$$MMR = 3.287/5$$

$$MMR = 0.66$$

With a CR of .92 and an MMR of .66, it becomes evident that the high CR is not solely attributed to the modal frequencies. Therefore, the CR indicates a substantial enhancement in reproducibility compared to the minimum level of .66, which demonstrates the adequacy of the MIIPSS.

The final criterion to conform to the Guttman scale is the CS, which indicates the proportion of responses that can be correctly predicted from the total summed score, thereby allowing for the relative frequencies with which different items are passed. Menzel (1953) developed the CS as a measure of a scale's ability to predict item responses in comparison to predictions based on marginal frequencies. The CS is the most important criterion to conform to the scale, which essentially tests the degree to which the data fits the model (Gothwal et al., 2009; Menzel, 1953). The CS is obtained by dividing percentage improvement (PI) by the difference between 1 and MMR. PI is the difference between the CR and the minimum marginal reproducibility (MMR). PI is an indication of the extent to which CR reflects the response patterns rather than the inherent cumulative interrelation of the variable used (Adams, Ashburn, Pickering, & Taylor, 1997).

$$PI = CR - MMR$$

$$PI = 0.92 - 0.66$$

$$PI = 0.26$$

The CS varies between 0 and 1. A CS value of ≥ 0.60 is accepted to confirm the validity of the Guttman scale (Manzel, 1953).

$$CS = PI/(1 - MMR)$$

The CS value calculated to test the adequacy of the MIIPSS is as follows:

$$CS = 0.26 / (1 - 0.66)$$

$$CS = 0.26 / 0.34$$

$$CS = 0.76$$

The CS value of 0.76 fulfils both desired requirements: (i) CS should be lower than 0.90 and CR, and (ii) CS should be between 0.60 and 0.80 (Stouffer et al., 1950) on an ideal Guttman scale. This confirms the adequacy of the MIIPSS.

Results

Responses from the 28 research participants were subjected to Guttman scalogram analysis. Regularity in the responses pattern of the Guttman Scalogram suggests that the responses on the MIIPSS do, indeed, follow a deterministic Guttman scale (i.e. if the interviewer was perceived to hold negative attitudes towards suspects, then there is a distinct possibility that such negative attitudes may lead to the interviewer displaying hostility towards the suspect). As evident in Table 4.5, the MIIPSS satisfies the essential criteria for classification as a valid Guttman scale because CS, CR, and MMR values fall within the desired range.

Discussion

The MIIPSS was created to evaluate the extent to which investigative interviewers exhibit prejudicial stereotyping towards suspects belonging to specific groups. The Guttman principle was applied to develop the MIIPSS because the author sought, firstly, to sequentially identify the factors that allow for the development of the scale. This scale, in turn, assesses whether negative attitudes are believed to be possessed by the interviewers towards the suspects. Secondly, the author aimed to distinguish between interviewers

Table 4.5 Evaluation of Guttman properties of the MIIPSS

Evaluation Criteria	*Value of the MIIPSS*
Coefficient of reproducibility (CR)	.92
Minimum marginal reproducibility (MMR)	.66
Percentage improvement (PI)	.26
Coefficient of scalability (CS)	.76

with different degrees of prejudicial stereotyping. The constructs in the MIIPSS meet all the requirements of a valid Guttman scale, and logically all the constructs relate to prejudicial stereotyping within the investigative interviewing context. The Guttman scalogram analysis of the MIIPSS provides a useful model to understand the processes and steps involved in the occurrence of perceived prejudicial stereotyping within the context of investigative interviewing. It could help to assess the level of apparent prejudicial stereotyping displayed by interviewers during investigative interviews.

It was hypothesised that if the interviewer has any perceived negative attitudes towards the suspect, this could be followed by judging the suspect based on this perceived negative attitude. As such, there is a distinct possibility that the interviewer could presume the suspect guilty based on perceived negative aspects and employ schemas by using alternative explanations to support existing negative beliefs. Once the interviewer has presumed the suspect guilty, the interviewer's expectation of guilt is considered likely to lead the interviewer towards a self-fulfilling prophecy. Consequently, this approach may lead (at its more extreme) to the interviewer demonstrating hostility towards suspects. A CR value of 0.92 and a CS value of 0.76 were found, indicating that patterns of items are cumulative and that the MIIPSS is a valid instrument of measurement. Because the CR exceeds 0.90, it can be predicted from the interviewee's response when they passed the 'more extreme' item that they also passed the 'less extreme' item. For example, if a guilt presumption (the third item in the MIIPSS) is perceived in an interview, it means that the interviewer used schemas (the second item in the MIIPSS) based on perceived negative attitudes (the first item in the MIIPSS) to arrive at the assumption that the suspect is guilty.

The MIIPSS can be used either by police supervisors to assess police interviewers' attitudes towards suspects or by interviewers themselves to monitor their own attitudes. Interviewers' attitudes can be measured by using the MIIPSS items in reverse order. For example, the measurement would begin when the interviewer recognises that they possess a hostile approach towards certain suspects. Given that a hostile approach is the fifth item on the MIIPSS, representing a more extreme negative attitude, the initial step towards improvement involves examining the fourth item on the MIIPSS, followed sequentially by the third, second, and first items.

The fourth item, 'self-fulfilling prophecy', is a 'false definition of the situation evoking a new behaviour which makes the originally false conceptions come true' (Merton, 2016, p. 477). This can happen when an interviewer fails to understand how their own belief has helped them construct a false reality (Biggs, 2009) and they become so focused on an issue/belief that no other information registers in their thoughts, which is known as tunnel vision (Findley & Scott, 2006). Tunnel vision is a product of multiple processes including cognitive distortions such as confirmation bias (Findley & Scott, 2006). Tunnel vision and confirmation bias can be the results of expectations of guilt (the third item on the MIIPSS).

If there is concern that an interviewer has presumed the suspect to be guilty before the interview, it can be identified by examining where those expectations of guilt came from, by asking such questions as these. Why did they presume the suspect to be guilty before the interview? What factors made the interviewer decide that the suspect was guilty? Do they assume every suspect to be guilty before the interview, or only those suspects who are suspected of a particular crime (such as knife crimes, sexual crimes, drug-related offences), or those who come either from a particularly notorious area, an ethnic minority, or who have been previously known to the police?

Such patterns that assign generalised characteristics to groups of suspects or groups of crimes without considering variations between individuals are known as schemas (second item on the MIIPSS) (Leyens, Yzerbyt, & Schadrom, 1994). They can result in unjustified negative attitudes towards a suspect based on his/her membership of a group, on being suspected of a particular crime, or belonging to a troublesome area. The interviewer's attitude towards a member of a certain group is, in part, based on the perceived positive and negative aspects of the group (i.e. the first item on the MIIPSS). By identifying the sources that contribute to interviewers' negative perceptions of certain groups and individuals suspected of specific offences, and by tracking how explanations that support such negative perceptions develop, interviewers could avoid presuming the suspects guilty before the interview. This would help them prevent tunnel vision and confirmation bias, which can compromise the investigative process.

Perceptions ⇆ Use of schemas ⇆ Guilt presumption ⇆ Self-fulfilling prophecy ⇆ Hostile approach

The MIIPSS allows both researchers and police interviewers to utilise its constructs in two ways. By using the MIIPSS, it is possible to identify the sequential factors that lead interviewers to possess extreme negative attitudes towards suspects.

Limitations

The Guttman scale is not without its limitations. A deterministic Guttman scale is ordinal. No information can be used to infer the intervals between constructs and participants. The scalogram analysis does not allow for enough variation in the construct being measured (Gothwal et al., 2009). While the MIIPSS identifies the sequential factors that potentially lead to interviewers' extreme negative attitudes towards suspects and distinguishes between interviewers with different degrees of prejudicial stereotyping, it is essential to remember that the MIIPSS is ordinal. Indeed, due to its bidirectional nature, the MIIPSS does not facilitate direct comparisons of prejudicial stereotyping levels exhibited by interviewers across different suspects. Instead, its primary focus lies in identifying and understanding the sequential factors that contribute to the development of negative attitudes towards suspects. Despite these apparent shortcomings, an important property of a Guttman scale is that a person's entire set of responses to all items can be predicted from the 'cumulative' score because the model is deterministic (Guttman, 1944).

It is also important to recognise that the causes of the presumption of guilt, self-fulfilling prophecy, and hostile approach do not necessarily arise only from prejudicial stereotyping based upon the suspect's membership in an ethnic, religious, or other minority group. But also could be due to other factors such as the particular nature of the crime (such as sexual crimes, paedophilia, or drug-related crimes), suspects' previous criminal record, or their being previously known to the police. Further, the interviewer's interpretations of any evidence held, or their schema, may well also have varying degrees of influence. Additionally, during the research interviews, the participants may have exaggerated their responses, which could have been affected by their personal biases against the police. Similarly, legal representatives' views may be affected by any social biases they may have held either towards or against the police or suspects (similarly, the researcher). Because participants were suspects from a minority community, a hard-to-reach group for voluntary study, the small sample size could limit the generalisability of this study. However, the responses from experienced legal representatives are triangulated with the suspects' responses, which is the strength of this research.

Further research

In the future, research that addresses the limitations of the present study by including a larger, more representative sample would be beneficial to test the present study's conclusions. Further, an examination of real-life police interviews (including cases with a number of legal outcomes) with those suspects (i) who are suspected of a particular crime (such as knife crimes, sexual crimes, drug-related offences), or (ii) who come from a particular notorious area, or (iii) who have been previously known to the police would be beneficial to test the present study's conclusions. Such research would also help to determine the implications of prejudicial stereotyping in greater detail within the context of investigative interviewing. Additionally, it would be beneficial for future research to compare the real-life police interviews with suspects from different communities to examine whether prejudicial stereotyping affected police interviewers' attitudes when they undertook the interviews with suspects from certain stigmatised minority communities and indigenous suspects.

Conclusions

Based on the Guttman analysis of the MIIPSS, the CR and CS values are evidence of a valid Guttman scale, which confirms the MIIPSS hypothesis. Thus, the findings of the present research constitute an important initial validation of the current scale. Researchers could use the MIIPSS as a tool to measure prejudicial stereotyping in investigative interviews. Further interviewers can also use the MIIPSS to examine their attitudes towards different groups or individuals suspected of different types of crimes. As a consequence, the MIIPSS not only enables researchers and police supervisors to measure police interviewers' possible negative stereotypes towards suspects, but the scale also may suggest why interviewers presume suspects are guilty before an interview. The MIIPSS also provides researchers with opportunities to assess police officers' prejudicial attitudes when conducting research more scientifically in either experimental or naturalistic settings.

Given the identification of five constructs of the MIIPSS, the following chapter will explore the perceptions of real-life Asian Muslim suspects concerning police interviewers' attitudes as perceived by these suspects when police officers undertook the task of interviewing them as the suspects of real-life crimes.

Acknowledgement

The study discussed in this chapter has been published as a research article in the journal *Police Practice and Research* and can be accessed using the following reference:

Rashid Ali Minhas, Dave Walsh, & Ray Bull (2017) Developing a scale to measure the presence of possible prejudicial stereotyping in police interviews with suspects: The Minhas Investigative Interviewing Prejudicial Stereotyping Scale (MIIPSS), *Police Practice and Research*, 18:2, 132–145, DOI: 10.1080/15614263.2016.1249870[1]

Note

1 www.tandfonline.com/doi/full/10.1080/15614263.2016.1249870

References

Adams, S. A., Ashburn, A., Pickering, R. M., & Taylor, D. (1997). The scalability of theRivermead Motor Assessment in acute stroke patients. *Clinical Rehabilitation*, *11*, 42–51. doi: 10.1177/026921559701100107

Anderson, L.W. (1981). *Assessing affective characteristics in the schools.* Boston: Allyn and Bacon, Inc.

Andrich, D. (1985). An elaboration of Guttman scaling with Rasch models for measurement. *Sociological Methodology*, *15*, 33–80.

Aronson, E., Wilson, T.D., & Akert, R.M. (1999). *Social psychology*. Third edition. NewYork: Longman.

Bailey, K. (2008). *Methods of social research*. Simon and Schuster, New York

Baldwin, J. (1992). Video taping police interviews with suspects – an evaluation. The HomeOffice. London Police Research Series Paper 1.

Bartlett, F. C. (1932). Remembering: An experimental and social study. *Cambridge:Cambridge University*.

Biggs, M. (2009). Self-fulfilling prophecies. In P. Bearman & P. Hedstrom, (Eds.) *TheOxford handbook of analytical sociology* (pp. 294–314), Oxford University Press, Oxford, UK.

Bradley, M. M., & Lang, P. J. (1994). Measuring emotion: the self-assessment manikin and the semantic differential. *Journal of Behavior Therapy and Experimental Psychiatry*, *25*, 49–59.

Brown, R., & Hewstone, M. (2005). An integrative theory of intergroup contact. *Advances in Experimental Social Psychology*, *37*, 255–343. doi:10.1016/S0065-2601(05)37005-5

Bull, R., & Cherryman, J. (1996). *Helping to identify skills gaps in specialist investigativeinterviewing*. London: Home Office.

Burns, N., & Grove, S. K. (1997). *The Practice of Nursing Research Conduct, Critique,&Utilization*. Philadelphia:W.B. Saunders and Co.

Charman, S. D., Kavetski, M., & Mueller, D. H. (2017). Cognitive bias in the legalsystem: Policeofficers evaluate ambiguous evidence in a belief-consistentmanner. *Journal of Applied Research in Memory and Cognition*, 6, 193–202.

Cherryman, J., & Bull, R. (2001). Police officers' perceptions of specialist investigativeinterviewing skills. *International Journal of Police Science & Management*, 3, 199–212.

Cherryman, J., Bull, R., & Vrij, A. (2000). *How police officers view confessions: Isthere still a confession culture*. Paper presented at the European Conference inPsychology and Law, Cyprus.

Clarke, C., & Milne, R. (2001). *National evaluation of the PEACE investigative interviewingcourse*. Police Research Award Scheme Report No. PRAS/149. London: HomeOffice.

Cliff, N. (1977). A theory of consistency of ordering generalizable to tailored testing. *Psychometrika*, *42*, 375–399. doi: 10.1007/BF02293657

Crano, W. D., & Brewer, M. B. (1973). *Principles of research in social psychology*. New York: McGraw Hill.

Dando, C. J., & Oxburgh, G. E. (2016). Empathy in the field: Towards a taxonomy ofempathic communication in information gathering interviews with suspected sexoffenders. *European Journal of Psychology Applied to Legal Context*, *8*, 27–33.

Denzin, N. K. (2017). *The research act: A theoretical introduction to sociological methods*. Routledge.

DeVellis, R. F. (2016). *Scale development: Theory and applications* 4th(Ed). California: Sage publications.

Dijker, A. J. (1987). Emotional reactions to ethnic minorities. *European Journal of Social Psychology* , *17*(3), 305–325. doi: 10.1002/ejsp.2420170306

Dwyer, E. E. (1993). Attitude scale construction: A review of the literature. Retrieved from ERIC database. (ED359201).

Edwards, A. L. (1957). *Techniques of attitude scale construction*. New York: AppletonCentury-Crofts, Inc.

Ekinci, Y., & Riley, M. (1999). The application of the Guttman scaling procedure in themeasurement of consumer behavior: A marketing myopia. *Journal of Travel and Tourism Marketing*, *8*, 295–309.

Findley, K. A., & Scott, M. S. (2006). The multiple dimensions of tunnel vision in criminalcases. *Wisconsin Law Review*, 2, 291–397.

Fishbein, M., & Ajzen, I. (1974). Attitudes towards objects as predictors of single andmultiple behavioral criteria. *Psychological Review*, *81*(1), 59. Retrieved from http://dx.doi.org/10.1037/h0035872

Fisher, R. J. (1993). 'Social desirability bias and the validity of indirect questioning'. *Journal of Consumer Research*, *20*, 303–315.

Gerbing, D. W., & Anderson, J. C. (1988). An updated paradigm for scale developmentincorporating unidimensionality and its assessment. *Journal of Marketing Research*, *25*(2), 186–192.

Gothwal, V. K., Wright, T. A., Lamoureux, E. L., & Pesudovs, K. (2009). Guttman scaleanalysis of the distance vision scale. *Investigative Ophthalmology & Visual Science*, *50*, 4496–4501. doi:10.1167/iovs.08-3330

Gudjonsson, G. (2003). *The psychology of interrogations and confessions*. Chichester: JohnWiley & Sons, Ltd.

Gudjonsson, G. H. (2018). *The psychology of false confessions: Forty years of science and practice*. John Wiley & Sons.

Guttman, L. (1944). A basis for scaling qualitative data. *American Sociological Review*, 9(2), 139–150. Retrieved from www.jstor.org/stable/2086306

Guttman, L. (1950). The principal components of scale analysis. *Measurement of Prediction*, 312–361.

Hattie, J. (1985). Methodology review: Assessing unidimensionality of tests and terms. *Applied Psychological Measurement,* 9, 139–164.

Heise, D. R. (1970). The semantic differential and attitude research. *Attitude Measurement*, *4*, 235–253.

Hill, C., Memon, A., & McGeorge, P. (2008). The role of confirmation bias in suspectinterviews: A systematic evaluation. *Legal and Criminological Psychology*, *13*, 357–371. doi: 10.1348/135532507X238682

Hoffman, C., & Hurst, N. (1990). Gender stereotypes: Perception or rationalization? *Journalof Personality and Social Psychology, 58,* 197–208. doi: 10.1037/0022-3514.58.2.197

Holmberg, U., & Christianson, S. Å. (2002). Murderers' and sexual offenders' experiences ofpolice interviews and their inclination to admit or deny crimes. *Behavioral Sciences & The Law*, *20*, 31–45. doi: 10.1002/bsl.470

Hurren, E., Kebbell, M., & Mazerolle, P. (2006). *An investigation into the effective andethical interviewing of suspected sex offenders*. Australian Institute of Criminology.

Irving, B. (1980). *Police interrogation: a case study of current practice:* Research StudyNo.2. Royal Commission on Criminal Procedure. London: HMSO.

Joshi, A., Kale, S., Chandel, S., & Pal, D. K. (2015). Likert scale: Explored and explained. *British Journal of Applied Science & Technology*, *7*(4), 396–403.

Kassin, S. M., Goldstein, C. C., & Savitsky, K. (2003). Behavioural confirmation in theinterrogation room: On the dangers of presuming guilt. *Law and Human Behaviour, 27,* 187–203. doi; 10.1023/A:1022599230598

Latham, G. P., Fay, C. H., & Saari, L. M. (1979). The development of behaviouralobservation scales for appraising the performance of foremen. *Personnel Psychology,* 32, 299–311.

Leyens, J. P., Yzerbyt, V., & Schadron, G. (1994). *Stereotypes and social cognition*. London:Sage.

Likert, R. (1932). A technique for the measurement of attitudes. *Archives of Psychology, 140,5–55.*

MacKenzie, S. B., Podsakoff, P. M., & Podsakoff, N. P. (2011). Construct measurementandvalidation procedures in MIS andandvalidation procedures in MIS behavioral research: Integrating newandexisting techniques. *MIS Quarterly,* 35, 293–334.

Manheim, H. L. (1977). *Sociological research: philosophy and methods*. Homewood, Ill. TheDorsey Press.

McGurk, B. J., Carr, M. J., & McGurk D. (1993). Investigative interviewing courses forpolice officers: An evaluation. Police Research Group Paper No. 4, London: Home Office.

Mclver, J. P. & Carmines, E. G. (1981*). Unidimensional scaling*. Beverly Hills, CA: Sage.

Menzel, H. (1953). A new coefficient for scalogram analysis. *Public Opinion Quarterly, 17*(2), 268–280.

Merton, R. K. (2016). The self-fulfilling prophecy. *The Antioch Review*, *74*, 504–521.

Milne, R, & Bull, R. (1999) *Investigative interviewing: Psychology and Practice.* Chichester:John Wiley & Sons Ltd.

Milne, R., & Bull, R. (2016). Witness interviews and crime investigation. *An introduction to applied cognitive psychology*, 175–196.

Minhas, R. A., Walsh, D., & Bull, R. (2017). Developing a scale to measure the presence of possible prejudicial stereotyping in police interviews with suspects: The Minhas Investigative Interviewing Prejudicial Stereotyping Scale (MIIPSS). *Police Practice and Research, 18*(2), 132–145.

Mortimer, A., & Shepherd, E. (1999). Frames of mind: Schemata guiding cognition andconduct in the interviewing of suspected offenders. In A. Memon & R. Bull (Eds.),*Handbook of the psychology of interviewing* (pp. 293–315). Chichester: Wiley.

Moser, C. A., & Kalton, G. (2017). *Survey methods in social investigation*. London: Routledge.
Moston, S., Stephenson, G. M., & Williamson, T. M. (1992). The effects of casecharacteristics on suspect behaviour during police questioning. *British Journal of Criminology, 32,* 23–40.
Mueller, D. J. (1970). Physiological techniques of attitude measurement. *Attitude Measurement*, 534–552.
Nickerson, R. S. (1998). Confirmation bias: A ubiquitous phenomenon in many guises. *Review of General Psychology* , 2, 175–220. doi: 10.1037/1089-2680.2.2.175
Oppenheim, A. N. (1966). *Questionnaire design and attitude measurement.* London: Heinemann.
Osgood, C. E. (1952). The nature and measurement of meaning. *Psychological Bulletin, 49*(3), 197. https://psycnet.apa.org/doi/10.1037/h0055737
Osgood, C. E., & Suci, G. J. (1955). Factor analysis of meaning. *Journal of Experimental Psychology, 50*(5), 325.
Osgood, C. E., Suci, G. J., & Tannenbaum, P. H. (1957). *The measurement of meaning. Urbana* : University of Illinois.
Oxburgh, G. E. (2011). *Developing a more effective framework for the investigativeinterviewing of suspected sex offenders* (Unpublished doctoral dissertation,University of Portsmouth).
Pearse, J., & Gudjonsson, G. (1996). Police interviewing techniques at two South Londonpolice stations. *Psychology, Crime and Law, 3*, 63–74. doi:10.1080/10683169608409795
Porier, G. W., & Lott, A. J. (1967). Galvanic skin responses and prejudice. *Journal of Personality and Social Psychology, 5*, 253–259
Selltiz, C., Wrightsman, L. S., & Cook, S. W. (1976). *Research methods in social research.* New York: Holt, Rinehart & Wnson.
Shawyer, A., & Milne, R. (2009). Investigative interviewing: Investigation, counter-fraud and behaviour. *2nd International Investigative Interviewing Research Group Conference, University of Teesside.*
Shepherd, E. & Milne, R. (1999). Full and faithful: Ensuring quality practice and integrity of outcomes in witness interviews. In A. Heaton-Armstrong, E. Shepherd & D. Wolchover (Eds.). *Analysing witness testimony: A guide for legal practitioners and other professionals*, 125–145. London: Black-stone Press Limited.
Shepherd, E. (1991). Ethical interviewing. *Policing*, 7, 42–60
Shepherd, E. (1993). Resistance in interviews; The contribution of police perception and behaviour. *Issues in Criminal and Legal Psychology, 18,* 5–12.
Stephan, W., & Stephan, C. W. (1985). Intergroup anxiety. *Journal of Social Issues, 41,* 157–175. doi: 10.1111/j.1540-4560.1985.tb01134.x
Stockdale, J.E. (1993). *Management and Supervision of Police Interviews.* Police Research Group. Home Office: London.
Stouffer, S.A., Guttman, L., Suchman, E.A., Lazarsfeld, P.F., Star, S.A., & Clausen, J.A. (1950). *Measurement and prediction,* vol 4 of *Studies in social psychology in World War II.* Princeton, NJ. Princeton University Press.

Straub, D., Boudreau, M. C., & Gefen, D. (2004). Validation guidelines for IS positivist research. *The Communications of the Association for Information Systems*, 13,63.

Thurstone, L. L., & Chave, E. J. (1929). *The Measurement of Attitude: A Psychophysical Method and Some Experiments with a Scale for Measuring Attitude Toward the Church*. University of Chicago Press: Chicago.

Trope, Y., Bassok, M., & Alon, E. (1984). The questions lay interviewers ask. *Journal of Personality, 52*, 90–105.

Uhlaner, L. M. (2005). The use of the Guttman Scale in the development of a family orientation index for smalltomedium-sized firms. *Family Business Review*, *18*, 41–56. doi: 90-371-0867-9

Venema, R. M. (2016). Police officer schema of sexual assault reports: Real rape, ambiguous cases, and false reports. *Journal of Interpersonal Violence*, *31*, 872–899.

Verhagen, T., van den Hooff, B., & Meents, S. (2015). Toward a better use of the semantic differential in IS research: An integrative framework of suggested action. *Journal of the Association for Information Systems,* 16, 108–125.

Walsh, D., & Bull, R. (2011). Benefit fraud investigative interviewing: A self-report study of investigation professionals' beliefs concerning practice. *Journal of Investigative Psychology and Offender Profiling*, *8*, 131–148. doi: 10.1002/jip.137

Walsh, D., & Milne, R. (2007). Perceptions of benefit fraud staff in the UK: Giving PEACE a chance?. *Public Administration*, *85*, 525–540. doi: 10.1111/j.1467-9299.2007.00645.x

Westie, F. R., & De Fleur, M. L. (1959). Autonomic responses and their relationship to race attitudes. *Journal of Abnormal and Social Psychology*, *58*, 340.

Williamson, T. (2006) *Investigative interviewing: Rights, research, regulation.* Devon: Willan Publishing.

Williamson, T. M. (1993). From interrogation to investigative interviewing; strategic trends in police questioning. *Journal of Community & Applied Social Psychology*, *3*(2), 8–99. doi:10.1002/casp.2450030203

Woodmansee, J. J. (1970). The pupil response as a measure of social attitudes. *Attitude Measurement. Chicago: Rand McNally*, 514–533.

Yoon, T. H., & Ekinci, Y. (2003). An examination of the SERVQUAL dimensions using the Guttman scaling procedure. *Journal of Hospitality & Tourism Research*, 27, 3–23.

Chapter 5

Perceptions of suspects from Muslim communities regarding police interviewing practices

A Qualitative Study

Introduction

The previous chapter identified five core constructs related to prejudicial stereotyping in investigative interviewing. These constructs include: (i) possessing negative perceptions, (ii) the use of schemas, (iii) guilt presumption, (iv) a self-fulfilling prophecy, and (v) a hostile approach. The Guttman scalogram analysis confirmed that these five constructs formed a valid Guttman scale. This suggests that police interviewers' attitudes could potentially transform into a hostile approach if they hold negative stereotypes about suspects based on factors such as ethnicity, race, geographic origin, or the type of crime involved. With these five constructs of the MIIPSS established, the current chapter aims to investigate how police interviewers' attitudes are perceived by real-life suspects within the 'suspect' community. This examination will shed light on the impact of these constructs on the interactions between law enforcement and suspects.

Research on investigative decision-making highlights that police investigators often rely on heuristics, which are sets of working rules they develop through practical experience gained from conducting investigations or day-to-day experiences (Smith & Flanagan, 2000). However, it's important to note that heuristics can sometimes lead to cognitive biases and mental errors, as indicated by previous studies (e.g. Rossmo, 2006). One particularly significant heuristic that has been linked to miscarriages of justice and investigative failures is known as 'tunnel vision', as identified by Snook and Cullen (2008). Tunnel vision can result from various processes, including cognitive distortions like confirmation bias (Rassin, 2018). Previous research has demonstrated that confirmation bias towards suspects' guilt during police interviews can lead to an 'accusatorial' style of interviewing. In this approach, police officers employ a confirmatory strategy to elicit confessions, as evidenced by the findings of Mortimer and Shepherd (1999). Furthermore, Kassin, Goldstein, and Savitsky (2003) observed that when investigators hold expectations of a suspect's

DOI: 10.4324/9781003366836-5

guilt, they tend to exhibit certain interview behaviours. These behaviours include: (i) asking more guilt-presumptive questions, (ii) engaging in persistent and coercive forms of questioning, and (iii) applying greater pressure on suspects to confess. These actions can potentially contribute to or result in false confessions, highlighting the critical need for addressing confirmation bias and its implications within investigative processes.

One of the most disturbing forms of biases within the criminal justice system revolves around prejudicial stereotypes regarding specific groups, as highlighted by Huggon (2012). These biases can target various aspects such as race, ethnicity, or an individual's group membership, extending beyond just these categories (Smith & Alpert, 2007). Prejudicial stereotypes are widely recognised as a significant source of bias that can introduce partiality into criminal trials (Huggon, 2012). In his seminal work, Allport (1954) proposed that prejudice is an inevitable and common consequence of the ordinary categorisation process, which includes stereotyping. Both negative stereotyping and prejudice have been identified as factors that can adversely impact police officers' pursuit of truth during investigations (Huggon, 2012; Williamson, 2006). This is especially concerning, considering that the official and stated goal of police interviews in England and Wales, governed by PACE (1984) legislation, is to uncover the truth. Recognising and addressing these issues is important to ensure that the pursuit of justice remains fair and unbiased within the criminal justice system.

The quality of an investigative interview can indeed be influenced by police officers' personal perceptions of individuals, places, and situations. Biases such as racism, sexism, and homophobia are well-recognised factors that can impact an individual's thought process, often without them being consciously aware of these biases (Stelfox, 2009). Among these biases, one of the most concerning within the criminal justice system is the presence of prejudicial stereotypes related to specific groups (Huggon, 2012). While these stereotypes can centre on race or ethnicity, they may also extend to bias against individuals based on their group membership. Prejudicial stereotypes are widely acknowledged as a significant source of bias in criminal trials (Huggon, 2012). Police officers, typically native-born citizens, have often spent a considerable amount of time immersed in their local social and cultural environments. This exposure can lead to the formation of stereotypes based on their society's collective knowledge and beliefs (Smith & Alpert, 2007). Whether these negative stereotypes operate at a conscious or unconscious level, there is an argument that repeated contact with perceived out-groups can further reinforce and solidify these negative stereotypes (Smith & Alpert, 2007). Given that police work frequently involves interactions with marginalised, minority, and socially disadvantaged groups (Maynard-Moody & Musheno, 2003), these repeated exposures can contribute to the development of negative stereotypes. In essence, it's important to acknowledge and address the potential impact of these biases and stereotypes within the context of investigative interviewing and the criminal justice system to ensure fair and impartial processes.

The present study

The current research examines the concept of the 'suspect' community, a term initially applied by Hillyard (1993) to describe the Irish in the United Kingdom during the era of the Prevention of Terrorism Act (PTA) in 1974. This concept has since been more recently applied to Muslims in the context of the global 'war on terror' (Awan, 2012; Breen-Smyth, 2014; Pantazis & Pemberton, 2009). In England and Wales, the 'war on terror' has been argued to have a detrimental impact on existing race relations policies. This negative impact is attributed to the introduction of new legislation, such as the Terrorism Act (TA) 2000, which grants wide discretionary powers for stop-and-search and arrest, the extension of pre-charge detention to 28 days in the TA 2006, and the use of control orders to detain individuals without trial.

These measures have led to the perception that Muslims are often cast as the 'enemy within' (Warsi, 2017). Moreover, recent research conducted by academics like Awan (2012, 2018); Breen-Smyth (2014); Cherney and Murphy (2016); Hickman et al. (2011); Hickman, Silvestri, and Thomas (2010); Mythen, Walkate, and Khan (2013), and Pantazis and Pemberton (2009) suggests the existence of a police bias against Muslims in the United Kingdom. This bias is arguably a direct consequence of state suspicion and various counterterrorism legislation, further categorising Muslims as a 'suspect' community. This research underscores the complex and controversial intersection of security policies, law enforcement practices, and community perceptions in the context of counterterrorism efforts, with a particular focus on how this affects the Muslim community in the United Kingdom.

The aims of the present study are, therefore, to

- investigate the perceptions and experiences of real-life Muslim suspects during police interviews when they are treated as suspects in criminal investigations.
- determine whether an individual's group membership, particularly belonging to stigmatised groups, influences the attitudes of police officers towards suspects. This influence will be observed through the

questioning style employed by police officers during interviews with suspects from these specific groups.

These aims outline the focus of the current research, which is to gain insights into how Muslim suspects perceive their interactions with law enforcement and to examine the potential impact of group-based biases on police questioning styles during interviews with suspects from marginalised or stigmatised communities.

Methods

Participants

The present research employed semi-structured interviews involving 22 individuals from the Asian Muslim community, all of whom had previously undergone police interviews as suspects in criminal investigations. Notably, all 22 participants were male, and they were drawn from four major cities in England: Bristol, London, Manchester, and the West Midlands. Sixteen of these participants were born in England, while the remaining six were migrants from Bangladesh, India, and Pakistan. The participants had all been subjected to police interviews as suspects at least once between 2010 and 2014. Their ages spanned from 18 to 50 years, with an average age of 31.32 years and a standard deviation of 9.48. Fourteen of the participants had been interviewed regarding a single offence, while the remaining eight had been interviewed on more than one occasion, either related to single or multiple offences. It's noteworthy that 11 of the participants had been convicted of the offences for which they were last interviewed, five had been released without charges, and six were awaiting trial at the time of this research. Importantly, none of the participants were believed to have any prior connection with each other, and none received any incentives or rewards for their involvement in the study. Additional details about the index offences of each participant can be found in Table 5.1.

Procedure

The recruitment process for participants involved several steps. Initially, the researcher reached out to their associates and asked if they knew individuals who had been interviewed by the police as suspects in a crime within the last five years. These associates were requested to provide the researcher's mobile phone number to potential participants. In some cases, the suspects themselves shared their contact information with the researcher. Through these initial contacts, the researcher successfully

Table 5.1 Index of suspected offences of the 22 participants

Participant No.	*Interview year*	*Age on event*	*No. of times interviewed*	*City*	*Index suspected offences*
01	1999.2011	18,30	2	West Midlands	Drugs/Suspected terrorism
02	2013	17	1	West Midlands	GBH
03	2012	18	1	West Midlands	Drugs (intent to supply)
04	2014	24	1	London	Human trafficking
05	2006,2010	34,38	2	West Midlands	GBH, Attempted murder
06	2014	46	1	London	Dangerous driving/Drugs
07	2011	18	1	West Midlands	Drugs
08	2014	48	1	Greater Manchester	Aiding a rape
09	2014	30	1	Greater Manchester	Fraud/Money laundering
10	2014	32	2	London	Fraud/ Money laundering
11	2011,2014	43,46	2	West Midlands	Suspected terrorism
12	2014	24	1	London	Sexual assault
13	2014	26	1	London	Sexual assault
14	2011	35	2	London	Human trafficking/money laundering
15	2011,2014	30,33	3	West Midlands	Drugs (intent to supply)
16	2011	19	1	West Midlands	Sexual assault
17	2013	26	1	Bristol	GBH
18	2012	34	1	West Midlands	GBH
19	2014	18	1	West Midlands	Drugs (intent to supply)
20	2013	28	3	West Midlands	Suspected terrorism
21	2014	21	1	Bristol	Drugs
22	2014	19	2	Greater Manchester	Money laundering

obtained agreement from 16 participants to participate in the study. Additionally, the researcher enlisted the assistance of a criminal lawyer, who asked some of their clients if they would be willing to take part in the research. Through this avenue, an additional six participants were recruited. This recruitment approach illustrates the researcher's efforts to connect with individuals who had relevant experiences in police interviews as suspects, thereby creating a diverse pool of participants for the study.

Having received ethical approval from the home university, the researcher arranged meetings with each of the participants, duly conducting semi-structured interviews in public places (for example, cafes and restaurants) throughout January–May 2015. All the participants were informed that their interview would be audio recorded (if they consented) and that they were assured anonymity, provided they did not make any indications to commit further offences or did not disclose information about a crime that they had committed (for which they had not yet been convicted). Twenty participants provided consent for their interviews to be audio-recorded (the other two agreed only to notes being taken of the interview manually). Participants first were asked to provide their own interpretations of their range of experiences and perceptions during an interview about the police interviewers' attitudes towards them. Each participant was asked the same standard set of questions, though where necessary, elaboration and clarification was provided.

Following the receipt of ethical approval from the home university, the researcher proceeded to schedule individual meetings with each of the participants. These interviews were conducted in public settings, such as cafes and restaurants, spanning from January to May 2015. Prior to the interviews, all participants were explicitly informed that their interviews could be audio-recorded if they provided their consent. Furthermore, they were assured of complete anonymity unless they indicated intentions to commit additional offences or disclosed information about a crime, they had committed but not yet been convicted for.

Out of the 22 participants, 20 consented to having their interviews audio-recorded, while the remaining two participants agreed to have their interviews documented through manual note-taking. In these interviews, participants were initially invited to share their interpretations and reflections on a range of experiences and perceptions related to police interviewers' attitudes towards them. Each participant was presented with the same standardised set of questions, with the researcher offering clarification or requesting elaboration as necessary to ensure a comprehensive understanding of their experiences and perceptions. This methodology ensured consistency in data collection and analysis across all participants.

Analytical framework

The current research adopted a thematic analysis approach for the examination of interview transcriptions. Thematic analysis is known for its flexibility, allowing for both inductive (data-driven) and deductive (theory-driven) approaches. This approach was chosen because it offers the opportunity to explore the data in two ways:

(i) inductively, by allowing themes to emerge naturally from the surface meaning of the data (Frith & Gleeson, 2004),
(ii) deductively, by examining the perceptions and experiences of suspects within the framework of the five constructs of the MIIPSS (Boyatzis, 1998; Crabtree & Miller, 1999).

Inductive analysis involves coding the data without imposing a pre-existing coding frame or the researcher's analytical preconceptions (Patton, 1990). This method ensures that the analysis remains open to the emergence of new themes and insights from the participants' experiences while also allowing for a structured examination of these experiences within the context of the MIIPSS constructs (see Chapter 4). By employing thematic analysis in this manner, the research aims to provide a comprehensive understanding of how suspects perceive their interactions with police interviewers, both through the exploration of naturally occurring themes and within the established framework of the MIIPSS constructs.

Indeed, deductive analysis in contrast to inductive analysis tends to be more driven by the researcher's theoretical or analytical interests in the subject matter. It is inherently more researcher-led and guided by pre-existing theories or concepts (Braun & Clarke, 2006). Deductive analysis is often employed when the research aims to provide a detailed examination of specific aspects of the data, rather than offering a broad, rich description of the overall data set. In a deductive analysis, a researcher might code data to address specific research questions that align with their theoretical framework. Alternatively, specific themes may evolve naturally during the coding process as a result of both the researcher's theoretical perspective and the content provided by the participants themselves (Miles & Huberman, 1994). In the context of the present research, the coding approach utilised a combination of both inductive and deductive elements of thematic analysis. Codes were derived from the researcher's theoretical understanding, aligning with the deductive approach, while also emerging from the participants' narratives and experiences, which align with the inductive approach. This dual approach allowed for a comprehensive examination of the data, considering both the researcher's theoretical framework and the insights provided by the participants themselves.

Thematic analysis can be approached in two main ways: the semantic approach and the latent approach. These approaches differ in their focus and the level of analysis:

(i) ***Semantic Approach***: In the semantic approach, themes are derived from the explicit or surface meaning of the data. Researchers identify patterns, topics, or ideas that are directly apparent from what participants have said or written (Braun & Clarke, 2006). This approach is concerned with the content and apparent meaning of participants' responses.
(ii) ***Latent Approach***: In contrast, the latent approach goes beyond the surface-level content of the data (i.e. what participants explicitly express) to uncover the underlying ideas, ideologies, and assumptions that shape and govern what people say. It delves into the deeper, often implicit, meanings and beliefs that influence individuals' statements (Boyatzis, 1998). The latent approach tends to be more constructionist in nature, seeking to understand how meanings and experiences are socially constructed and shaped by sociocultural contexts and structural conditions (Burr, 2006).

From a constructionist perspective, thematic analysis that focuses on 'latent' themes does not primarily concern itself with individual motivations or perceptions. Instead, it aims to theorise the broader sociocultural and structural factors that enable and influence the accounts provided by individuals. This approach recognises that meaning is not inherent within individuals but is shaped by the larger social and cultural context in which they exist. In summary, the choice between a semantic or latent approach in thematic analysis depends on the research goals and whether the emphasis is on surface-level content or the underlying, often more complex, meanings and assumptions within the data.

In contrast, from an essentialist/realist perspective, there is an assumption of a straightforward, largely unidirectional relationship between language, meaning, and experience. It is believed that language reflects and enables individuals to articulate their meanings and experiences (Potter & Wetherell, 1987; Widdicombe & Wooffitt, 1995). Given this essentialist/realist stance, the analysis in the present research took a semantic approach. This approach is well suited for examining and understanding the explicit content of what participants say or write, emphasising the direct interpretation of their responses without delving extensively into the underlying ideologies or assumptions. The choice of a semantic approach is consistent with the present research framework, as it aligns with the essentialist/realist perspective that assumes a straightforward relationship between language, meaning, and experience, facilitating a more direct interpretation of participants' accounts.

Inductive analysis

In the present research, themes were identified based on the 'explicit or surface meaning of data' (Braun & Clarke, 2006, p. 84), adopting an inductive analysis approach (Boyatzis, 1998). The initial step involved a comprehensive review of the transcribed interviews to gain familiarity with the data. Subsequently, during a second reading, the researcher conducted a line-by-line coding to assign each sentence a code that captured its primary essence.

The coding process followed the guidelines for conducting thematic analysis outlined by Braun and Clarke (2006). Initially, all the data was coded, and these codes were later merged into larger units, grouping those that shared similar content meaning. The researcher then proceeded to sort these different codes into potential themes, collating all the relevant coded data extracts within the identified themes and subthemes for each interview.

In the current research, a theme was defined as the smallest unit capable of meaningfully expressing the codes it contained. From the individual summary sheets, the researcher constructed an overall list of themes. These themes were subsequently refined and grouped into clusters, resulting in the formation of two superordinate themes: (i) the legal framework underlying the police interview context and (ii) participants' perceptions of the interviewing practices.

Deductive analysis

The researcher employed the thematic analysis approach to examine the attitudes of interviewers as perceived by the research participants. In the case of deductive analysis, five constructs from the MIIPSS (as outlined in Chapter 4) were designated as a priori categories, and the method of category allocation was utilised.

To implement this method, the researcher thoroughly reviewed each interview transcript. He then utilised the five MIIPSS constructs as coding categories, examining whether: (i) any of these constructs were evident in each transcript; (ii) they aligned with the descriptions of these constructs provided in Chapter 4; and (iii) they could identify any evidence of specific constructs within the transcripts. The examination of each construct is presented in the results section under the superordinate theme of 'perceived attitudes of the interviewers as held by the suspects'.

Inter-rater reliability

After completing the coding process of the transcriptions, the researcher sought an independent PhD researcher with expertise in thematic analysis to code a randomly selected set of ten transcripts. The independent rater worked with clean copies of the transcriptions, working independently and without knowledge of the researcher's initial coding results.

To assess the inter-rater reliability in identifying the three themes mentioned earlier—namely, the legal framework underlying the police interview context, participants' perceptions of interviewing practices, and perceived attitudes of the interviewers as held by the Muslim suspects—Cohen's kappa was employed. The analysis revealed a Cohen's kappa value of 0.91, indicating a strong level of agreement (Fleiss, 1981).

Results

The findings are discussed and presented under these main themes: (i) the legal framework underlying the police interview context; (ii) participants' perceptions of interviewing practices; and (iii) the perceived attitudes of the interviewers as held by the Muslim suspects. For each of these themes, this chapter constructed an analytical narrative and included extracts from the transcripts to provide illustrative examples.

The legal framework underlying the police interview context

Within this superordinate theme, this chapter explores two distinct subthemes that align with research participants' perceptions of the legal framework surrounding police interviews:

(i) Section 76 and Section 78 of PACE (1984): In this subtheme, this chapter delves into the participants' perspectives on the application of Section 76 and Section 78 of PACE.
(ii) Explaining Legal Procedures: This subtheme focuses on how research participants perceive the explanations of legal procedures during police interviews.

The examination of these subthemes paves the way for a deeper understanding of research findings.

Section 76 and section 78 of PACE (1984).

Section 76 of PACE (1984) deals with challenges to the admissibility of confessions and directs the court to exclude confession evidence obtained by oppression in circumstances likely to make the confession unreliable. Section 78 of PACE (1984) provides further safeguards against police malpractice. It allows the courts to exclude any evidence that would otherwise be admissible against a defendant felt to have been unfairly induced. None of the participants described any instances that evidently indicated a violation of either Section 76 or Section 78 of PACE.

For example, participant (08) stated:

> I was given time to comment. They treated me alright; they didn't misbehave towards me.

Building on the previous insights into Section 76 and Section 78 of PACE, it's noteworthy that all the participants shared a common view that they were treated better during the interviews as compared to during their arrest and custody arrangements. For example, participant (13) described it in this way:

> Overall my experience in all three (arrest, custody, and interview) was not pleasant, but I would say the interview was much better. Due to the police officers were not wearing a uniform I did not feel intimidated. I was not asked any irrelevant question.

Explaining the legal procedures

Continuing the exploration of participants' experiences, it's important to note that at the beginning of the interview, police interviewers explained the purpose of the interview. They also mentioned the legal rights that the suspects had, according to all the participants. For example, participant (16) reported,

> I mean, the initial questions were making sure I understood my charges, why I'd been brought there and what rights I had, you know, like the right to remain silent and the right to legal representation.

Participants' perceptions of interviewing practices

Within this superordinate theme, this section explores three distinct subthemes that align with participants' perceptions of the techniques employed by police interviewers during interviews:

(i) Participants' Perceptions of Interviewers' Communication: This subtheme delves into how participants perceive their interviewers' communication with them.
(ii) Effects of Evidence on Participants' Denials and Confessions: This subtheme focuses on the effects of evidence on participants' denials and confessions during interviews.
(iii) Use of Tactics Employed by Interviewers: This subtheme examines the tactics employed by interviewers as perceived by the participants.

The examination of these subthemes provides valuable insights into the techniques employed by police interviewers and their impact on participants' perceptions.

Participants' perceptions of their interviewer's communication (rapport) with them

In exploring participants' experiences during police interviews, it is notable that 16 of the participants described their interactions with police interviewers as uncomfortable and characterised by an unfriendly atmosphere. For example, participant (16) reported,

> They started off with the whole what my rights are, what I can do, what I cannot do and then straightaway they got into it, right you have been arrested for [...], give us your side of the story, why did this happen, what was going on?

Similarly, participant (06) stated,

> No, I mean, like I said, it was all done professionally. At no point was anybody overly aggressive to me, but they were not placid either. It was, sort of, right tell us, you know, what you have got to say for yourself basically.

Another participant (05) described it in this way:

> So, when I went to the interview they started throwing the questions at me instead of listening to me.

In contrast, six of the participants reported a more positive experience, noting that their interviewers communicated with them in a friendly manner. These participants reported that police interviewers explained all the procedures before the interview. Furthermore, the interviewers followed those procedures throughout the interview. For instance, participant (19) described his experience this way:

> When I was arrested and taken to the police station, I thought I would be mistreated, but overall, my experience in the police station was pleasant. At the police station, I was introduced to the interviewers. I was told that they would be interviewing me. They did not ask me any questions that I would feel pressured. I was given enough time to answer, and I was not interrupted during the entire interview. Before the interview, I was given full information on what and what time I would be interviewed and what procedures would be taken, and they followed all of the procedures throughout the interview.

Effects of evidence on participants' denials and confessions during interviews

Building on an examination of participants' perceptions and confession patterns, it's important to note that six of the participants perceived the evidence held by the police against them as strong. Out of these six participants, five stated that they did not attempt to deny their guilt to the police. They all shared a common reason for confessing: a belief that the police officers would be able to prove their guilt due to the strong evidence against them. Participant (06), perhaps, best encapsulates this:

> I was caught in the act [...] I mean, I can say this [...] I was guilty, and I did go in with a guilty plea [...] it was a mistake that is what's happened, nothing, yes, I wanted to confess to it.

Continuing this exploration of participants' confession decisions during their interviews with police, participant (22) shared that he initially denied his guilt but later decided to confess when he believed the police had gathered enough evidence to prove his guilt. He stated,

> Slowly, slowly, pulling out loads of evidence and then obviously [...] but then when they come out with the evidence, I knew that if I carried on lying I am going to get sent to trial and I am going to get, like, extra years on my sentence, even though I got told I got two years. I would be looking five, five and a half, but then obviously they sorted it out of Crown Court they go just knock it down to two if you plead guilty and obviously reduce my sentence, so that's it, better start talking, isn't it? I just admitted to everything, I said, yes, I done it and then...

In contrast, 16 of the participants held a different perspective. They believed that the evidence against them was either very weak or non-existent. Importantly, these are the same participants who also mentioned that police officers were not friendly towards them. These participants stated that police interviewers exerted pressure and wanted them to confess when they were not involved in any wrongdoings (or evidence against them was either very weak or did not exist at all). For example, participant (11) said,

> There was no evidence against me; evidence did not exist. It was one-way traffic. They tried to contain me and re-enforce their version.

Moreover, participant (04) stated,

> There was no evidence; they did not present any evidence other than a witness statement. The witness was the accomplice of the main suspect. He was given witness protection by the police. Whatever he said against me, police believed him blindly, and I was charged on the basis of his statement.

Tactics employed by the interviewers as perceived by the participants

Fourteen of the participants shared a common experience. They perceived that repetitive and guilt-presumptive questions dominated the questioning during the interview. These are the participants who also indicated there was a lack of good communication (rapport) between them and the interviewers, and they perceived that the evidence against them was weak or didn't exist at all. For example, participant (05) reported,

> When you come in there, you're already, like you had been charged already. It shouldn't be like that. I should have a chance to express myself and to give my event of what happened.

Further, participant (15) stated,

> Like, for example, something happened, and they are making out it's me and then trying to turn my words around and saying, you were there this time that happened it was you. Trying to make everything into a different story, what's happened and make it into a different...

A number of these participants stated that police interviewers exerted pressure on them during interviews. For instance, participant (22) described his situation in this way:

> Yes, twisting the questions and twisting my words. If I am saying something, he'll twist it saying that he did not just say something else, then he wants me to say what he's saying, but it did not work, and then I start shouting a bit.

Nevertheless, eight of the participants stated that police interviewers asked relevant questions. These particular participants emphasised that the purpose of the questioning throughout the interview seemed to be to know their part of the story. For instance, participant (13) stated,

> My interviewers were interested in getting my part of the story. They did not try to accuse me or treat me badly.

Participant (18) described his experience like this:

> I think I'm lucky in that case I have good police interviewers. I would say they asked me fair questions.

Furthermore, a couple of participants who had been interviewed by the police on multiple occasions, both with and without legal representation, emphasised the importance of having a legal representative. They described that when they did not have legal representation, police officers asked them repetitive and guilt-presumptive questions. For instance, participant (15) stated:

> When the solicitors are there, they only ask the basic questions. When the solicitors are not there, they go into it differently really. With the solicitor, they ask you the same questions, and you speak to the solicitor, he does it properly without the solicitor there they keep going on and on.

Perceived attitudes of the interviewers as held by the Muslim suspects

This superordinate theme is comprised of five subthemes which are consistent with the participants' perceptions concerning the police officers' attitudes towards them. These subthemes are: (i) possessing negative perceptions; (ii) use of schemas; (iii) guilt presumption; (iv) self-fulfilling prophecy; and (v) hostile approach.

Possessing negative perceptions

Building on the previous chapter's findings, it's evident that interviews may be significantly influenced by negative perceptions held by police interviewers, particularly when suspects identify one or more of the following factors during the interview: (i) the interviewer's perceived attitudes towards them were negative; (ii) there was a lack of empathy, and (iii) there was an absence of good communication (or rapport) between the suspect and the interviewer.

When reflecting on their perceptions of police officers' attitudes, 17 of the participants believed that police officers held negative attitudes toward them. The majority of these participants perceived the police interviewers as unfriendly during the interview and believed that their attitudes were biased. For instance, participant (02) stated,

> They are always biased and negative towards you because obviously, they are interviewing you. They want you to fall into their trap, isn't it? In the interview, they are negative all the way.

Further, participant (05) described this as,

> A tense moment, not a very good experience, I was treated unfairly as I walked in.

Use of schemas

As discussed in the previous chapter, police interviewers may exhibit negative attitudes towards suspects for various reasons, which can be attributed to:

(i) Suspects' group membership,
(ii) Suspects' race,
(iii) Suspects' religious beliefs,
(iv) The specific nature of the crime (e.g. sexual offences, paedophilia, or drug-related crimes), or
(v) Suspects' prior criminal record, if known to the police.

Over two-thirds of the participants (68.2 per cent) cited several factors contributing to police officers' negative attitudes towards them, namely: (i) being previously known to the police, (ii) ethnicity, (iii) religion, (iv) police culture, and (v) specific crime-related location. Each of these factors will now be discussed in detail.

PREVIOUSLY BEING KNOWN TO THE POLICE

Among the participants who had been interviewed by the police on multiple occasions, five individuals mentioned that the perceived negative attitudes from police officers could be attributed to their prior criminal record. For example, participant (22) stated,

> I have had a case where I have been beaten up by a gang, and I have been hurt, wounded, and I have taken the case to the police, they did not take it any further. They said this case could not go to court. Even though I had a witness, they said we could not take it to court, we do not trust you, because of your criminal record.

Moreover, participant (15) described his situation like this:

> Got a grudge, no, they just do not like me. Well, some of them were. I got arrested in (police station name) and (town name) police are no good. Yes, some police are good, the rest...

Further, participant (02) encapsulated his experience in this way:

> I do not know, probably my colour. There's no respect. I have been in trouble with the police a few times, so they know your faces, do you know what I mean?

ETHNICITY

Thirteen participants stated that police officers' perceived negative attitudes towards them might be attributed to their ethnicity. For instance, participant (21) mentioned

> There's a certain mindset, or there's a certain belief system, you know, amongst some of the police officers which actually they feel that you know, perhaps people of like Asian Muslim background ethnicity are the enemy, are the criminals.

Another, participant (03), described it in this way:

> You see, we are scum. Before it used to be the Black, but now it's the Asian more scum. I think Muslims and Asians are being targeted everywhere; media, news, police. Most media, all this 9/11, this war against terrorism and all that it plays a big role in it.

RELIGION

Seven participants believed that police interviewers' perceived negative attitudes towards them could be linked to their religious background. For example, participant (07) reported,

> Yes, as I mentioned before, the one officer, you know, when he was saying things like your kind or your type of person and, you know, it was fairly obvious that he was discriminating. But, then afterwards it became apparent to me when he commented that I'd rather interview a Bob over an Abdul any day. It became very apparent that it had to do with my race and religious background, so it was very clear at that point.

Participant (17) claimed he had been wrongly accused and falsely convicted of a serious offence. He went on to describe that at one stage of the investigation, he became so fearful that police officers might connect him to terrorism offences because of his religious background. He stated,

> I thought they were very cooperative with me in the beginning, but as time passed, I realised that the only thing they wanted was to get me convicted. I think my religious background played an important part and they thought I could be a terrorist. However, I was tricked, trapped, and deceived.

He further described the experience:

> The overall attitudes of the police interviewers were very negative towards me, they were committed to proving me guilty, and they wanted to send me to prison. And this was mainly due to my Islamic background and sporting a beard. That's why I became so scared that they would link me with terrorism offences.

POLICE CULTURE

Four of the participants thought that it is a matter of police culture (in holding negative attitudes towards anyone who is suspected of committing a crime). For instance, participant (09) stated,

> That's the way they are brought up in the camp. Even if it's an Asian police officer, it's the same attitude. If he's White or Black or whatever, they have all got the same attitude. It's the uniform. It's the power, and that's why.

Participant (19) encapsulated it as,

> 'hey take advantage of their authority. Every police officer just wants to win the case. They always look at you as if you have done something wrong. It is not always like that, is it? But it's the way, the police are.

SPECIFIC CRIME-RELATED LOCATION

Five participants described instances where police officers might hold negative attitudes if an individual is of Asian descent and the alleged crime is drug-related in a specific location. For example, Participant (16) reported,

> Basically, I lived in a very Muslim Asian area, and the area was known to have problems with the police. You know, drug dealing happens everywhere. Because it was an Asian area, it was that sort of profile, they had [...] I was a student. I was doing a law degree myself at the time, but they did not even know any of that. As far as they were concerned, what it felt like was just another guy brought off the street and they were not willing to even talk to me.

Participant (22) described it like this:

> When you see copper, they'll be like this, like that, or they'll be like, oh, what you got on you today class A or class B? They say it partly, like. Obviously, people sell drugs around here and obviously the Asians and Muslims, and these lot just think because one Asian Muslim is doing it, all the Asian Muslims are doing it in the area.

Guilt presumption

As revealed in the previous chapter, interviewers might have presumed a suspect's guilt if the suspect exhibited one or more of the following behaviours during their interview:

(i) The interviewer asked guilt-presumptive questions, displaying confirmation bias.
(ii) The interviewer posed provocative questions.
(iii) The interviewer employed bluffing tactics.
(iv) The interviewer demonstrated inflexibility, failing to adjust their stance in light of new information from the interviewee.
(v) The interviewer responded to the suspect's behaviour with destabilising, disturbing, or confusing non-verbal reactions.

Fourteen participants believed that police officers presumed their guilt from the outset of the interview. Many of these participants mentioned that, after explaining the legal procedures, the officers proceeded to ask questions aimed at proving their guilt. For instance, participant (05) reported,

> Like as soon as I came in, they treated me like I was guilty of the crime, not giving me a chance to prove my innocence. When I went to the interview, they started throwing the questions at me, instead of listening to me, when I should have had a bit more chance for them to understand the story.

Another, participant (11) stated,

> They treated me as if I am a convicted criminal, repeated accusations. They used jargon and tried to suppress me technically.

These participants reported that police officers repeatedly posed guilt-presumptive questions. For instance, participant (09) reported,

> No, because they kept asking the same question and then he starts raising his voice, so you know that he wants to get it out of you, but if I do not know the truth, then how can I tell them something.

Another, participant (10) reported this as,

> When they did ask me harsh questions, my solicitor got involved and told them that he did not need to answer that. So, yeah, a few times there were situations where my solicitor got involved, and he noticed there was a bit more pressure from them on me. But they got a way of doing, even they cover themselves as well.

Self-fulfilling prophecy effect

As was noted in the previous chapter, interviews could be influenced by police interviewers' self-fulfilling prophecies when interviewers:

(i) Overemphasised the evidence.
(ii) Disregarded evidence that could have favoured the suspect or at least not implied guilt.
(iii) Exaggerated or downplayed the nature of the offence.
(iv) Repeatedly accused the suspect of the crime(s).
(v) Continuously asked leading questions.

Ten participants perceived that the police officers: (i) exaggerated the evidence; (ii) ignored the evidence that could have gone in their favour (or at least not supported any belief of guilt); (iii) maximised the nature of the offences; and (iv) repeatedly accused them of the crime. A number of these participants described the police officers' presumption of guilt even though there was no evidence to connect them to the crime. These participants perceived that the police officers still tried to connect them to the crime with 'irrelevant' evidence. For example, participant (06) described his experience in this way:

> See, in terms of, like, the evidence, see some evidence was obviously brought into the interview room, which some of it was really like irrelevant, something [...] I mean, obviously, I do not want to go into details, but something that [...] you know, because they did search my house, you know, and they found a few things which were totally irrelevant, was totally not connected to the crime at all. In fact, there was nothing at all. That was nothing to do with them. But, I felt that they were trying to make links. Make links which are stupid links, and I just laughed, and I said, no, and even those things, you know, they had no weight to them. It's just, like, trying to make mountains out of molehills. That's why, you know, the CPS did not even bother taking it seriously, but the police just for the sake of it...

Another, participant (11), stated,

> Muslim plus Asian is an ingredient to criminality in their eyes. They already made up their mind that I was guilty, and their approach was authoritative. They manipulated the questions to as much extent as they could. They wanted me to get charged.

Further, participant (02) reported,

> They want to believe what they want to believe, no matter what I say. I am a criminal in their eyes.

Six of these participants reported that police officers were so determined to charge them that they disregarded evidence that could have supported the suspects' innocence. For example, participant (5) reported,

> All the evidence was short, CCTV, that was missing. They presented the evidence which was all against me and nothing in my defence. My solicitor asked for that, but we never got it. I do not know what circumstances, maybe it was what colour I am, ethnicity group I am, or maybe they just like that, they try to get all the evidence against me.

Three participants reported that police officers exaggerated and reached conclusions that exceeded what the evidence warranted. These participants explained that although the Crown Prosecution Service (CPS) successfully charged them, the court later dropped the case due to insufficient evidence against them. For example, participant (01) stated,

> Because when I got done for the drugs, there were no drugs found on me, and they are still saying those drugs are you. They got their own version saying you went there and you are a drug dealer, which I was not. They got their own version. So, I had to go to court, and at the end the court dropped it.

Hostile approach

As mentioned in the previous chapter, an interviewer's approach may turn hostile if they (i) come across as oppressive, such as instances of undue pressure, bullying, or constant challenges; and/or (ii) pose persistent and coercive questions during the interview. During the interview, eight of the participants perceived that the police officers had displayed hostility towards them. For instance, participant (17) described his experience like this:

> He kept repeating the question about the diary, again and again, I started smiling. The police officer shouted, Stop smiling, I am serious about these questions. My solicitor intervened. The police officer lost his temper with him too and shouted, You do not need to intervene, let the suspect talk. Then they stopped the interview.

Whereas, participant (18) reported his on his situation in the following way:

> However, during the third interview, the interviewers were very persistent, and they asked me such questions that I felt that they were pressurising me to say something and go against my solicitor's advice. In the third interview, they just wanted me to confess and say that I have done this. They were pushing me to speak up and confess.

Further, participant (11) described his experience this way:

> 'Police interviewers' behaviour towards me was very dehumanising and threatening. I felt powerless as the interviewers were in actual power and controlling everything, they are control freaks'.

When reflecting on the police officers' attitudes during interviews, a couple of participants described it as aggressive and threatening. For instance, participant (06) offered this description:

> Because he was losing his cool, you know his posture. I noticed he started leaning back, you know, raising his chin, raising his voice, and he started flapping his hands about and stuff, you know. It was not very pleasant. He came across as very aggressive. I do remember at one point he slammed his fist on the table, do you understand?

Discussion

The present chapter investigated the perceptions of Asian Muslim suspects regarding the potential use of negative stereotypes by police interviewers. Additionally, this chapter sought to determine whether interviewers employ tactics that deviate from the current guidelines for police interviewing practices in England and Wales, as outlined in the PACE Code C. Building upon the five constructs identified in the previous chapter through analysis of the MIIPSS (as discussed in the previous chapter), this chapter also delves into whether these suspects perceive the presence of prejudicial stereotypes during police interviews. If such perceptions exist, the present chapter explored the extent to which these perceived prejudicial stereotypes translate into discriminatory behaviour.

Based on findings in relation to the legal framework that governs police interviews, it becomes evident that police interviewers demonstrate a high level of awareness regarding the significance of legal and procedural aspects. The PACE Act has established a standardised and structured set of procedures that police interviewers must adhere to; failure to do so could result in the interview being deemed inadmissible in court. All participants reported that, at the outset of the interview, the police officers explained the purpose of the interview and outlined the legal rights the participants possessed. Interestingly, participants shared a common perception that they were treated more respectfully during their formal interviews compared to their interactions at the time of arrest or during custody arrangements. It is apparent that there has been overall improvement in the standards of police interviewing, particularly concerning legal and procedural matters, since the introduction of the PACE Act and the PEACE model. This aligns with the findings of earlier studies, as demonstrated by Clarke and Milne (2001); Clarke, Milne, and Bull (2011); and Griffiths and Milne (2006).

Additional findings, regarding participants' perceptions of interviewing practices, reveal that in interviews characterised by poor rapport, participants perceived police officers as tending to accuse them directly or indirectly right after explaining the legal procedures. In such interviews, participants described their experience as agonising, indicating a hostile atmosphere. This finding raises concerns about whether these interviews provided a suitable foundation for open and productive conversations, a fundamental principle of the investigative interview model in which police officers are trained. Research in the field suggests that poor rapport building is associated with an increased risk of police interviewers failing to elicit comprehensive and reliable accounts from interviewees (Walsh & Bull, 2012). In this study, just under two-thirds of the participants reported poor communication, indicating that they felt their interviews were agonising and confrontational. This aligns with the findings of Walsh and Bull (2012), who also found that poor rapport building is linked to an increased risk of police interviewers failing to obtain comprehensive and reliable accounts—a primary objective of police interviews in England and Wales. Therefore, the findings of this research suggest that in interviews marked by poor rapport, police interviewers may obtain incomplete accounts, lacking crucial information or evidence that could assist in determining the innocence or guilt of the individuals involved.

Furthermore, the present research revealed a significant trend: when participants perceived that the evidence against them was strong, they were more inclined to confess to their guilt. Conversely, when participants believed or perceived that the evidence was weak or non-existent, they consistently denied their involvement and refuted any accusations. This finding aligns with earlier research, notably the pre-PEACE studies conducted by Moston, Stephenson, and Williamson (1992) and Baldwin (1993), which observed a similar pattern. There are two plausible explanations for these findings. Firstly, it's possible that these particular participants perceived the evidence against them as weak. Consequently, they felt it was challenging for the police interviewers to establish their guilt, leading them to deny involvement. Secondly, when police officers lacked strong evidence, they tended to repeat the original accusations and ask more guilt-presumptive questions in an attempt to obtain confessions. Consequently, these interviews often lacked rapport, as participants emphasised that police interviewers exerted pressure and sought confessions even when they had not engaged in wrongdoing or when the evidence against them was weak or non-existent.

The third qualitative theme, related to prejudicial stereotyping, is a novel contribution to this research. After developing the MIIPSS constructs, the researcher applied these constructs to examine whether police interviewers held negative stereotypes towards suspects and, if so, to what extent these perceived negative stereotypes manifested as discriminatory behaviour (Minhas, Walsh, & Bull, 2017). When participants were asked about their perceptions of police officers' attitudes, the majority (82 per cent) indicated that they perceived police interviewers' attitudes as negative. These negative attitudes were attributed to various factors, including: (i) the participants being previously known to the police (33 per cent); (ii) their ethnicity (60 per cent); (iii) their religious beliefs (32 per cent); (iv) aspects of police culture (14 per cent); or (v) the specific crime-related location (23 per cent). This fixed and overgeneralised belief about a particular group or class of people is known as stereotyping, as defined by Fiske and Durante (2016).

Negative stereotypes are among the most concerning biases within the criminal justice system, with a particular focus on race or ethnicity (Huggon, 2012). The persistence of negative stereotypes inevitably leads to prejudice (Devine, 1989). According to the Social Identity Theory's explanation of the social foundation of such stereotypes, group membership serves to enhance self-esteem. Consequently, individuals often exhibit a preference for in-group members (those similar to themselves) over out-group members (those different from themselves) (Tajfel & Turner, 1979). The cumulative findings from current research, which highlight the impact of negative stereotypes based on ethnicity, religion, or specific crime locations leading to guilt presumption and self-fulfilling prophecies, align with previous research (Devine, 1989; Huggon, 2012; Tajfel & Turner, 1979). They collectively suggest that the use of negative stereotypes can have detrimental effects on interviews, especially when suspects hail from stigmatised out-group communities. These findings support this assertion, with over 59 per cent of the suspects perceiving negative attitudes from police interviewers based on their racial and religious background.

To what extent can negative stereotypical attitudes translate into discriminatory behaviour? Nearly two-thirds of the participants in the current study perceived that police interviewers posed guilt-presumptive questions, and they attributed this to the influence of negative stereotypes. Previous research has shown that guilt-presumptive questions can create a self-fulfilling prophecy effect (Hill et al., 2008; Kassin et al., 2003). Alarmingly, almost half of the participants believed that their interviews could be influenced by police officers' self-fulfilling prophecies. Consequently, this approach, characterised by guilt presumption and self-fulfilling prophecy effects, may have led interviewers to exhibit hostility or discrimination towards suspects, as our previous chapter's findings revealed. Additionally, one-third of the participants reported instances of interviewers' discriminatory behaviour.

During the present study, several suspects claimed that police officers disregarded evidence that could have favoured their case. Existing research indicates that confirmation bias and tunnel vision may be more prevalent in investigative processes when the suspect comes from a stigmatised community (Roach & Trotter, 2004). The experience in previous Irish cases highlights how tunnel vision can contribute to various system failures, such as police negligence, misconduct, and the failure to discover or disclose exculpatory evidence (Findley & Scott, 2006).

Future research is necessary for two primary reasons: (i) to validate the conclusions drawn in the present study and (ii) to explore whether, in real-life investigations, police officers overlook or fail to disclose exculpatory evidence when dealing with suspects from the 'suspect' community. Furthermore, it is crucial to compare and contrast the experiences of suspects from different communities to gain a more comprehensive understanding of the implications of prejudicial stereotypes during investigative interviews. Considering that the present study focused on suspects from the 'suspect' community, specifically Asian Muslims, it is evident that additional research is needed to comprehensively comprehend the extent and consequences of negative stereotypes within the context of investigative interviews involving suspects from various communities.

However, it is important to approach these data with caution. Some of the unsatisfactory findings may not necessarily be linked to race or religion but could be attributed to police mishandling, which might have been voiced regardless of the suspect's ethnicity or religious background.

Limitations

Semi-structured interviews, commonly used to assess people's perceptions, are susceptible to errors due to cognitive and motivational biases, primarily relying on self-reports (Ehrlich & Rinehart, 1965). During these interviews, there is a risk that suspects may exaggerate their responses or allow their biases against the police to influence their answers. To counteract potential biases, the researcher took several precautions. Firstly, it was ensured that none of the participants had any prior knowledge of one another or of the researcher. This was achieved by avoiding recruitment methods that would allow participants to refer others. Additionally, participants were selected independently to reduce the risk of shared biases. Moreover, in the current study, participants recalled events from up to five years before their interviews. Such a time-lapse can affect the accuracy of memories, and participants might have consulted with others during this intervening period. These interactions could lead to memory distortions or source monitoring errors. To address this concern, the present study considered the influence of time delay and external consultations on the reliability of participants' recollections.

While the sample size was small, it's essential to acknowledge that the participants belonged to a minority community traditionally considered hard to reach for research purposes. However, despite the small sample, thematic saturation was evident, suggesting that a larger sample might not have provided significantly more insights. It's important to recognise that the superordinate themes presented in this study are the result of the researcher's interpretations of the data. These interpretations could potentially be influenced by biases, either against the police or the suspects involved in the study. To address this concern, the present study assessed inter-rater reliability using Cohen's kappa, which yielded a strong coefficient of 0.91. This high level of agreement among raters suggests that researcher bias may not have unduly influenced the interpretation of the data.

Conclusions

The present study's findings indicate that negative stereotypes based on suspects' ethnicity or religion can lead to discriminatory behaviour when interviewing suspects from out-groups. However, it is challenging to determine whether these racial or religious stereotypes operate consciously or unconsciously. From a theoretical perspective, unconscious racial stereotyping may provide an explanation for police interviewers' discriminatory behaviour, as such negative stereotypes can develop through repeated contact with an out-group and subsequently guide perceptions in future encounters (Smith & Alpert, 2007). Given the potential and serious consequences of racial and religious stereotypes, which may result in discriminatory behaviour during interviews, it is imperative to argue for further training of police officers. This training should aim to make them more aware of the implications of these negative stereotypes to improve their interviewing performance, case outcomes, and community cohesion.

To adopt a holistic approach, the following chapter examines the perceptions of legal representatives. These professionals may be present during suspect interviews, and it is important to assess whether they perceive any prejudicial stereotyping that might lead police officers to engage in discriminatory behaviour when interviewing Muslim suspects.

Acknowledgement

The study discussed in this chapter has been published as a research article in the *Journal of Policing, Intelligence and Counter Terrorism* and can be accessed using the following reference:

Rashid Minhas, Dave Walsh, & Ray Bull (2017) An exploration of perceptions of real-life suspects' from the Asian Muslim community relating to the police interviewing practices in England, *Journal of Policing, Intelligence and Counter Terrorism*, 12:2, 158–174, DOI: 10.1080/18335330.2017.1355103[1]

Note

1 Copyright © Macquarie University, reprinted by permission ofTaylor & Francis Ltd, www.tandfonline.com on behalf of Macquarie University.

References

Allport, G. W. (1954). *The nature of prejudice*. Cambridge, MA: Addison-Wesley.

Awan, I. (2012). 'I Am a Muslim Not an Extremist': How the Prevent Strategy Has Constructed a'Suspect' Community. *Politics & Policy*, 40(6), 1158–1185. DOI:10.1111/j.17471346.2012.00397.x

Awan, I. (2018). 'I never did anything wrong'–Trojan Horse: a qualitative study uncovering the impact in Birmingham. *British journal of sociology of education, 39*(2), 197–211.

Baldwin, J. (1993). Police interview techniques: Establishing truth or proof?. *British Journal of Criminology*, 33, 325–352.

Boyatzis, R. E. (1998). *Transforming qualitative information: Thematic analysis and code development*. London: Sage.

Braun, V., & Clarke, V. (2006). Using thematic analysis in psychology. *Qualitative Research in Psychology*, 3, 77–101. DOI:10.1191/1478088706qp063oa

Breen-Smyth, M. (2014). Theorising the 'suspect community': counterterrorism, security practices and the public imagination. *Critical Studies on Terrorism*, 7(2), 223–240. Doi:10.1080/17539153.2013.867714

Burr, V. (2006). An introduction to social constructionism. London: Routledge.

Cherney, A., & Murphy, K. (2016). Being a 'suspect community' in a post 9/11 world–The impact of the war on terror on Muslim communities in Australia. *Australian & New Zealand Journal of Criminology, 49*(4), 480–496.

Clarke, C., & Milne, R. (2001). *A national evaluation of the PEACE Investigative Interviewing Course*. London: Home Office.

Clarke, C., Milne, R., & Bull, R. (2011). Interviewing suspects of crime: The impact of PEACE training, supervision and the presence of a legal advisor. *Journal of Investigative Psychology and Offender Profiling*, 8, 149–162. DOI: 10.1002/jip.144

Crabtree, B., & Miller, W. (1999). Using codes and code manuals: A template organizing style of interpretation. In B. F. Crabtree & W. L. Miller (Eds.), Doing qualitative research (2nd ed.) (pp. 163–177). Thousand Oaks, CA: Sage Publications

Devine, P. G. (1989). Stereotypes and prejudice: their automatic and controlled components. *Journal of Personality and Social Psychology*, 56, 5. DOI:10.1037/00223514.56.1.5

Ehrlich, H. J., & Rinehart, J. W. (1965). A brief report on the methodology of stereotype research. *Social Forces*, 43, 564–575. Doi: 10.2307/2574464

Findley, K. A. & Scott, M. S. (2006). The Multiple Dimensions of Tunnel Vision in Criminal Cases. Wisconsin Law Review, Vol. 2, 2006; Univ. of Wisconsin Legal Studies Research Paper No. 1023. Available at SSRN: https://ssrn.com/abstract=911240

Fiske, S. T., & Durante, F. (2016). Stereotype content across cultures. *Handbook of Advances in Culture and Psychology*, 6, 209–258.

Fleiss, J. L. (1981). The measurement of interrater agreement. *Statistical Methods for Rates and Proportions*, 2, (pp. 212–236).

Frith, H., & Gleeson, K. (2004). Clothing and embodiment: Men managing body image and appearance. *Psychology of Men & Masculinity*, 5, 40.

Griffiths, A., & Milne, R. (2006). Will it all end in tiers? Police interviews with suspects in Britain. In T. Williamson (Ed.) Investigative Interviewing, pp. 167–189. London: Routledge.

Hickman, M., Silvestri, S., & Thomas, L. (2010). The Construction of 'Suspect' Communities in Britain 1974–2007: Comparing the Impact on Irish and Muslim Communities Interim Report, Preliminary Findings, March. London: ISET.

Hickman, M.J., Thoms, L., Silvestri, S., & Nickels, H. (2011) 'Suspect Communities'? Counter-terrorism policy, the press, and the impact on Irish and Muslim communities in Britain: A Report for Policy Makers and the General Public. London Metropolitan University

Hill, C., Memon, A., & McGeorge, P. (2008). The role of confirmation bias in suspect interviews: A systematic evaluation. *Legal and Criminological Psychology*, 13, 357–371. doi:10.1348/135532507X238682

Hillyard, P. (1993). *Suspect Community: People's Experiences of the Prevention of Terrorism Acts in Britain*. London: Pluto Press.

Huggon, W. G. (2012). *Subtle bias in legal decision making: How attitudes and social norms affect primary and peripheral targets* (Unpublished Doctoral dissertation, University of Toronto). Toronto

Kassin, S. M., Goldstein, C. C., & Savitsky, K. (2003). Behavioral confirmation in the interrogation room: on the dangers of presuming guilt. *Law and Human Behavior*, 27(2), 187. Doi.org/10.1023/A:1022599230598

Maynard-Moody, S., & Musheno, M. (2003). *Cops, teachers, counselors: Stories from the front lines of public service*. Ann Arbor: University of Michigan Press.

Miles, M. B., & Huberman, A. M. (1994). *Qualitative data analysis: An expanded sourcebook*. London: Sage.

Minhas, R., Walsh, D., & Bull, R. (2017) Developing a scale to measure the presence of possible prejudicial stereotyping in police interviews with suspects: The Minhas Investigative Interviewing Prejudicial Stereotyping Scale (MIIPSS). *Police Practice and Research: An international Journal*, 18, 132–145 Doi:10.1080/15614263.2016.1249870

Mortimer, A., & Shepherd, E. (1999). *Frames of mind: Schemata guiding cognition and conduct in the interviewing of suspected offenders*. In A. Memon & R. Bull (Eds.), Handbook of the psychology of interviewing, pp. 293–315. Chichester: Wiley.

Moston, S., Stephenson, G. M., & Williamson, T. M. (1992). The effects of case characteristics on suspect behaviour during police questioning. *British Journal of Criminology*, 32, 23–40.

Mythen, G., Walklate, S., & Khan, F. (2013). 'Why should we have to prove we're alright?': Counter-terrorism, risk and partial securities. *Sociology*, *47*(2), 383–398.

Pantazis, C., & Pemberton, S. (2009). From the 'old' to the 'new' suspect community examining the impacts of recent UK counter-terrorist legislation. *British Journal of Criminology*, 49, 646–666. DOI: 10.1093/bjc/azp031

Patton, M. Q. (1990). *Qualitative evaluation and research methods* (2nd ed.). Newbury Park, CA: Sage.

Police and Criminal Evidence Act 1984 (PACE) codes of practice. Home Office. GOV.UK. 26 March 2013. Retrieved 1 December 2022 www.gov.uk/guidance/police-and-criminal-evidence-act-1984-pace-codes-of-practice

Potter, J., & Wetherell, M. (1987). *Discourse and social psychology: Beyond attitudes and behaviour*. London: Sage

Rassin, E. (2018). Reducing tunnel vision with a pen-and-paper tool for the weighting of criminal evidence. *Journal of Investigative Psychology and Offender Profiling*, 15(2), 227–233.

Roach, K., & Trotter, G. (2004). Miscarriages of Justice in the War against Terror. *Penn State Law Review*, 109, 967.

Rossmo, D. K. (2006). Criminal investigative failures: avoiding the pitfalls. FBI Law Enforcement Bulletin, Oct, 2006. Washington

Smith, M. R., & Alpert, G. P. (2007). Explaining police bias a theory of social conditioning and illusory correlation. *Criminal Justice and Behavior*, 34, 1262–1283. Doi:10.1177/0093854807304484

Smith, N., & Flanagan, C. (2000). The Effective Detective: Identifying the skills of an effective SIO. Home Office, Policing and Reducing Crime Unit, Research, Development and Statistics Directorate. London

Snook, B., & Cullen, R. M. (2008). Bounded rationality and criminal investigations: Has tunnel vision been wrongfully convicted. *Criminal Investigative Failures*, 71–98.

Stelfox, P. (2009) *Criminal Investigation: An introduction to principles and practice*. Cullompton: Willan

Tajfel, H., & Turner, J. C. (1979). An integrative theory of intergroup conflict. In W. G. Austin & S. Worchel (Eds.), The social psychology of intergroup relations (pp. 33–47). Monterey, CA: Brooks/Cole.

Walsh, D., & Bull, R. (2012). Examining rapport in investigative interviews with suspects: Does its building and maintenance work? *Journal of Police and Criminal Psychology* 27, 73–84. Doi:10.1007/s11896-011-9087-x

Warsi, S. (2017). *The enemy within: A tale of Muslim Britain*. London: Penguin UK.

Widdicombe, S., & Wooffitt, R. (1995). *The Language of Youth Subcultures: Social Identity in Action*. London: Harvester Wheatsheaf.

Williamson, T. (2006). Investigative interviewing and human rights the war on terrorism. In T. Williamson (Ed.) Investigative interviewing, (pp. 3–22). London: Routledge.

Chapter 6

Perceptions of English defence lawyers on police interviewing practices

An in-depth exploration

Introduction

Following the discussion of the development of the MIIPSS in Chapter 4, the previous chapter examined the attitudes of police interviewers as perceived by Asian Muslim suspects. It was revealed that when police interviewers hold prejudicial stereotypes based on suspects' ethnicity or religious beliefs, it can lead to discriminatory behaviour. To take a more comprehensive approach, the current chapter delves into the perceptions of legal representatives who were present during suspect interviews. It is essential to gather legal representatives' viewpoints to assess whether they observe any prejudicial stereotyping that could potentially lead to discriminatory behaviour on the part of police interviewers when dealing with Muslim suspects. This study is groundbreaking, as to the best of the author's knowledge, no prior research has explored the views of legal representatives regarding police interviews with suspects in England and Wales.

Background

Research has reported a decrease in the use of coercive techniques in England and Wales following the introduction of the PEACE interviewing model (Bull, 2014). This model is recognised for providing a planned, fair, and ethical approach to interviewing, with the potential to enhance the likelihood of a fair trial (Shawyer & Milne, 2009). To ensure this fairness, the European Court of Human Rights has recently determined that suspects are entitled to access legal advice both before and during interviews (Art. 6 ECHR). This landmark decision, established in the Salduz case law (*Salduz v. Turkey*, ECtHR 27 November 2008, no. 36391/02), has prompted legal reforms across various European countries, enabling lawyers to offer legal counsel to suspects before and during interviews. It's worth noting that in England and Wales, the practice of providing legal

DOI: 10.4324/9781003366836-6

advice before and during interviews has been in place since the implementation of PACE in 1986 (Bull, 2014).

The National Training Package for Investigative Interviewing (National Crime Faculty (NCF), 1998) addresses the central topic of legal representation within the context of investigative interviews. It makes explicit reference to the prerequisites outlined in Code of Practice C (PACE, 1984), which encompass several key aspects:

(i) The police should inquire into the reasoning behind a suspect's refusal to seek legal advice.
(ii) The role and responsibilities of a legal representative during the interview process.
(iii) The specific conditions under which a legal representative may be excluded from the interview room.

Furthermore, the NCF provides guidance to police interviewers on how to navigate the changes introduced by legal representatives under the Criminal Justice and Public Order Act (1994) (Smith, 1995). In the post-PACE period, particularly since 1986 when it became mandatory for all police interviews with suspects conducted in stations to be audio-recorded, there has been noticeable evidence indicating an increase in suspects requesting and being granted access to legal representation both before and during police interviews (Irving & McKenzie, 1989). In the study conducted by Sanders et al. (1989), it was revealed that approximately one-quarter of the suspects examined were granted access to a legal representative either before or during the interview process. This statistic highlights a significant aspect of the evolving landscape of suspects' rights during police interviews. Furthermore, another noteworthy shift in the attitudes of police officers towards the rights of suspects can be attributed, in part, to their training in the PEACE interviewing method. The PEACE training approach emphasises not only making suspects aware of their right to legal representation but also actively encouraging suspects to exercise this right. This represents a notable departure from previous practices, reflecting a more comprehensive approach to ensuring suspects are informed about and able to utilise their legal rights during the interview.

The role of legal representation during police interviews with suspects has become a subject of intense scrutiny, particularly in the aftermath of well-publicised miscarriages of justice that have been brought before the Court of Appeal. One striking example of this legal scrutiny can be seen in the case of the Cardiff Three, where the Court of Appeal played a pivotal role in overturning their convictions. In its judgement, the Court of Appeal made a significant observation about the importance of legal representation in the pursuit of justice. The Court of Appeal remarked:

> The solicitor who sat in on the interview seems to have done that and little else [...] It is of the first importance that a solicitor fulfilling the exacting duty of assisting a suspect during the interviews should follow the guidelines and discharge his (sic) functions responsibly and courageously.
>
> (R. v. Paris, Miller, Abdullahi (1993) 97 Cr. App. R. 99)

Furthermore, previous research has raised significant concerns about the limited and ineffectual involvement of legal representatives during police interviews. In a study conducted in the post-PACE era, Baldwin (1993) made a noteworthy discovery: legal representatives often played a negligible role when representing suspects in police interviews. Baldwin argued,

> It was curious to note from the videotapes, for example, how often legal representatives remained in silence at interviews when one might have anticipated some intervention from them.
>
> (Baldwin, 1993, p. 345)

McConville et al. (1994) conducted a comprehensive examination of legal representation in police interviews and discovered a significant trend. In nearly half of the cases they investigated, legal advisers encouraged suspects to respond to or cooperate with police questioning. However, they also noted a prevalent reluctance on the part of legal representatives to actively support suspects during these interviews. Clarke and Milne (2001) delved into the influence of legal representation on the performance of police interviewers. Analysing 174 real-life interviews, they found no discernible differences in the performance of police officers when comparing interviews with and without a legal representative (Clarke, Milne, & Bull, 2011). This suggests that the presence of a legal representative may not directly impact the outcome of the interview process. However, it's worth noting that Clarke et al. (2011) did identify a distinct effect—the presence of a legal representative seemed to diminish the willingness of suspects to engage with the police. In other words, when a legal representative was present, suspects were more inclined to remain silent during the interview.

In response to the concerns and recommendations outlined by the Royal Commission on Criminal Justice (RCCJ), the Law Society initiated a scheme to accredit legal representatives who were not qualified solicitors. This proactive step aimed to address criticism regarding the prevalence of such individuals attending police stations and being the sole source of advice and assistance for suspects in detention and during interviews. The accreditation scheme involved the development of a series of police station training manuals tailored specifically to legal representatives, with the objective of elevating the standards of legal advisory services. Furthermore, the Law Society revised its guidelines to provide a more comprehensive understanding of the expected role of a legal representative during an interview (Newton, 1999).

The primary content of the training manuals, aptly titled 'Becoming Skilled' (Shepherd, 1996), consisted of a comprehensive set of guidelines specifically designed for the provision of custodial legal advice. These guidelines delineated the five fundamental aims of skilled defence:

(i) To meticulously investigate the prosecution's case, gathering information essential for both the current and future conduct of the client's defence.
(ii) To prevent the client from providing evidence that might inadvertently bolster the prosecution's case.
(iii) To exert influence on the police, either to dissuade them from charging the client due to insufficient evidence or to discourage them from seeking admissions from the client.
(iv) To persuade the police to acknowledge the client's innocence.
(v) To strategically position the client for the most favourable outcome in the event of charges, whether that means securing a not guilty verdict or obtaining mitigation for a guilty plea.

These guidelines explicitly communicated that being a legal representative entails much more than passive observation during an interview to ensure fair representation. They underscored the importance of a proactive approach, where intervention and advice to suspects are employed when necessary.

The present study

As revealed in Chapter 4, the influence of a police interviewer's negative attitudes towards a suspect from a particular group can manifest in various ways. Specifically, it was observed that such attitudes could lead to one or more of the following behaviours:

(i) Asking excessive, repetitive, and guilt-presumptive questions.
(ii) Making declarative statements rather than asking open-ended questions.
(iii) Exaggerating the strength of the evidence against the suspect.
(iv) Disregarding exculpatory evidence that could potentially work in the suspect's favour.

These negative behaviours have significant implications for the fairness of police interviews. In the preceding chapter, it was discovered that a substantial proportion of suspects perceived the presence of these problematic behaviours during their interactions with police officers. More than half of the suspects reported experiencing repetitive guilt-presumptive questioning, the exaggeration of evidence against them, or the dismissal of evidence that could have supported their innocence. This perception often coincided with the suspects' perception of a hostile approach from the police officers.

Following on findings from the previous chapters, the main aim of the present study is, therefore, to

- Examine the legal representatives' perceptions concerning police officers' attitudes towards suspects from ethnic minorities, particularly Muslims, and
- Examine what legal representatives' actions were if they reported observing: (i) any negative behaviours towards suspects; or (ii) whether the officers asked repetitive, and guilt-presumptive questions; or (iii) whether the officers ignored or exaggerated the evidence; or (iv) whether the officers made statements inviting suspects to agree with them rather than asking questions.

Methods

Participants

The present study conducted semi-structured interviews with 15 male legal representatives, all of whom possessed extensive experience in representing suspects from diverse ethnic backgrounds across England and Wales. Notably, three of these legal representatives were associates of the researcher and, in turn, facilitated contact with an additional 12 criminal defence lawyers. All participants boasted a wealth of experience in representing suspects during police interviews, with their relevant backgrounds spanning from three to 30 years (mean = 8.6 years, standard deviation = 9.1 years). The age range of the participants varied from 32 to 60 years, with an average age of 42.7 years (standard deviation = 15.8 years). During the interviews, which had a duration ranging from 35 to 90 minutes, the average interview time was approximately 50 minutes. It is worth noting that 11 of the legal representatives who took part in this study had each represented more than 1,000 suspects throughout their careers, underscoring the depth of their experience in this field. Importantly, none of the participants received any form of incentive or reward for their participation.

Procedure

Recruitment for this study involved a multistage process, primarily facilitated by three defence lawyers who were associates of the researcher. Initially, these three associates were tasked with reaching out to their fellow criminal defence lawyers and providing them with the researcher's contact information. Subsequently, those lawyers who expressed a willingness to participate were directly contacted by the researcher, resulting in the successful recruitment of eight additional defence lawyers during the first round of recruitment. Following this initial recruitment phase, the researcher further expanded the pool of participants by requesting the already recruited defence lawyers to approach their colleagues and encourage their participation. Through this approach, an additional four defence lawyers were recruited, contributing to the total of 15 participants in the study.

After obtaining ethical approval from the researcher's home university, he scheduled individual meetings with each of the participants. These semi-structured interviews took place in the participants' offices, spanning from March 2015 to January 2017. It was made explicitly clear to all participants that the interviews would be audio-recorded, provided they consented, and that their anonymity would be rigorously upheld throughout the study. Out of the 15 participants, nine granted consent for their interviews to be audio-recorded, while the remaining six preferred to have only manual notes taken during the interviews. To initiate the interviews, participants were invited to share their personal interpretations of their extensive experiences and perceptions related to investigative interviews, particularly focusing on the attitudes of police officers towards their clients, including Muslim suspects. Each participant responded to the same standardised set of questions, ensuring consistency in the data collection process. Whenever necessary, the researcher offered elaborations and sought clarifications to ensure a comprehensive understanding of the participants' perspectives.

Analytical framework

The analytical framework employed in this study is centred around a thematic analysis of interview transcriptions. In this approach, the codes used were a combination of both inductive and deductive coding, drawing inspiration from both the researcher's theoretical understanding and the insights provided by the participants themselves (Miles & Huberman, 1994). The current research approach aligns with an essentialist/realist perspective, and consequently, the analysis in this study adopted a semantic approach, as advocated by Boyatzis (1998). This approach aims to uncover and understand the explicit meanings and themes derived from the interview data.

Inductive analysis

In the present study, themes were identified from the 'explicit or surface meaning of the data' (Braun & Clarke, 2006, p. 84), which is a semantic approach (Boyatzis, 1998). The first step of the inductive analysis involved an initial reading of the research interview transcripts to gain familiarisation with the data. In the second reading, line-by-line coding was undertaken to ascribe each sentence to a code that described the main essence of the sentence.

In the present study to code the data, the guidelines for conducting a thematic analysis constructed by Braun and Clarke (2006) were followed. Initially, all the data was coded, and codes were merged into larger units organising those that seemed similar in meaning content. This was followed by sorting the different codes into potential themes and collating all the relevant coded data extracts within the identified themes and subthemes for each interview. The researcher used these codes for coding of final four of the 15 transcripts to elucidate the codes and link them to each other. At this point, saturation had occurred, meaning that no new codes emerged and, therefore, the researcher did not seek to interview further defence lawyers and data collection ceased.

In the present study, a theme was defined as the smallest unit that in a meaningful way could express the codes that were included in it. From the individual summary sheets, an overall list of themes was constructed. Themes were refined and grouped into clusters to form following the superordinate theme of legal representatives' perceptions concerning the interviewing practices.

Deductive analysis

This approach to thematic analysis was employed by the researcher to examine the perceptions of legal representatives regarding the attitudes of police interviewers towards Muslim suspects. For deductive analysis, five constructs from the MIIPSS (as detailed in Chapter 4 of this book) were considered as a priori categories. Therefore, the method used was category allocation. The five constructs of the MIIPSS are as follows: (i) possessing negative perceptions; (ii) use of schema; (iii) guilt presumption; (iv) self-fulfilling prophecy; and (v) hostile approach. The researcher carefully reviewed each interview transcript, using these five constructs as coding categories, to determine whether any of these constructs were evident in each transcript. Essentially, the analysis involved identifying the themes present in the transcripts, consulting the descriptions of each MIIPSS construct (as defined in Chapter 4), and assessing whether there was any evidence of a specific construct in the transcripts. The examination of each construct is presented in the results section under the superordinate theme of 'attitudes of the interviewers towards Muslim suspects as perceived by the legal representatives'.

Inter-rater reliability

After completing the coding process for the transcriptions, the researcher enlisted the assistance of an independent PhD researcher who possessed a well-established understanding of thematic analysis. This external rater was tasked with coding a randomly selected set of seven interview transcripts. The rater worked with clean copies of the transcripts independently and was unaware of the researcher's coding results. To assess the inter-rater reliability of identifying the two superordinate themes, namely (i) legal representatives' perceptions concerning the interviewing practices and (ii) attitudes of the interviewers towards Muslim suspects as perceived by the legal representatives, Cohen's kappa was employed. The analysis revealed a Cohen's kappa value of 0.92, indicating a strong level of agreement between the two sets of scores (Fleiss, 1981).

Results

The findings are discussed and presented under the two main themes: (i) legal representatives' perceptions concerning the interviewing practices; and (ii) attitudes of the interviewers towards Muslim suspects as perceived by the legal representatives. An analytical narrative was constructed, and extracts from the transcripts are presented to illustrate each of these two superordinate themes.

Legal representatives' perceptions concerning the interviewing practices

This overarching theme comprises four subthemes that align with participants' observations regarding police interviewing practices. These subthemes encompass (i) Legal representatives' perceptions of police interviewers' tactics; (ii) Legal representatives' views on the relationship between ethnicity and charging decisions; (iii) Legal representatives' observations of the negative portrayal of the Muslim community in police interviewers' attitudes; and (iv) Police interviewers' attitudes in both affluent and deprived areas.

Legal representatives' perceptions concerning the tactics employed by the police interviewers

Nine participants reported that police interviewers deliberately make legal representatives wait in the police station for as long as possible, which they perceive as an attempt to 'frustrate them'. This deliberate delay, as participants pointed out, can sometimes lead to suspects not receiving the quality of advice they should. For instance, participant (06) stated,

> So, the fact is that previously the payment structure was on an hourly basis, so if a solicitor sat there and gave proper advice and went through every bit of evidence and it took the time it would not be an issue because you get paid hourly. Now that it's a fixed fee structure, whether you are there for an hour or five hours, it's still the same fee that you are getting. And, unfortunately, what I think is happening is that people are not taking the same amount of time and care to give advice because they want to get out as quickly as possible, because at the end of the day, it's a business. I do think that some police officers try to manipulate the situation. That is a tactic sometimes used, make solicitors wait outside for ages, et cetera, and will make solicitors wait, so they get annoyed and they don't want to be there any longer.

Seven participants reported that in some cases, police interviewers try to persuade suspects that their legal representatives will take too long to arrive. They suggest to suspects that conducting a 'quick interview' with them will expedite their release from police detention. For example, participant (13) encapsulated this situation as

> A very common tactic that police use is to tell suspects that solicitors are going to take hours, take too long to get there and just come up quickly have an interview, you will be out of here very quickly and when suspects do not have solicitors they are more prone to making admissions where they would not necessarily make those admissions if they were legally represented, but there you have it. I do not think that has anything to do with ethnicity. I think that's a very common practice.

Twelve participants reported that in volume crimes, police interviewers disclose all the evidence they have, while in serious crimes, they tend to withhold information from solicitors. For example, participant (14) described such a situation:

> But in the most serious cases, police will normally withhold information back from lawyers before [...] well, they withhold information back to a certain extent, they want to know what the client has to say before they disclose any evidence.

Legal representatives' perceptions concerning the association between ethnicity and charging decision

Eight participants reported instances where they observed that a suspect's ethnicity appeared to influence police officers' decisions on whether to pursue charges. For example, participant (01) described it this way:

> I have represented clients up and down the country. Birmingham, there was a time where there were lots of Black people, and magistrate courts were full of Black people. They just disappeared. But, now there are more and more Asian Muslims or Eastern Europeans. I would say that if they [police] find an Eastern European, say a petty theft or a small amount of class A drugs, say low-level theft maybe £20, £30, they would let it go. But if they find an Asian Muslim youth with such a theft or a small amount of class A they will definitely charge him.

Participant (14) reported this circumstance as follows:

> There are certain areas in Birmingham where it's not only Asians dealing; there are other communities also involved in dealing. However, they are [police] more concerned into Asian Muslim areas. Perhaps they believe that loads of Asians are involved in dealing, and it would be easier to arrest them, to meet their targets.

Moreover, participant (09) described such a situation as,

> It's already in their mind that, obviously he must have done something and how should we get it out, if the suspect is known Asian Muslim or known Black. Whereas, if a suspect is a typical White person, the question would be whether or not he has done it and then attitudes when deciding whether just to caution them or charge them. The attitude towards a White person would be very different. Let me give you an example. I went to the police station to represent a client, and there was a CCTV footage, a White girl, entered in a shop, started throwing

> things from the shelf, broke a bottle of vodka, threw it on the till, the guy on the till was Asian. You could see clearly in the footage that he was bleeding, a big long cut on his face. I thought that she would be charged with serious offences, for example, drunken disorderly, assault, but the sergeant said to me that if she pleads guilty, which she has to because it's all on CCTV, we will caution her and send her to alcohol rehab. I was really surprised obviously. In the best interest of my client I could not tell the sergeant to charge her, and she was cautioned and sent to rehab.

However, four participants reported that, while representing their clients in police interviews, they observed the police officers treating suspects fairly, irrespective of their ethnicity. For example, participant (10) reported,

> I would not want to tar the whole police force with the same brush. I think the police force does generally do a good job, relatively speaking and then given all the pressures that they have. But, the police forces are also aware of Islamophobia, you cannot say that they are not aware of Islamophobia. How much of it they suffer from themselves is something that needs to be quantified. However, I have never observed police interviewers treated my client unfairly due to his/her ethnicity or religion.

Legal representatives' perceptions concerning the negative portrayal of the Muslim community on police interviewers' attitudes

Ten participants noted that police officers' attitudes could be influenced by public perception. For instance, participant (15) described this circumstance as follows:

> Some of those prejudices, unfortunately, are against Muslims, and police officers see it day in and day out, and they have their prejudices too. We are all human. We are all affected by what is in the public eye, what is in the media, which unfortunately taints the rest of us, and people do see Islam or Muslims in a bad way, and people cannot get past their own prejudices. And, people fear what they do not know, what they do not understand and sometimes those fears play a big part as well. Well, at the moment like I said, the political hot potato is grooming, so Asian men who happen to be Muslims having sexual relations with a White woman automatically the police officer will probably ask the question of grooming or looking to groom. Whereas if it's a White male and a White female in the same situation, that may not cross their mind. So, I think again people are influenced with what's going on or what is [...]

> it's a political hot potato at the moment, so I think that does affect the way police work, yes.

Further, participant (01) reported,

> I had an Asian Muslim client who was arrested for endangering an aircraft. The way he endangered the aircraft was that he flashed a laser light at a police helicopter and got arrested. The custody sergeant did not know what that offence was. However, his first reaction was because the suspect was a Muslim, because he was from an ethnic minority area, the first reaction in the police station was that they had a suspect related to terrorism offences. When I went to the police station, they already thought that he was a terrorist and we had got a terrorist at the police station. I did not know much about this particular offence at that time. I looked through the magistrate court guide and could not find anything; then I asked the sergeant, and he replied, Oh, these are special legislations, I think you need to find it in the Terrorism Act. However, another sergeant, who had dealt with such incidents before, said that if he admitted, we would send him to the magistrate court, and that's what happened. My client went to the magistrate court; he was fined £80. I was really shocked to see this in the local newspaper the next morning, On the front page, a Muslim was fined £80 for endangering an aircraft. It was not a report that he was fined £80. It was a report that emphasised, look, he has done such a heinous crime, and he has been let off with just an £80 fine.

Eight participants stated that incidents related to terrorism might have had an impact on police investigations involving Muslim suspects. For instance, participant (07) reported,

> They may because the media is very strong and influential, right, and at the end of the day everybody is a human being [...] there is a terrorist incident a few days ago in France, 12 people have unfortunately been killed, right, and obviously the people would suspect these people, that a minority or society is breeding terrorism. But, then again the media is strong, they influence the society, and other societies and when there is an obvious [...] it would be unfair to them, how do they know [...] if there are 20 Muslims there, how do they know that one is a terrorist, and the others are not, right, because they will suspect all the society, which you have got to be fair to them as well, because you have got to see their point of view as well. They have got children; they have got families. Yes, they are professional, they have got to do their job right and if one particular society keeps on doing something like that,

> then obviously, they will have the perception, they will have all this. If one society is committing robberies, they will know that, oh, yes, this community is involved in terrorism, robberies, cases like in Rotherham, I think, or Rochdale.

Further, participant (12) characterised this situation in the following way:

> Well, I am sure that whatever is part and parcel of the general information which is available from the television or the internet or the newspapers and so forth affects police officers just as much as it affects anybody else in society. It's just that they are in a different position, and they have to deal with people and so forth, and any bias they have does far more damage. They are well trained to recognise even their own biases and so forth, one hopes at least, and they are able to contain that and not let it interfere with the investigation. But, then again, like the rest of society, they too are human beings, and sometimes they will not be able to do that, or it will affect their questioning. Unfortunately, I have observed that in fact, this affects their investigations and questioning.

Additionally, four participants described how such portrayals could also influence the attitudes of Muslim police officers towards Muslim suspects. For example, participant (06) related this situation in the following way:

> In my experience, if you have an Asian Muslim police officer, just so that he can show to his employers, to the police, that he is not biased, he would be harder on Asian clients. Asian suspects than he would on White suspects, just so that he is not accused of being racist in favour of the Asians. So, it's almost like a double negative.

Police interviewers' attitudes in affluent and deprived areas

Ten participants reported that they had observed police officers displaying more hostile attitudes in deprived areas compared to affluent areas. These participants also noted that police officers tend to ask guilt-presumptive questions when conducting interviews with individuals from deprived areas. For example, participant (01) stated,

> In my observations, there are police stations that they do have stereotypical branding and attitudes are different in different areas, particularly in London. These attitudes are different in south London deprived areas where the predominately Black community lives, for example, Brixton and that area. If you are in Brixton police station, Brixton has

> a reputation and the officers there are convinced that they are dealing with the most hardened criminals. They perceive, they arrest, and they investigate differently. They question them differently. Their attitudes are different. Whereas, if you come down to [...] if you go farther south towards a slightly more affluent area, attitudes are very different. Interview techniques are different. So, that's my opinion. I have represented clients up and down the country.

Further, participant (06) encapsulated such observations like this:

> If you have a police station which deals predominately with middle-class White people, there is a different kind of policing that is needed, and crime is probably perceived not as prevalent, or certain types of crime are not as prevalent, for example, the better parts of Sutton, nice parts of Edgbaston. Whereas if you contrast that with deprived areas, for example, a police station which deals with ethnic minorities, such as Small Heath, Sparkhill, or Sparkbrooke, where there is a lot of Asians, and they deal day in day out with Asian suspects, prisoners, then I think that they are [...] that does affect them, that does affect the way they police them because of that, because of the experiences they have.

Seven participants stated that in certain localities, they have observed police interviewers' attitudes towards suspects from minority and Muslim communities being potentially influenced by prejudicial stereotyping. For instance, participant (14) described the situation this way:

> In certain parts of the country, for example, in (city name) or in (city name) or (location) side, they do not get many Asians or Muslim suspects and when they do get Asian Muslim suspects, they have got that particular stereotypical impression of them that either they are involved in terrorism-related offences, money laundering, drugs or they must be involved in something dodgy.

Four participants reported that in predominantly ethnic minority and deprived areas, police officers' attitudes differ not only towards suspects but also towards their legal representatives. For instance, participant (05) encapsulated this, saying,

> There are variations in attitudes between certain police stations, deprived and affluent areas, or police officers might have a certain reputation. I would not say it is everywhere, but I would say in particular police stations, especially in predominantly ethnic or deprived areas,

> even the legal representative when you turn up to the police station, their attitudes are also negative towards you. You can feel this. You are going to represent a suspect from an ethnic minority, and you are a solicitor from an ethnic minority.

Attitudes of the interviewers towards Muslim suspects as perceived by the legal representatives

This superordinate theme comprises five subthemes that align with participants' perceptions of police officers' attitudes toward Muslim suspects. These subthemes include: (i) possessing negative perceptions; (ii) the use of schema; (iii) guilt presumption; (iv) the self-fulfilling prophecy; and (v) a hostile approach.

Possessing negative perceptions

As was noted in Chapter 4, interviews may be affected by police officers' negative *perceptions towards suspects from certain groups*, if research participants reported observing (i) the interviewer's perceived attitudes towards the interviewee were negative; or (ii) there was a lack of empathy; or (iii) there was an absence of a good relationship (or rapport) between the suspect and the interviewer.

Nine participants reported observing instances where interviews appeared to be influenced by police interviewers' negative attitudes towards Muslim suspects. The majority of these participants noted that during such interviews, police interviewers were unfriendly and displayed biased attitudes toward their clients. For instance, participant (02) stated,

> I have observed when representing Muslim clients that some officers have got attitude problems and it affects interviews badly, so I would say it's the officer's problem, not as a whole.

Seven participants reported observing instances of non-verbal expressions of negative attitudes, such as police officers 'nodding their heads' or 'shrugging their shoulders', possibly in an attempt to make their Muslim clients uncomfortable. For example, participant (14) described this in the following way:

> You can see their expressions. The majority of the interviews are audio-recorded, you can observe their attitudes and expressions, and they are not friendly, they look anxious, annoyed...

Moreover, participant (12) characterised this by saying,

> I observed negative attitudes on many occasions, but it's hard to explain. A lot depends on who the police officer is. Some police officers probably have that, but they do not bring it to the forefront, it's all done behind closed doors, manipulate evidence, etc. They would not bring it to the forefront because they know if they bring it to the forefront they will be in trouble.

Nine participants reported that, based on their observations, they believe that the specific nature of the crime may impact police interviewers' attitudes towards a suspect. For instance, participant (13) stated,

> Some suspects will be treated differently; if they are drug addicts or alcoholics or drug dealers, they would be charged differently. Recently in the news regarding the sexual offences in Rochdale, the Asians, that's obviously put a bit of a spanner in the works, given a bit of a bad name to the Asian Muslim suspects who are arrested for sexual offences.

Participant (14) encapsulated this situation like this:

> A native wearing a suit sitting in a police station is different, a guy wearing typical gear with a beard, their attitude is different because in police officers' mind, he is culturally different, so he has more reasons to be on the wrong side.

Moreover, participant (09) reported on this by saying,

> Well, I have heard people say that the police is institutionally racist. I have heard that saying many times, by many people. So, when you have got prejudice, you know, to the grassroots in that way, then there are. Unfortunately, it stems down, does not it, to all the smaller stations, et cetera. But, yes, I think it is prevalent throughout, unfortunately, the force, but maybe more so in some areas than others. I certainly think that a lot of police officers abuse their power. I have in the past been stopped by police officers. I have a nice car; I am an Asian Muslim man. If I am travelling late at night in Birmingham in a nice car, unfortunately, it might attract attention. But, when they speak to me, and they realise that I am not a drug dealer from certain areas of Birmingham, then they soon get the message, but they stop nonetheless.

Use of schema

As Chapter 4 revealed, possible reasons for police officers' negative attitudes towards suspects may include (i) the suspect's group membership; (ii) the suspect's ethnicity; (iii) the suspect's religious beliefs; (iv) the suspect's previous criminal history; (v) the specific nature of the crime (such as sexual crimes, paedophilia, or drug-related crimes); or (vi) the location associated with the crime.

Eight participants perceived that, in some instances, police officers' negative attitudes towards suspects could be attributed to the suspects' ethnicity. These participants emphasised that they believed police interviewers treated suspects negatively because of their ethnicity. For example, participant (06) stated,

> Unfortunately, from my point of view a lot or probably 80 per cent plus of the people that I represent are from the Asian Muslim ethnic origin, unfortunately, but there you have it. So, the way I have [...] the way some police officers view Asian suspects is that they are guilty before they have even been tried. The police officers view them as guilty because they are Asian. It's quite clear sometimes that they are not information gathering. They are trying to prove a case against them.

Furthermore, participant (02) described this situation like this:

> Police officers make the assumption on the basis of a suspect's ethnicity that in their opinion they committed a particular crime. That's their opinion. It's not evidence. It doesn't hold any weight in court. I give you an example; domestic violence where husband and wife have an argument; the wife calls the husband on the police, he gets arrested, and then says he has probably beaten her because she has got a lot of bruises. Again, that is not only the Asian community or a certain ethnicity. It would be across the board. But if it's an Asian suspect, they assume that he is guilty, he committed the crime. With the drugs it's more they do the drugs if a young guy is driving a flashy car. Then if they arrest him, they will start asking him questions, and they would automatically assume that he is a drug dealer if he is Black or Asian.

Seven participants reported that, based on their observations, they occasionally felt that police interviewers displayed negative attitudes towards their clients, possibly attributing these attitudes to their clients' Muslim background. Participant (07) reported,

> Whether they are able to contain their own prejudices or not, I am not saying police officers do not have prejudices; they, like the rest of society, will also have prejudices and will have their own preferences. How much they are able to contain them depending on the type of offence that they are dealing with, or the ethnicity of the person they are dealing with, or the religion of the person they are dealing with is a different matter altogether. There are, of course, instances where I felt that their [suspect] ethnicity or their religion had affected the interview, or their explanation being understood or even being registered, was adverse to their interests because of their Muslim background.

Guilt presumption

As demonstrated in Chapter 4, interviewers may presume a suspects is guilty when they: (i) ask guilt-presumptive questions (i.e. questions displaying the interviewer's confirmation bias); (ii) pose provocative questions; (iii) employ bluffing tactics; (iv) exhibit inflexibility (e.g. fail to adjust their stance in light of new information received from the interviewee); or (v) respond to the suspect's behaviour with destabilising, disturbing, or confusing (non-verbal) reactions.

Eight participants reported that, on multiple occasions, they had observed police officers presuming their clients' guilt right from the beginning of the interview. These participants reported the police officers asked repetitive questions to try to prove a case against their clients. For instance, participant (05) reported,

> Obviously interviews are tape-recorded in the presence of a solicitor or appropriate adult. They cannot be that hostile or cannot go overboard and do things which are not appropriate. But, as I said, the attitude is that, yes, we are convinced you have done it, so why do not you tell us. If he is a non-Asian or not a Black person, if he says, well, I did not do it, or I was somewhere else, they would just take it. They would just take his words. However, with a Black or an Asian or a Muslim, they will keep on questioning, and with these clients, interviews are normally longer than usual.

Another, participant (11) encapsulated this issue by saying,

> When a suspect is Black or Asian, they come to the interview with the assumption that they are guilty before they have even been tried. They can be quite pressurising at times. I think that comes with experience. Some police officers will just repeat the questions where clients would

> not give them answers; again experience will bring that. Experienced police officers they might have a slightly different harsh technique of asking questions, but those are the senior officers, so they are trained better because they have been in the job for a long time and they know all the tricks of the trade. In some aspects, it depends on what the offence is, usually that can make a difference.

Self-fulfilling prophecy

Chapter 4 also revealed that interviews could be influenced by police interviewers' self-fulfilling prophecies if interviewers: (i) gave excessive weight to the evidence; (ii) disregarded evidence that could have favoured any suspect, or at least not suggested guilt; (iii) either exaggerated or downplayed the nature of the offence; (iv) repeatedly accused interviewees of the crime(s); or (v) consistently posed leading questions.

Six participants reported that, while representing their clients during investigative interviews, they observed one or more of these behaviours. Among these participants, three described instances where police officers presumed their clients' guilt despite the absence of evidence connecting them to the crime. These participants noted that the police officers attempted to link their clients to the crime using 'irrelevant' evidence. For example, participant (02) described such circumstances in this way:

> Some police officers get overexcited and ask questions which are not relevant because there is no evidence, they make the assumption that in their opinion the suspect had committed this crime. That's their opinion. It's not evidence. It does not hold any weight in court. I have seen interviewers exert pressure on suspects even when a solicitor is present. As solicitors we will intervene and tell the police officers to take a step back and we prevent that because we have a duty to look after our clients' rights.

Three participants reported that, on several occasions, they felt that police officers had exaggerated the evidence and drawn conclusions that went beyond what the evidence justified. These participants noted that despite the Crown Prosecution Service (CPS) charging their clients, the court ultimately dropped the cases due to insufficient or non-existent evidence against them. For example, participant (04) reported,

> I would not say it's racism; I believe it's about police priorities or a political hot potato. I am not a Muslim; if you are talking about ethnic minorities or Muslims, I give you an example. I have seen a police officer

> who was from the same race as my client, the same religion as my client. He was coming up with every piece of evidence which might align with his belief to get a conviction for my client. On the other hand, every piece of evidence that my client was submitting in his defence, that particular police officer was making every effort to exclude it. He took it too far; it was annoying to me as well being the defence lawyer, the way he was dealing with that particular investigation. The matter could have been resolved without going to the court, but we ended up in the court, and finally, the honourable judge dismissed that case.

Further, participant (02) reported,

> When they are investigating or interviewing a Muslim suspect, it depends if they are investigating an offence where there is terrorism-related suspicion or money laundering. I have seen that they are convinced that, yes, he has done something wrong and how should we get it out.

Four participants reported instances where they observed police officers asking repetitive questions to their clients. As participant (05) reported,

> Only in certain cases sometimes the questions put to a suspect, it's very repetitive. In such instances, although I pause the interview as a result of repetitive questions, police officers would come up with, for example, this is completely a new question, but actually, that's not a new question. It's the same as the previous question. You can understand where they are coming from if you are in that environment…

Another, participant (14), reported,

> I had a client where somebody went to the police and said that it has come to their knowledge that my client is involved in a conspiracy to kidnap a police officer. It was also in the news a few weeks ago, before Christmas. In fact, my client had nothing to do with it; he was not aware of anything. He was affiliated with a mosque, he had a beard, and he was a bit active in the mosque. Police arrested him, took him to the police station, and interviewed him. It was also in the news that a Muslim suspect was arrested for conspiracy to kidnap a police officer. He did not have a clue. After interviewing he was released with no further action. He had absolutely no idea, and now the police are in the process of making further inquiries and arresting those who made this complaint. As I said, this is typical […] because he was a Muslim, he goes to the mosque, he must have a reason to kidnap somebody.

Hostile approach

Interviewers may be considered hostile if they: (i) appear oppressive (e.g. exhibit undue pressure, bullying, or continual challenges); and/or (ii) ask persistent and coercive questions during the interview (as discussed in Chapter 4).

All participants stated that in every interview, they remain alert to questions that may be oppressive, aggressive, offensive, insulting, or threatening. Five participants reported instances of oppression, such as (i) the continued repetition of questions to which answers had already been given or to which a 'no comment' response had been provided; (ii) officers raising their voices or becoming angry; or (iii) frequent interruptions of the suspect by the officer. These participants indicated that they promptly intervened when they sensed that the interview was becoming oppressive. Due to the persistence of such behaviour, they sought to suspend the interview and made representations to the custody officer or senior officer. For instance, participant (07) described this situation in the following way:

> That police officer was very aggressive, and his attitude was not the one he was going to ask questions. He was so angry with my client; if he had a chance, he could have punched him, he was very aggressive, he whispered something which we were unable to hear, and even the tapes did not pick it up. I think he would have been in trouble. Because I believe he said something very negative and racial.

Discussion

The present study aimed to investigate legal representatives' perceptions of whether police interviewers appear to employ negative stereotypes when dealing with suspects from stigmatised groups. Firstly, this study explored whether police officers utilised tactics misaligned with the current ethos of police interviewing practices in England and Wales, as outlined in the PACE Code C, and as described in the framework officers have been trained in, known as the PEACE model. Secondly, the current study delved into how legal representatives responded when they observed deviations from PACE guidelines, such as excessive repetition of questions or police officers making statements and seeking agreement from suspects instead of asking questions. Finally, building upon the five constructs of the MIIPSS identified in Chapter 4, the present study examined whether legal representatives perceived that police interviewers displayed negative stereotypes towards Muslim suspects and the extent to which these perceptions translated into hostile and discriminatory behaviour.

Based on the findings regarding legal representatives' beliefs concerning the tactics used by police interviewers, it appears that police interviewers employ various tactics, including: (i) making legal representatives wait longer, and (ii) attempting to persuade suspects to undergo interviews without legal advice. The PACE Act legally imposes a standardised and structured set of procedures to which police interviewers must adhere, with the risk of the interview being ruled inadmissible in court if they fail to do so. Following the introduction of PACE, there was evidence suggesting that more suspects requested and were granted legal advice (Irving & McKenzie, 1989). Additionally, PEACE interviewing training emphasised not only making suspects aware of their right to legal representation but also encouraging suspects to exercise that right (Bull, 2014). In light of the reported observations by legal representatives, if police interviewers are indeed employing such tactics, they may be in breach of the PACE Act and the ethos of the PEACE model. This includes actions such as making legal representatives wait unnecessarily or pressuring suspects to forgo legal advice before an interview.

More than half of the participants expressed the belief that police officers are more inclined to seek charges from the CPS if a suspect is of Black or Asian Muslim ethnicity. These participants emphasised that this inclination is even stronger when the investigation involves alleged drug offences, leading them to believe that Black or Asian Muslim suspects are more likely to face charges compared to their White counterparts. These findings suggest that legal representatives' perceptions include suspicions about the ethnicity of suspects influencing decisions regarding whether to seek charges from the CPS. Furthermore, participants also noted their perceptions of negative portrayals of the Muslim community in the media, which they believed could impact police officers' attitudes towards Muslim suspects. These participants stressed that the focus on terrorism-related offences and, more recently, the association of sexual offences with Asian Muslims may have exacerbated the impact of such stereotypes on police investigations.

Negative racial and religious stereotypes can significantly contribute to biased decisions concerning members of certain stigmatised minority groups (Mears, Stewart, Warren, & Simons, 2017; Correll et al., 2007; Fazio, Jackson, Dunton, & Williams, 1995). The portrayal of individuals from these stigmatised groups through negative stereotypes can strongly influence how people interact with members of these communities (Mears et al., 2017). These negative stereotypes are automatically activated when exposed to individuals from stigmatised groups, potentially impacting the decisions made by police officers (Banaji & Greenwald, 1995; Devine, 1989; Fazio et al., 1995; Macrae & Bodenhausen, 2000). In the present study, one-third of the participants reported observing instances where the ethnicity and religion of a suspect seemed to play a crucial role in officers' decisions to seek charges against the suspect. These participants recounted witnessing cases in which a White suspect was released, while a charge was sought against an Asian Muslim suspect for a similar alleged offence.

When police officers are exposed to negative behaviours exhibited by individuals from certain minority groups, they may overestimate the prevalence of these behaviours, thereby reinforcing pre-existing stereotypes (Hamilton & Gifford, 1976). Prejudicial stereotyping is likely a consequence of unconscious stereotyping, re-emerging either through a differential presentation of group criminality or due to the illusory correlation phenomenon. Consequently, police officers may overestimate the pervasiveness of negative behaviours within stigmatised communities (Smith & Alpert, 2007). This may explain why suspects from stigmatised communities are charged more frequently.

Additionally, it was found that some participants perceived differences in police officers' attitudes when suspects originated from deprived areas. More than half of the participants believed that police officers treated suspects from deprived areas, irrespective of their ethnicity, in a less favourable manner compared to those from more affluent areas. Police officers may hold the belief that individuals from deprived areas are more likely to be involved in criminal activity (Bowling, 2018; Bowling & Phillips, 2007), which can influence their attitudes towards suspects from such neighbourhoods. Just as police officers' perceptions of suspects from deprived areas can impact their attitudes, the negative portrayal of the Muslim community in public discourse (e.g. being more likely to be associated with crimes such as terrorism or sexual offences) may similarly affect police officers' attitudes. This offers an alternative explanation for why legal representatives perceived suspects from stigmatised communities as being charged more frequently.

The second qualitative theme of 'perceived prejudicial stereotyping' emerged as a novel aspect in the present study. When reflecting on their perceptions of police officers' attitudes, two-thirds of the participants reported observing instances of police interviewers displaying negative attitudes towards Muslim suspects. These participants believed that these negative attitudes towards their clients might stem from either their ethnicity or their religious beliefs.

Furthermore, when exploring legal representatives' beliefs regarding whether police officers were perceived to judge suspects as guilty based on perceived negative attitudes (as discussed in Chapter 4), more than half of the participants reported observing instances where police interviewers presumed the suspect's guilt and asked guilt-presumptive questions. These participants noted that such presumption of guilt could be attributed to: (i) the suspect's ethnicity; (ii) the suspect's religion; or (iii) the specific nature of the crime, including sexual crimes, drug offences, or terrorism-related offences.

One-third of the participants reported observing instances of self-fulfilling prophecies displayed by police interviewers. The self-fulfilling prophecy is described as a 'false definition of the situation evoking a new behaviour which may make the originally false conceptions come true' (Merton, 2016, p. 477). This phenomenon can occur when an interviewer fails to recognise how their own beliefs have contributed to the construction of a false reality. In such cases, interviewers become excessively focused on an individual or incident, often to the exclusion of other pertinent information. In the present study, it was found that police officers, on occasion, were believed by participants to have (i) asked repetitive questions; (ii) exaggerated the strength of evidence; or (iii) become so fixated on charging the suspect that they disregarded evidence that could have supported the suspect's case. This investigative approach can result in tunnel vision, a product of various processes, including cognitive distortions such as confirmation bias (Findley & Scott, 2006). Limited existing research suggests that tunnel vision may be more prevalent in the investigative process when the suspect comes from a stigmatised community (Hall, Hall, & Perry, 2016; Roach & Trotter, 2004). This may offer an additional explanation for why suspects from stigmatised communities are charged more frequently.

To what extent can negative stereotypical attitudes result in discriminatory behaviour? In the present study, nearly two-thirds of legal representatives reported observing police interviewers asking suspects guilt-presumptive questions, indicating their belief that police officers had adopted negative stereotypes. Additionally, it was found that nearly a third of the participants believed that, on certain occasions, interviews with Muslim suspects may have been affected by what they perceived as police officers' self-fulfilling prophecies. Furthermore, a quarter of the legal representatives mentioned instances where they perceived interviewers displaying hostile and discriminatory behaviour towards their Muslim clients.

Limitations

Semi-structured interviews, commonly employed to assess participants' perceptions, are susceptible to errors stemming from cognitive and motivational biases, as they rely on self-reports (Ehrlich & Rinehart, 1965). During the semi-structured interviews conducted for the present study, legal representatives may have provided exaggerated responses or responses influenced by their own biases, whether directed against the police or the suspects. Furthermore, as participants recalled events, sometimes from several years prior, concerning their diverse experiences, there is a possibility that time delays may have affected their memories or that they may have engaged in discussions with others during the intervening period, potentially leading to memory distortions or source monitoring errors. Future researchers should aim to minimise time delays between police interviews and research interviews to mitigate the potential impact of these factors.

While the sample size in this study was relatively small, it is important to acknowledge the difficulty in reaching legal representatives for voluntary research participation, as they have traditionally been a challenging group to engage (and as far as it is known, this study is the first to gather legal representatives' views within the context of investigative interviewing of suspects). However, it's worth noting that thematic saturation was achieved, indicating that a larger sample may not have provided substantially different insights. It is also important to recognise that the superordinate themes presented in this study are the result of the researchers' interpretations of the data, which could potentially be influenced by biases, whether against the police or legal representatives. Nevertheless, the presence of a strong Cohen's kappa value of 0.92 between raters suggests that such biases may not have significantly influenced the interpretations.

Additionally, future studies could benefit from comparing and contrasting the experiences of legal representatives regarding investigative interviewing with various populations. The present study focused specifically on investigative interviewing of suspects from the Muslim community, and extending this research to different demographic groups would provide a more comprehensive understanding of the implications of prejudicial stereotyping within the context of investigative interviewing and criminal investigations.

Conclusions

The present study highlighted participants' reports of police interviewers employing tactics that, if accurate, could potentially contravene both the PACE and the ethos of the PEACE model. These tactics included making legal representatives wait unnecessarily and attempting to persuade suspects to undergo interviews without legal representation. Furthermore, participants in the study believed that negative portrayals in the media could significantly influence police interviewers' attitudes towards Muslim suspects. They suggested that terrorism-related offences and the association of sexual offences with Asian Muslims might exacerbate the impact of such stereotyping on the outcome of investigations. This aligns with previous research indicating that negative stereotypical portrayals of individuals from certain minority groups can strongly influence how people behave towards members of these groups (Hall et al., 2016; Mears et al., 2017). Additionally, participants perceived that police interviewers were more likely to seek charges against suspects of Black or Asian Muslim ethnicity. For instance, participants recalled instances where White suspects were treated more leniently than Asian Muslim suspects, despite the alleged offences being of a similar nature.

Given the beliefs reported in the present chapter, the following chapter will delve deeper into the question of whether suspects' ethnicity or religious background can indeed influence police officers' judgements. It will explore whether such judgements, when investigating similar crimes involving suspects from different community groups, could ultimately impact the outcome of a criminal investigation.

Acknowledgement

The study discussed in this chapter has been published as a research article in the *Journal of Policing, Intelligence and Counter Terrorism* and can be accessed using the following reference:

Rashid Minhas & Dave Walsh (2021) Prejudicial stereotyping and police interviewing practices in England: an exploration of legal representatives' perceptions, *Journal of Policing, Intelligence and Counter Terrorism*, 16:3, 267–282, DOI: 10.1080/18335330.2021.1889016[1]

Note

1 Copyright © Macquarie University, reprinted by permission of Taylor & Francis Ltd, www.tandfonline.com on behalf of Macquarie University.

References

Baldwin, J. (1993). Police interview techniques: Establishing truth or proof? *British Journal of Criminology*, 33, 325–352.

Banaji, M. R., & Greenwald, A. G. (1995). Implicit gender stereotyping in judgments of fame. *Journal of Personality and Social Psychology*, *68*, 181–192.

Bowling, B. & Phillips, C. (2007). Disproportionate and discriminatory: reviewing the evidence on police stop and search. *Modern Law Review, 70*, 936–961.

Bowling, B. (2018). Pulled over: how police stop define race and citizenship. *Policing and Society*, 28, 1–4.

Boyatzis, R. E. (1998). *Transforming qualitative information: Thematic analysis and code development*. London: Sage.
Braun, V., & Clarke, V. (2006). Using thematic analysis in psychology. *Qualitative Research in Psychology*, *3*, 77–101. DOI:10.1191/1478088706qp063oa
Bull, R. (2014). *Investigative interviewing*. New York, Springer.
Clarke, C., & Milne, R. (2001). *National evaluation of the PEACE investigative interviewing course*. Police Research Award Scheme Report No. PRAS/149. London: Home
Clarke, C., Milne, R., & Bull, R. (2011). Interviewing suspects of crime: The impact of PEACE training, supervision and the presence of a legal advisor. *Journal of Investigative Psychology and Offender Profiling*, 8, 149–162. DOI: 10.1002/jip.144
Correll, J., Park, B., Judd, C. M., Wittenbrink, B., Sadler, M. S., & Keesee, T. (2007). Across the thin blue line: Police officers and racial bias in the decision to shoot. *Journal of Personality and Social Psychology, 92,* 1006–1023. http://dx.doi.org/10.1037
Devine, P. G. (1989). Stereotypes and prejudice: their automatic and controlled components. *Journal of Personality and Social Psychology*, *56*, 5. DOI:10.1037/00223514.56.1.5
Ehrlich, H. J., & Rinehart, J. W. (1965). A brief report on the methodology of stereotype research. *Social Forces*, *43*, 564–575. Doi: 10.2307/2574464
Fazio, R. H., Jackson, J. R., Dunton, B. C.,&Williams, C. J. (1995).Variability in automatic activation as an unobtrusive measure of racial attitudes: a bona fide pipeline? *Journal of Personality and Social Psychology*, *69*, 1013–1027.
Findley, K. A. & Scott, M. S. (2006). The Multiple Dimensions of Tunnel Vision in *Criminal Cases. Wisconsin Law Review,* Vol. 2, 2006, 291; University of Wisconsin Legal Studies Research Paper No. 1023. Available at SSRN: https://ssrn.com/abstract=911240
Fleiss, J. L. (1981). The measurement of interrater agreement. *Statistical Methods for Rates and Proportions*, *2*, 212–236.
Hall, A. V., Hall, E. V., & Perry, J. L. (2016). Black and blue: Exploring racial bias and law enforcement in the killings of unarmed black male civilians. *American Psychologist*, *71*, 175–186.
Hamilton, D. L., & Gifford, R. K. (1976). Illusory correlation in interpersonal perception: A cognitive basis of stereotypic judgments. *Journal of Experimental Social Psychology*, *12*, 392–407. www.gov.uk/guidance/police-and-criminal-evidence-act-1984-pace-codes-of- practice
Irving, B., & McKenzie, I. K. (1989). *Police Interrogation: The Effects of the Police and Criminal Evidence Act, 1984*. Police Foundation.
Macrae, C. N., & Bodenhausen, G. V. (2000). Social cognition: Thinking categorically about others. *Annual Review of Psychology*, *51*, 93–120.
McConville, M., Hodgson, J., Bridges, L., & Pavlovic, A. (1994). *Standing Accused: The organisation and practices of criminal defence lawyers in Britain.* Oxford: Oxford University Press.
Mears, D.P., Stewart, E.A., Warren, P.Y. & Simons, R.L., (2017). Culture and formal social control: The effect of the code of the street on police and court decision making. *Justice Quarterly*, *34*, 217–247.

Merton, R. K. (2016). The self-fulfilling prophecy. *The Antioch Review*, 74(3), 504–521.
Miles, M.B. and Huberman, A.M. (1994). *Qualitative data analysis: An expanded sourcebook*. California: Sage
Newton, T. (1999). *Reducing miscarriages of justice: police training and the development of 'ethical' interviewing* (Doctoral dissertation, University of Wales. Cardiff)
Police and Criminal Evidence Act 1984 (PACE) codes of practice". *Home Office*. GOV.UK. 26 March 2013. Retrieved 1 December 2017
Roach, K., & Trotter, G. (2004). Miscarriages of Justice in the War against Terror. *Penn State Law Review*, *109*, 967.
Sanders, A., Bridges, L., Mulvaney, A., & Crozier, G. (1989). *Advice and assistance at police stations and the 24 hour duty solicitor scheme*. London: Lord Chancellor's Department.
Shawyer, A., & Milne, R. (2009). Investigative interviewing: Investigation, counter-fraud and behaviour. *2nd International Investigative Interviewing Research Group Conference, University of Teesside*.
Shepherd, E. (1996). *Becoming skilled*. London: Law Society.
Smith, A. 1995: *The Criminal Justice and Public Order Act 1994. The public order elements*. Criminal Law Review January, 19–27
Smith, M. R., & Alpert, G. P. (2007). Explaining police bias: A theory of social conditioning and illusory correlation. *Criminal Justice and Behavior*, *34*, 1262–1283.

Case Cited

Miller, Paris and Abdullahi R v Miller, Paris and Abdullahi (1993). 97 Criminal Appeal Reports 99.

Chapter 7

Impact of racial and prejudicial stereotypes on the outcome of criminal investigations

Introduction

The preceding chapters have delved into the intricate role of racial and prejudicial stereotypes within the realm of investigative and interviewing processes. This exploration has spanned various dimensions, from analysing stop-and-search practices to examining the dynamics of investigative interviews. In particular, the examination of Asian Muslim suspects and their interactions with police officers, as well as insights from defence lawyers, has illuminated how a suspect's ethnic and religious background can lead some police officers down the path of guilt presumption, self-fulfilling prophecies, and, in certain instances, even hostility and discriminatory behaviours. Furthermore, it was noted that these perceptions extend to suspects and lawyers, who have, at times, perceived ethnicity and religious background as factors influencing police officers' judgements.

Building upon this foundation, this chapter embarks on a rigorous analysis. It draws upon a crisp-set qualitative comparative analysis of interviews conducted with real-life police officers. The primary aim of the current study is to investigate whether these prejudicial stereotypes can indeed influence the outcome(s) of a criminal investigation. Specifically, it was inquired whether similar crimes, when investigated, yield different outcomes when the suspects come from different community groups. By examining these nuanced aspects, the current study aims to shed further light on the intricate interplay between stereotypes, investigative processes, and the ultimate results of criminal investigations.

Background

Previous research on unconscious racial stereotypes has cast doubt on individuals' ability to make impartial decisions when it comes to members of certain minority groups (Correll et al., 2007; Fazio, Jackson, Dunton, & Williams, 1995; Mears, Stewart, Warren, & Simons, 2017).

DOI: 10.4324/9781003366836-7

This body of work suggests that deeply ingrained prejudicial stereotypes against individuals from specific minority groups significantly influence people's behaviour towards them. Notably, these stereotypes are often subconscious, meaning that even individuals who overtly profess to be fair-minded may exhibit biases at an implicit level (Lammers & Staple, 2011). These negative stereotypes tend to be automatically activated when individuals encounter members of stigmatised groups, potentially affecting their decisions, even when they consciously wish to remain unbiased (Banaji & Greenwald, 1995; Devine, 1989; Fazio et al., 1995; Greenwald, 1992; Macrae & Bodenhausen, 2000).

Certain ethnic minorities often fall victim to negative stereotypes that attribute to them characteristics supposedly predisposing them to criminal behaviour (Correll et al., 2007). Notably, within the context of policing, these stereotypes can be deeply ingrained, as Ware (2007) argues, especially in the case of young Black men who are often stereotyped as dangerous criminals. These pervasive negative stereotypes may significantly impact how individuals within the criminal justice system, including police officers and judges, interact with suspects from these ethnic minorities (Lammers & Staple, 2011). The decisions made by these actors within the criminal justice system carry profound consequences for all parties involved. Recent research underscores the troubling fact that racial stereotypes can even influence critical decisions, such as a police officer's choice to use lethal force. For instance, studies have suggested that an officer's decision on whether to use lethal force when confronting a potentially armed suspect may be influenced by the suspect's ethnicity (Correll et al., 2007; Hall, Hall, & Perry, 2016).). These findings underscore the pressing need for addressing and confronting the impact of racial stereotypes within the criminal justice system, as they can have far-reaching and sometimes life-altering ramifications for individuals from ethnic minority backgrounds.

Another potential explanation for racial stereotyping by police officers is the concept of illusory correlation (Smith & Alpert, 2007). In essence, illusory correlation refers to the perception of a relationship between two sets of events that are either less associated or correlated to a lesser degree than one might think (Chapman, 1967). The notion of illusory correlation initially emerged from the work of Hamilton and Gifford (1976), who observed that individual subjective experiences could reinforce socially transmitted stereotypes by linking distinctive behaviours with minority communities. In the context of law enforcement, this means that when police officers encounter negative behaviours exhibited by individuals from minority groups, they may overestimate the prevalence of such behaviours, thereby reinforcing pre-existing racial stereotypes (Mullen & Johnson, 1990). Smith and Alpert (2007) propose that racial profiling may be a consequence of unconscious racial stereotyping, resurfacing either due to differential exposure to criminality within certain groups or as a result of the illusory correlation phenomenon. Consequently, this process may lead police officers to overestimate the frequency of negative behaviours among minority citizens (Hall et al., 2016). In essence, illusory correlation serves as a cognitive mechanism that can inadvertently perpetuate and intensify racial stereotypes within the context of law enforcement.

Moreover, the inherent nature of police work often leads officers to have frequent interactions with members of minority and socially disadvantaged communities, which are disproportionately affected by complex social issues such as unemployment, poverty, and housing challenges (Maynard-Moody & Musheno, 2003). This close engagement between law enforcement and these communities is a critical aspect of policing in many societies. Smith and Alpert (2007) put forth the argument that police officers often reflect the general public from which they are recruited. It could be contended that when a community becomes constructed as a 'suspect' within public discourse, it may have a profound impact on the criminal investigative process concerning the members of this 'suspect' community. This influence is rooted in the fact that police officers are drawn from the very communities they serve, potentially sharing some of the negative stereotypes that may prevail in the broader societal discourse. The implications of this connection between police officers and the communities they serve are complex and multifaceted. It raises questions about the potential influence of community perceptions and stereotypes on policing practices and the need for strategies to address and mitigate any biases that may emerge.

Building upon the research studies discussed earlier, it becomes evident that stereotypes are cognitive constructs residing within the minds of perceivers, shaped by their knowledge, beliefs, and expectations about identifiable social groups (Mackie, Hamilton, Susskind, & Rosselli, 1996). In this context, it is worth noting that during the initial stage of abductive reasoning (Fahsing & Ask, 2016), negative stereotypes can come into play when officers are faced with decisions regarding a particular suspect. This occurs as a result of their pre-existing mental images associated with the group to which the suspect belongs (Darley & Gross, 1983). Abductive reasoning marks the inception of any inquiry, where investigators seek to formulate explanatory hypotheses that can later be assessed (Fahsing & Ask, 2016). As Peirce (1965) aptly stated, 'Abduction is the process of forming explanatory hypotheses' (p. 172). This implies that unconscious stereotypes can be activated within the decision-making processes of police officers. Once activated, these negative stereotypes can exert influence over decisions related to a suspect's profile and perceived culpability. It is important to note that such activation does not necessitate overt endorsement of the stereotype (Correll et al., 2007). In light of these insights, the current chapter embarks on an investigation to ascertain whether any prejudicial stereotyping based on suspects' ethnicity or religious background could exert an impact on police officers' investigative decision-making and, consequently, on the outcome(s) of a criminal investigation. By delving into this complex interplay between stereotypes and law enforcement, the present study aims to shed further light on the dynamics of policing in diverse communities.

The present study

The present study contributes to the literature on prejudicial stereotyping within the context of criminal investigations in several significant ways. Firstly, it involves real-life police officers and seeks to determine whether prejudicial stereotyping, rooted in a suspect's background, exerts an influence on their investigative decision-making.

Secondly, as observed in the previous chapter, legal representatives perceived police interviewers as more inclined to pursue charges against suspects of Asian Muslim ethnicity. These legal professionals stressed that negative portrayals of the Muslim community in the media may have played a role in shaping police interviewers' attitudes towards Muslim suspects. Consequently, the present study will also investigate whether a suspect's Muslim background significantly impacts the outcome(s) of a criminal investigation, shedding light on the potential consequences of such perceptions.

Lastly, the current study employs an innovative methodological approach, crisp-set qualitative comparative analysis (csQCA). This method allows the author to identify the causal relationship between racial/religious stereotypes and the associated outcomes of a criminal investigation, providing a unique perspective on this complex issue.

By exploring these dimensions, the current research aims to deepen our understanding of the dynamics surrounding prejudicial stereotyping in criminal investigations, with the potential to inform policy and practices aimed at promoting fairness and equity within the criminal justice system.

Methods

Materials and procedures

To investigate whether stereotyping of 'suspect' communities influences police officers' investigative decision-making, the current study involved conducting semi-structured interviews with 20 serving police officers from a single police organisation in England. During these individual interviews, each police officer was presented with the same scenario. However, the scenarios differed only in the name of the suspect. For one-half of the sample, the scenario referred to an indigenous person from the United Kingdom (Scenario A), while for the other half, the scenario described a suspect with an obviously Muslim name (Scenario B). The following written scenario was presented to the officers:

Scenarios

> You have been required to interview, an adult male named *person*, who is suspected of supplying class A drugs.[1] You have one statement from a reliable witness, and a small amount of class A drugs were recovered. There is no other previous criminal intelligence available relative to the suspect. You have sufficient grounds under the Police and Criminal Evidence Act (1984) to interview the suspect. (Where the named *person* in scenario A is Richard Fisher, and in Scenario B is Muhammad Ali)

To investigate the potential influence of a suspect's name on police officers' decision-making, the current study utilised scenarios during semi-structured interviews. Each police officer participating in the study was randomly assigned to either Scenario A or Scenario B, ensuring equal usage of each case scenario.

In response to their assigned scenario, each police officer was asked to provide insights into the following key aspects:

(i) How they would prepare and plan the interview.
(ii) The possible points they would seek to prove during the investigation.
(iii) Their opinion on the strength of evidence presented in the scenario, which they rated as either strong or weak.
(iv) Their suggested outcome for the investigation.

Participants

The present research conducted in-depth interviews with a sample of 20 serving police officers from a single force. Of the participants, 17 were male. Each interview had an approximate duration of 30 minutes. Participants in the study had substantial experience in conducting interviews with suspects, with an average of 8.88 years of experience (SD = 4.96 years). Their ages ranged from 23 to 56 years, with an average age of 36.47 years (SD = 8.68). Importantly, all participants reported receiving formal training in the interviewing of suspects.

Procedures

In order to gain access to the relevant police organisation for the current research, an external research application was completed and submitted. Subsequently, the police management assigned an inspector and a sergeant as the main contacts for the study. The initial step involved a meeting between the police inspector and the researcher to discuss the research aims and objectives. During this meeting, the researcher delivered a brief presentation outlining the study's goals. Following this discussion, an interview schedule was prepared and sent to the first contact, who then forwarded it to the police management for formal approval. After obtaining approval from both the police organisation and the researcher's home university, the sergeant, acting as the main contact, proceeded to allocate dates for interviews with police officers. The actual interviews were conducted between September 2015 and December 2015.

The selection of participants for the study was carried out by the police sergeant and inspector. The participants were divided into two groups: Scenario A and Scenario B.

Scenario A Participants (Numbers 1–3, 7–9, 13–14, 19–20):

- Of these participants, nine were male.
- Their ages ranged from 23 to 44 years, with an average age of 37.5 years (SD = 7.37).
- Their experience in the field varied from one to 14 years, with an average of 8.8 years (SD = 4.37).

Scenario B Participants (Numbers 4–6, 10–12, 15–18):

- Of these participants, eight were male.
- Their ages spanned from 26 to 56 years, with an average age of 36.7 years (SD = 9.49).
- Their experience ranged from two to 16 years, with an average of 9.6 years (SD = 5.22).

All participants were informed of their right to anonymity and confidentiality prior to the interviews. Detailed information regarding the rank, age, and relevant experience of each officer was recorded. Each officer responded to the same standardised set of questions during the interview, with opportunities for elaboration and clarification when necessary. After each recorded interview, transcripts were prepared, forming the foundation for data examination and analysis.

Analytical framework

To analyse the data and develop explanatory accounts regarding police officers' decisions to charge suspects with either possession of class A drugs or possession with intent to supply class A drugs, the current research employed a specific analytical technique—csQCA. This approach involves systematic and logical comparisons of cases to identify the unique combinations of logical factors associated with a given outcome (Ragin, 2008). In the context of our research, csQCA was chosen because it allows for a comprehensive investigation into the conditions under which specific combinations of logical factors lead to the outcome of interest. This method aligns perfectly with current research objectives, which seek to uncover the pathways that influence police officers' decision-making processes when faced with the choice of charging suspects with varying degrees of drug-related offences. By applying csQCA, the current study gains deeper insights into the intricate dynamics at play within police decision-making and explores the nuanced factors that drive their choices between these two distinct criminal charges—a critical aspect of our study.

Qualitative comparative analysis (QCA)

Qualitative comparative analysis (QCA), a case-oriented approach developed over 25 years ago by Ragin (1987, 2008), has gained widespread recognition and acceptance as a valuable methodology in the social sciences. In recent years, the use of QCA in research design has experienced rapid growth, and the methodology itself continues to evolve and be refined (Rihoux & Marx, 2013).

QCA is an analytical technique that employs systematic and logical case comparisons, grounded in the principles of Boolean algebra, to identify unique combinations of explanatory variables associated with a particular outcome (Musheno, Gregware, & Drass, 1991). It operates by discerning 'causal regularities'—that is, it identifies key combinations of necessary and sufficient properties, referred to as 'conditions', in QCA terminology, that lead to specific phenomena, known as 'outcomes', in QCA terminology (Rihoux & Ragin, 2008). In essence, QCA provides a methodological framework for exploring complex causal relationships, offering valuable insights into the interplay of various factors in producing specific outcomes.

QCA is widely recognised as one of the significant methodological innovations of recent decades (Gerring, 2001). It is built upon the binary language originally developed by George Boolean in the mid-1800s—a language that also serves as the mathematical foundation of computer technology (Stokke, 2007). QCA utilises Boolean algebra, a system that doesn't manipulate numbers but rather organises logical expressions to create configurations of circumstances associated with specific outcomes, such as the decision to charge or caution a suspect. This approach combines elements of both qualitative and quantitative methods but is firmly rooted in the qualitative tradition, emphasising the uniqueness and significance of each case. In contrast to conventional statistical methods, which rely on a probabilistic approach to examine the average effects of variable changes, QCA operates on a deterministic understanding of causality. It explores the connections between attributes and outcomes within sets and set relationships. The goal of QCA is parsimony, aiming to identify the smallest number of condition combinations that lead to the explained outcome (Ragin, 1987; Soulliere, 2005).

QCA is a tool for the systematic comparison of cases. The result of a QCA analysis, an explanatory model which contains one or more causal paths to the explained outcome, is based on a constant dialogue between theory and evidence. QCA forces the development of a model based on theoretical information and selected variables, on the one hand, and empirical information on these variables in the context of specific cases, on the other hand (Marx & Dusa, 2011). The goal of this systematic comparative case strategy is to 'integrate the best features of the case-oriented approach with the best features of the variable-oriented approach' (Ragin, 1987, p. 84). This approach consists of three central features: (i) development of an explanatory model; (ii) exploration and discovery of similarities and differences in outcomes across comparable cases by comparing configurations of conditions; and (iii) identification of causal regularities that are parsimonious using systematic Boolean analysis (Marx & Dusa, 2011; Ragin, 1987; Rihoux & Ragin, 2008). Also, QCA simplifies the analysis by dropping irrelevant factors. When two combinations that lead to an outcome are identical on all but one condition, that condition becomes irrelevant in the context of the other condition and can be eliminated, thereby reducing two combinations into one and simplifying the analysis (Cress & Snow, 2000).

Crisp-set qualitative comparative analysis (csQCA)

Crisp-set qualitative comparative analysis (csQCA), as introduced by Ragin (1987), was initially presented as an approach to understanding macro-social phenomena, encompassing entire societies and institutions. However, the versatility of csQCA extends beyond macro-social analyses, making it suitable for exploring micro-social phenomena, including small groups and interactions (Soulliere, 2005).

The core technique of csQCA revolves around the matching and contrasting of cases, with the aim of eliminating negligible or trivial conditions. This process highlights the minimum necessary and sufficient conditions required to explain the occurrence or non-occurrence of a particular outcome (Ragin, 1987). The systematic reduction of complex expressions into shorter combinations of conditions is referred to as 'minimisation', and it is accomplished through the application of Boolean algorithms (Rihoux & Ragin, 2008). The csQCA is a powerful analytical method that can be applied to a wide range of social phenomena, from large-scale societal dynamics to small-scale group interactions. It provides a means to distil complex relationships into parsimonious configurations of conditions, facilitating a deeper understanding of causal patterns.

In the realm of csQCA, the process of minimisation can be performed with or without the consideration of logical remainders. Logical remainders represent potential configurations of causal conditions that, while logically possible, may not be observed as empirical cases due to limitations in selection or the non-existence of such cases at the time of the study (Ragin, 2004). When researchers conduct minimisations with logical remainders, they aim to achieve parsimonious or 'short' solutions (Winand, Rihoux, Robinson, & Zintz, 2013). In essence, this approach allows for the exploration of every conceivable configuration of causal conditions, given the conditions under consideration, which can lead to a specific outcome.

The significance of csQCA lies not only in its ability to uncover multiple pathways to an outcome (Cress & Snow, 2000) but also in its capacity to identify the simplest combinations of factors that consistently result in a particular outcome. In this way, csQCA offers researchers a robust tool for navigating the complexity of causal relationships and pinpointing the key contributors to specific outcomes.

Performing a csQCA, in general, requires nine following distinct steps (Marx & Dusa, 2011, p. 106):

1. Deciding what outcomes need to be investigated.
2. Selecting the cases for analysis with sufficient variations regarding the outcome.
3. Listing the most significant conditions, which might contribute to an explanation of the outcome.
4. In a csQCA both the presence and absence of a condition or outcome are meaningful. It requires dichotomous data (1/0). This implies that for each case an explanatory condition is coded '1' if the condition is present for that case and '0' if the condition is absent in that case.
5. Coding each condition for each case and bring this information together in a data matrix.

6. Analysing the data matrix by specifying an explanatory model and resolving contradictions.
7. Transforming the data matrix to produce a truth table.
8. Analysing the truth table and generate the most parsimonious explanation based on the minimisation procedure which is available in csQCA.
9. Interpreting the resulting explanatory models, which allows researchers to identify mechanisms that link explanatory conditions to an outcome. The last step may allow researchers to identify mechanisms which link explanatory conditions to an outcome.

The implementation of csQCA to the present study

In the analytical comparison of two sets of interviews, the current research employed a csQCA. In csQCA, each interview is treated as a holistic configuration of causal conditions rather than a collection of variable scores. This approach is distinct in that it does not assume that the effect of an explanatory variable remains constant regardless of the values of other variables (Rantala & Hellström, 2001; Soulliere, 2005). QCA, including csQCA, operates on the fundamental principle that variables exert their influence in combination with other variables (Rihoux & Ragin, 2008). As articulated by Ragin (1993), 'no value on any variable (categorical or interval) can be understood in isolation, but only in the context of the values of other relevant variables' (p. 306). This foundational perspective underscores the importance of examining how conditions interact and cooperate to produce specific outcomes. QCA serves as a bridge between qualitative and quantitative approaches, providing a holistic and comprehensive framework often sought in social research. This framework enables researchers to consider the broader context in which behaviours and phenomena occur (Rantala & Hellström, 2001). By embracing the interplay of variables within complex configurations, QCA facilitates a deeper understanding of the multifaceted nature of causal relationships.

The csQCA was the chosen analytical approach for this research due to its unique ability to identify both the necessary and sufficient conditions for an outcome. This characteristic aligns with a deterministic understanding of causality, making csQCA particularly well suited for addressing questions related to cause and outcome (Marx & Dusa, 2011). The research objective was to explore whether a suspect's Muslim name 'causes' a different 'outcome' in a criminal investigation. Analysing a complex set of interviews, csQCA proved to be an ideal choice because the focus was on identifying configurations of causal conditions regarding how a suspect's background influences an outcome, rather than quantifying the individual influence of single variables such as age, experience, or gender on a dependent variable.

Compared to traditional statistical procedures like regression and ANOVA, csQCA takes a different approach by emphasising the analysis of set relations rather than correlations. This methodology offers a closer link to theory, which can be more challenging to achieve with conventional quantitative methods that primarily analyse matrices of bivariate correlations (Marx & Dusa, 2011). In this research, factors like the age, gender, training, or experience of police officers might indeed exert varying degrees of influence on individual cases. However, these factors do not affect the core objective of understanding whether a suspect's Muslim name could influence the outcome of a criminal investigation.

Selecting outcomes and conditions

Outcomes

In the csQCA methodology, the first crucial step involves selecting the outcomes and causal conditions (Coverdill & Findley, 1995). The present study conducted 20 semi-structured interviews with police officers, during which each was asked to envision the possible outcomes of the investigation based on the evidence presented in a given scenario. The officers suggested two distinct outcomes:

1. Charging the suspect with only possession of class A drugs.
2. Charging the suspect with possession and intent to supply class A drugs.

The current research aimed to understand the factors influencing the decision to 'charge with possession and intent to supply class A drugs' as opposed to 'charge with only possession of class A drugs'. It was anticipated that comparing these two outcomes would reveal different combinations of justifications. Thus, these selected outcomes formed the basis for csQCA analysis.

Thus, the selected outcomes for csQCA for the present research are as follows.

Outcome 1: charge with possession of class A drugs (CWP)
Outcome 2: charge with possession and intent to supply class A drugs (CWPIS)

Causal conditions

To identify the possible causal conditions associated with different outcomes in a criminal investigation scenario, the current study's approach was to allow the data to reveal relevant causal conditions, maximising descriptive validity (Britt, 1997). These conditions would then be cross-checked against the relevant UK legislation, specifically the PACE Act, which outlines requirements for the questioning of suspects. The csQCA typically involves a preliminary stage (Soulliere, 2005) that relies on either theoretical deductions or standard forms of qualitative data analysis (Coverdill & Finlay, 1995). The present study sought to pinpoint the potential causal conditions that might influence police officers' investigative decision-making regarding whether to charge suspects with possession only or with possession and supplying class A drugs. To accomplish this, preliminary coding was conducted using the grounded theory methodology developed by Glaser and Strauss in 1967.

Grounded theory analysis

Grounded theory, as introduced by Glaser and Strauss in 1967, is widely recognised as one of the most rigorous methods for conducting preliminary or exploratory research, particularly in areas with limited existing knowledge (Walton, 1999). In the present research, grounded theory was employed to analyse the factors influencing police officers' investigative decision-making. This methodology was chosen because it is not constrained by pre-existing theories and instead aims to generate or develop a plausible theory grounded in the data (Braun & Clarke, 2006).

Grounded theory offers the flexibility needed for analysing and conceptualising the data in the current research context (Strauss & Corbin, 1997). Since there was no existing model that delineated the influence of negative stereotyping on investigative decision-making, it became essential to develop one. This approach helped identify the causal conditions that may exert an influence on police officers' decision-making processes.

The researcher adopted a grounded theory approach (Glaser & Strauss, 1967), for the analysis of transcripts. Grounded theory analyses are primarily designed to uncover theories within the data itself (Charmaz, 2006). The grounded theory analysis commenced with open coding, a process characterised by the labelling of each line of data without any predetermined theoretical constraints. This approach allowed for an open and unrestricted exploration of the data, free from pre-existing theories. The researcher meticulously reviewed the transcripts, line by line, coding events to capture the participants' narratives. The resulting codes were then organised into categories and subjected to the constant comparison method—a fundamental aspect of grounded theory. This method involves comparing codes with each other to aid in the conceptualisation of the data (Glaser & Strauss, 1967).

During this phase, codes that did not exhibit meaningful connections with other codes were omitted, as they were not deemed to hold core relevance. This process led to a reduction in the number of codes, while enriching their conceptualisation of the data (refer to Figure 7.1 below). Subsequently, these codes were used for the coding of the final four of the 20 transcripts, shedding further light on their interrelationships. At this juncture, data saturation was achieved, indicating that no new codes emerged. Consequently, there was no need to seek authorisation from the police for additional interviews, and data collection was concluded.

In the final stage of the analysis, the codes were subjected to a deeper examination to identify the core process that linked them. This process aimed to uncover the essential steps and processes crucial to the decision-making of police officers. The codes were initially organised into three main categories that encapsulated various aspects of the data. Next, the text associated with these codes was systematically extracted, organised by category, and subjected to multiple iterations of reading. During this iterative process, a constant comparison was maintained both between and within the text segments to identify the key processes related to the specific steps involved in decision-making during and after an investigative interview.

Ultimately, a core variable emerged—a statement that best captured the essence of what transpired in the data. The core variable emerged as a statement that best captured what was going on in the data, and that could account for the categories identified and the codes within them. Additionally, subcore variables emerged, representing stages within the core process. These subcore variables encompassed the previous categories and their respective properties, providing a comprehensive understanding of the analysis.

Grounded theory results

The theory developed in this analysis culminated in the identification of a core category: 'factors influencing officers' investigative decision-making during an interview'. This core category serves as the overarching explanatory framework that accounts for all other codes and categories, providing a comprehensive understanding of the analysis. Within this core category, a three-stage process emerged, depicting the officers' decision-making process when deciding whether to charge with possession (CWP) or charge with possession and intent to supply (CWPIS) concerning suspects. These three stages include: (i) perceptions about evidence; (ii) points to prove; and (iii) decision to search suspects' premises under S.18 of PACE Act (1984).[2] The components of this three-stage process are shown in Figure 7.1.

Perceptions about evidence

When responding to the provided scenario, officers mentioned various types of evidence that could be utilised during interviews, primarily the witness statement and the recovered drugs. They noted that such evidence could serve multiple purposes, including challenging statements made by the suspect and potentially eliciting further information from the suspect. Furthermore, officers who anticipated the witness as trustworthy tended to perceive that the evidence against the suspect was robust enough to secure a conviction for possession with intent to supply class A drugs. One officer (13) put it this way,

> Evidence is quite strong because I have got a small amount of drugs and a reliable witness, so, yes, I have got enough to get a conviction.

In contrast, officers who expressed a need for additional information about the witness, such as assessing the witness's reliability or determining whether there were any prior associations between the witness and the suspect, tended to perceive the strength of the evidence against the suspect as weak.

For example, the officer (03) put it this way,

> It's very difficult because it does not say what the witness has seen. We have got a reliable witness, but what have they seen, what have they said? It's difficult that is for supply anyway, I mean, and the amount of drugs is relevant [...] it's reasonably weak evidence I would think at the moment, good evidence to possession.

Points to prove

During the interview process, officers highlighted several legal points that needed to be proven, including the suspect's sources of income, the amount paid for the drugs, the origin of the funds, ownership of the drugs, witness reliability, and the suspect's whereabouts at the time of arrest, among others. Importantly, it was observed that the likelihood of officers aiming to prove either possession of class A drugs (P) or possession with intent to supply class A drugs (PWIS) was closely linked to their perception of the strength of the evidence.

Officers were more inclined to pursue charges of possession with intent to supply when they perceived the evidence as robust and compelling. For example, one officer (19) put it like this:

> You have got strong evidence there, then it's so much easier I would say. With little or no evidence, then you have got massive bits of doubt in

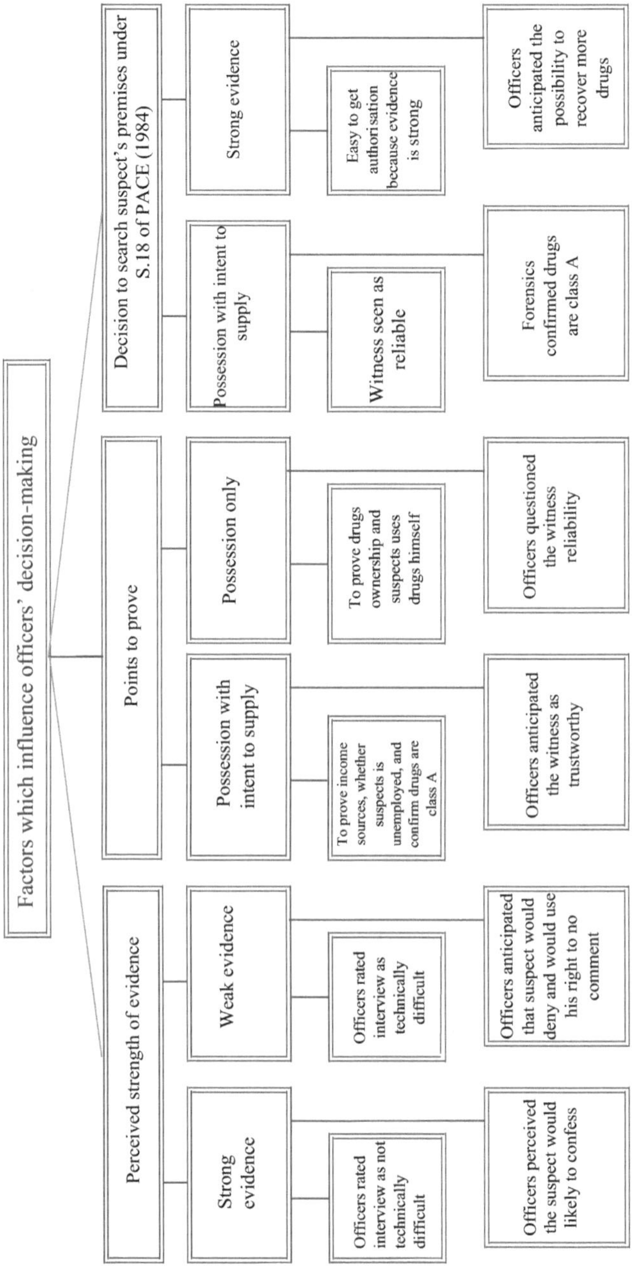

Figure 7.1 A grounded theory—factors which possibly affect officers' investigative decision-making.

> there. I would be hoping for a charge with intent to supply because of the fact that we have got a reliable witness and recovered drugs.

In contrast, officers who perceived the evidence's strength as weak indicated that their approach would be to conduct the interview with the aim of proving possession only. For instance, one officer (05) encapsulated this situation in this way:

> Well, obviously a small amount of drugs and one witness, so we are not going to be looking at possession with intent, so we are just going to be looking at a simple possession of Class A drugs.

The decision to search the suspect's premises under Section 18 of the PACE Act (1984)

In line with their decisions to prove either possession of class A drugs (P) or possession with intent to supply class A drugs (PWIS), 15 of the officers indicated their intention to seek authority from their relevant senior police officers under Section 18 of the PACE Act 1984 to search the suspect's home address(es) potentially in search of more drugs. This further underscores the connection between the officer's decision-making process and their approach to handling the case. For example, one officer (16) characterised this situation this way:

> I would because he's got class A on him. To me, yes, that's a section 18. You arrest him, and you do a section 18 because potentially he might have some more. Yes, I would section 18 because....

The theory—factors which influence officers' investigative decision-making

As a result of grounded theory analysis, it was discovered that the perceived strength of evidence plays a central role in the investigative process. Moreover, it became evident that the perceived strength of evidence not only influences the entire structure of the interview but also determines subsequent lines of inquiry. The degree to which evidence is perceived as strong or weak directly impacts whether an officer will aim to establish possession of class A drugs or possession with intent to supply class A drugs. If an officer deems the evidence to be strong, they are likely to conduct the interview with the goal of proving possession with intent to supply. Conversely, if the evidence is perceived as weak, the officer is more inclined to focus on establishing possession only. Consequently, a police officer's decision regarding the execution of a Section 18 search may also be influenced by the perceived strength of evidence and the specific elements that need to be proven. If an officer conducts an interview to establish 'possession with intent to supply class A drugs', there is a distinct possibility that they will seek authorisation from their relevant inspector under Section 18 of the PACE Act 1984 to search the suspect's residence(s) in an effort to recover additional drugs.

Trustworthiness of the theory

To limit the introduction of bias into the analysis and bolster the validity of the theory developed, several measures were implemented. First, the scenarios were deliberately kept broad, enabling police officers to respond in their own words. This was achieved by using open-ended questions, as opposed to inquiries that might be perceived as leading or biased towards the researcher's expected findings. Second, the interviews were conducted by the researcher with the assistance of police officers who possessed first-hand investigative interviewing experience. It is noteworthy that, at the time of the study, the researcher had no practical experience in conducting investigative interviews. This lack of practical experience was considered beneficial in preventing preconceived notions from influencing the research process. Third, to further ensure the validity of the categories developed, a PhD student with a strong background in qualitative research conducted a formal validity check on the empirical data. These categories encompassed perceptions about evidence, points to prove, and decisions related to searching suspects' premises under Section 18 of the PACE Act (1984). The PhD researcher, who possessed extensive knowledge of qualitative research, coded ten randomly selected transcriptions (five from each scenario). Inter-rater reliability was assessed using Cohen's kappa, resulting in a Cohen's kappa value of 0.91. This high value indicates a robust level of agreement between the two sets of scores, demonstrating strong agreement (Fleiss, 1981).

Causal conditions

As a result of the grounded theory analysis, several causal conditions were identified that have the potential to influence officers' decision-making during criminal investigations. These factors, when taken into account, can significantly impact the overall outcome of such investigations. The following causal conditions were revealed:

1. **The suspect's name:** entails information about the suspect's name. The scenarios which were given to police officers were with a suspect named either Richard Fisher (**RF**) (Scenario A) or Muhammad Ali (**MA**) (Scenario B).

2. **The strength of evidence (SE):** contains information about officers' opinions concerning the evidence. During the analysis of interviews, officers' opinion concerning the strength of evidence was found as a causal condition, which may be contributing towards the outcome of criminal investigations.
3. **Legal points to prove:** entails information about the legal points to prove suggested by the police officers in response to the given scenarios. As a result of grounded theory analysis, it was identified that police officers suggested they will investigate this crime to prove either only possession of class A drugs (P) or possession with intent to supply class A drugs (PWIS). These two points to prove the offence appeared as causal conditions that may well contribute to the outcomes.
4. **The decision to search the suspect's premises under Section 18 of the PACE Act 1984 (S18S):** the police officers' decision about exercising Section 18 powers at the suspect's premises was found as a causal condition, which may also contribute to the outcome.

Dichotomous coding and data matrix

In csQCA, once outcomes and causal conditions have been identified, the next step involves the preliminary coding of all variables implicated in the analysis, as outlined by Ragin (1987). Due to the constraints of Boolean algebra, which allows for only two values ('0' and '1'), csQCA necessitates that both causal conditions and outcomes should be dichotomous. This dichotomisation is achieved by coding the causal conditions and outcomes based on their presence/absence, yes/no, strong/weak, or similar criteria. The dichotomous coding for outcomes was as follows:

- For the first outcome, a decision to charge with 'only possession of class A drugs' was denoted by '1', while the decision not to charge was denoted by '0'.
- For the second outcome, a decision to 'charge with possession and intent to supply class A drugs' (CWPIS) was indicated by '1', whereas the decision not to charge was represented by '0'.

Similarly, the dichotomous coding of the causal conditions was indicated by '1' where these causal conditions were present and by '0' where they were absent.

Truth table analysis

To apply Boolean algebra as a technique for qualitative comparison, it is essential to construct a raw data matrix known as a 'truth table'. This table

Table 7.1 Truth table of six causal conditions and two outcomes

Causal Conditions						*Outcomes*	
RF	*MA*	*PWIS*	*P*	*S18S*	*SE*	*CWPIS*	*CWP*
1	0	1	1	1	0	0	1
1	0	0	1	0	0	0	1
1	0	0	1	0	0	0	1
1	0	1	1	1	0	0	1
1	0	1	1	1	1	0	1
1	0	0	1	0	0	0	1
1	0	1	1	0	0	0	1
1	0	1	1	1	1	0	1
1	0	0	1	0	0	0	1
1	0	1	1	1	1	1	0
0	1	1	1	1	1	1	0
0	1	1	1	1	1	1	0
0	1	1	1	1	0	0	1
0	1	1	1	1	1	1	0
0	1	1	1	1	0	0	1
0	1	1	1	1	1	1	0
0	1	1	1	1	1	1	0
0	1	1	1	1	1	1	0
0	1	1	1	1	0	0	1
0	1	1	1	1	1	0	1

RF *= Richard Fisher;* ***MA*** *= Muhammad Ali;* ***PWIS*** *= Possession with intent to supply;* ***P*** *= Possession only;* ***S18S*** *= Section 18 search;* ***SE*** *= Strength of evidence;* ***CWPIS*** *= charge with possession and intent to supply;* ***CWP*** *= charge with possession*

serves to summarise the patterns of outcomes associated with various configurations of causal conditions, as described by Ragin (1987). In essence, a truth table catalogues different combinations of causal conditions and records the corresponding values of the outcome variable for cases falling into each combination. Table 7.1 illustrates the truth table representing officers' decisions regarding whether to charge with only possession of class A drugs (CWP) or to charge the suspect with possession and intent to supply class A drugs (CWPIS).

The present study employed the fs/QCA (version 3.0) software package for conducting csQCA analysis (Ragin & Sean, 2014). Initially, a preliminary csQCA analysis, using minimisations with logical remainders in the fs/QCA software, was conducted. This analysis aimed to match and contrast the selected causal conditions to eliminate negligible, redundant, and trivial determinants. The process of paired comparison ultimately led to the identification of causal combinations linked to the desired outcome (Ragin, 2008).

Subsequently, the fs/QCA software automatically selected the smallest number of these combinations necessary to cover all the positive instances of the outcome. In the truth table containing the six key causal conditions, no contradictory configurations were found. Instead, six unique configurations of conditions were associated with each outcome, each having a distinct outcome value. Therefore, based on the analysis of 20 cases, it can be inferred that these causal conditions are sufficient to explain the factors that may influence officers' decision-making in criminal investigations.

The outcome of the minimisation process yields a prime-implicant equation (Ragin, 2008). This equation serves as a concise representation that summarises the data in the truth table, utilising only the logically essential prime causal conditions (Ragin, 2008). Consequently, this equation offers a robust foundation for bridging theoretical concepts (Coverdill & Finlay, 1995). It succinctly describes the various combinations of conditions associated with a specific outcome, facilitating the development of logically derived theories about the nature of the phenomenon under investigation (Soulliere, 2005).

During the truth table analysis conducted using the fs/QCA software, three solutions are presented: (i) a 'complex' solution that avoids the use of any counterfactual cases (rows without cases 'remainders'); (ii) a 'parsimonious' solution, which allows for the inclusion of any remainders that lead to simpler (or fewer) combinations; (iii) an 'intermediate' solution, which incorporates the remainders that withstand counterfactual analysis based on theoretical and substantive knowledge, typically provided by the user. Ragin (2008) suggests that the intermediate solutions are the most suitable. Consequently, the present research employed intermediate solutions for analysis.

Results

The analysis conducted using the fs/QCA (version 3.0) software on the truth table yielded the following results, offering insights into the factors that may influence a police officer's decision regarding whether to charge a suspect with possession and intent to supply class A drugs (CWPIS) or with possession only (CWP).

Pathway to police officers' decision to charge the suspect with possession of class A drugs (CWP)

Utilising the configured cases, the fs/QCA analysis of the truth table generated the following minimisation equations that explain officers' decisions to charge the suspect with possession only. Pathways to CWP:[3]

$$CWP = RF*P*se$$

$$CWP = MA*PWIS*P*S18S*se$$

$$CWP = RF*P*se + MA*PWIS*P*S18S*se$$

Key: RF = Richard Fisher; P = Possession; se = Strong Evidence; MA = Muhammad Ali; PWIS = Possession with intent to supply; S18S = Section 18 search

The two equations provided above offer a logically minimal representation of the various combinations of factors associated with the outcome CWP. Essentially, these equations convey that possession (P) is a sufficient condition for a police officer to charge a suspect with possession. Due to their nature as logical statements, these two recipes for CWP can be factored. Consequently, this intermediate solution can be factored to highlight the presence of possession of class A drugs (P) in both equations:

$$CWP= P.(RF+MA*PIS*S18S*)$$

Key: P = Possession; RF = Richard Fisher; MA = Muhammad Ali; PWIS = Possession with intent to supply; S18S = Section 18 search

The above expression indicates that police officers may decide to CWP if they investigated for only possession of class A drugs combined with either: (i) a suspect named Richard Fisher or (ii) the combination of a) a suspect named Muhammad Ali, b) possession with intent to supply, and c) execution of Section 18 search at the suspect's address(s).

Pathways to police officers' decisions to charge the suspect with possession and intent to supply class A drugs (CWPIS)

The analysis again used the coding outcomes presented in the truth table. Using the configured cases, the fs/QCA software produced the following minimised equations of officers' decision to charge the suspect with possession and intent to supply class A drugs (CWPIS). The analysis produced the following pathway to the police officers' decision regarding CWPIS:

$$CWPIS = MA*SE$$

$$CWPIS = MA*rf*PWIS*P*S18S*SE$$

$$CWPIS = MA*SE+MA*rf*PWIS*P*S18S*SE$$

Key: MA = Muhammad Ali; SE = Strong Evidence; rf = Richard Fisher; PWIS = Possession with intent to supply; P = Possession; S18S = Section 18 search

As in the analysis of the CWPIS outcome, this specifies, in a logically minimal way, the different combinations of factors that are linked to the outcome of CWPIS. Because they are logical statements, these two recipes for CWPIS can be factored. As such, this intermediate solution can be factored to show the suspect named Muhammad Ali (MA), and strength of evidence as strong (SE) is present in both equations:

MA*SE (PWIS*P*S18S)

Key: MA = Muhammad Ali; SE = Strong Evidence; PWIS = Possession with intent to supply; P= Possession; S18S = Section 18 search

In essence, this equation outlines the circumstances under which police officers may choose to charge a suspect with both possession and intent to supply class A drugs. Specifically, if the suspect's name is Muhammad Ali and the police officers perceive the strength of evidence as strong, they may proceed with pressing charges. In simpler terms, the decision to charge the suspect hinges on the perceived strength of evidence. This equation essentially clarifies that police officers will consider the evidence strong when Muhammad Ali's name is involved, potentially leading to charges for possession and intent to supply class A drugs.

In summary, police officers may opt to CWPIS when they perceive the strength of evidence as strong, provided the suspect's name is Muhammad Ali and either of the following conditions is met: (i) the officer's investigation points to possession with intent to supply class A drugs, or (ii) the officer decides to execute a Section 18 search at the suspect's addresses.

As outlined in Table 7.2, when presented with scenario A, where the suspect was named RF, three out of ten officers perceived the evidence strength as strong, while seven officers perceived the evidence strength as strong when the suspect's name was MA. In scenario B, involving the suspect MA, six officers indicated that MA would be charged with both possession and intent to supply class A drugs, whereas, in the RF condition, only one police officer stated that RF would face charges for both possession and intent to supply.

The results also reveal that in the case of MA, all of the officers decided to conduct interviews related to the more serious matter of possession with intent to supply class A drugs, with the majority of these officers perceiving the evidence strength as strong. On the other hand, when dealing with RF, six

Table 7.2 Officers' responses to causal conditions and their stated outcomes of the investigation

Causal conditions and outcomes	*MA*	*RF*
Strong Evidence	70%	30%
Investigated possession with intent to supply class A drugs	100%	60%
Section 18 search	100%	50%
Charge with only possession of class A drugs	40%	90%
Charge with possession and intent to supply class A drugs	60%	10%

officers chose to conduct interviews concerning possession with intent to supply class A drugs, but most of them perceived the evidence strength as weak.

Additionally, it was observed that all of the officers opted to execute a Section 18 search (under the PACE Act 1984) at MA's address(es), while only half of the officers made the same decision in the case of RF. Table 7.2 provides a detailed representation of officers' responses to the causal conditions and their stated investigation outcomes.

Discussion

The present chapter sought to examine whether police officers who may have developed negative stereotypes towards members of the 'suspect' community (i.e. Muslims) may use their discretionary authority to act on those feelings and whether these negative stereotypes could influence investigative decision-making and the outcome of a criminal investigation. Using a comprehensive analysis of semi-structured interviews through grounded theory and csQCA, the present study identified two distinct pathways that influence officers' decisions regarding the outcome of criminal investigations. The grounded theory analysis of interview transcriptions revealed six causal conditions that form the foundation of these two pathways. The first pathway, leading to what this chapter refers to as CWP (i.e. the decision to charge a suspect with possession of class A drugs), hinges on two critical causal conditions:

(i) The officer's focus is on investigating possession of class A drugs.
(ii) The suspect's name is RF.

On the other hand, the second pathway, CWPIS (i.e. the decision to charge a suspect with possession and intent to supply class A drugs), relies on a different set of two key causal conditions:

(i) The police officer's perception of the strength of the evidence is strong.
(ii) The suspect's name is MA.

These findings suggest that the suspect's name and the perceived strength of evidence marked as 'strong' played pivotal roles in officers' investigative decision-making. These factors significantly influenced their choice of investigative paths and considerations related to the legal aspects of the case.

The findings of the current study indicate that in the MA condition, more than twice as many officers perceived the evidence as strong compared to those in the RF condition. This suggests that officers tended to reinforce their initial hypotheses regarding the case, specifically concerning their perception of the evidence's strength. In doing so, they appeared to disregard or diminish conflicting evidence within the available materials (Fahsing & Ask, 2016). Unconscious racial stereotypes can influence individuals within the criminal justice system, leading them to 'focus on a suspect, selectively choose, and filter evidence that supports a conviction, all while overlooking or suppressing evidence that suggests innocence' (Findley & Scott, 2006, p. 292). This implies that negative racial stereotyping rooted in the suspect's background may have influenced police officers to perceive the evidence as 'strong' in the MA condition when compared to the RF condition.

When comparing the pathways to both outcomes, the suspect's name emerged as the most influential factor in officers' investigative decision-making when determining their lines of inquiry and the elements to establish charges. For instance, in the case of MA, all officers opted to conduct an interview related to the more severe charge of possession with intent to supply class A drugs, citing a perception of strong evidence. This discovery highlights the possible impact of negative stereotypes associated with specific groups on investigative decision-making, potentially leading to discriminatory behaviour by police officers towards suspects from stigmatised groups.

Consequently, in the MA condition, six times as many officers expressed their intent to charge the suspect with possession and intent to supply class A drugs compared to those in the RF condition. When police officers perceived the strength of evidence as strong, signifying their desire to corroborate their initial hypothesis that MA was more likely involved in drug supply, they also indicated their readiness to allocate additional resources to substantiate his guilt. Notably, in the RF condition, only half of the sample chose to exercise the powers outlined in Section 18 of the Police and Criminal Evidence Act 1984 (PACE), whereas all officers in the MA condition opted for the exercise of such powers.

Previous research has demonstrated that confirmation bias towards a suspect's wrongdoing during police interviews often results in an 'accusatorial' interviewing style, where officers employ a confirmatory strategy to elicit confessions (Hill et al., 2008; Mortimer & Shepherd, 1999). This approach can, in turn, contribute to or result in false confessions (Kassin, Goldstein, & Savitsky, 2003). Consequently, investigations of this nature may be particularly susceptible to miscarriages of justice when officers become fixated on charging the suspect and are willing to allocate additional resources to validate their initial hypothesis regarding the suspect's wrongdoing.

Within the realm of criminal investigations, the initial phase of abductive reasoning entails rigorous problem recognition, problem framing, and option generation (Fahsing & Ask, 2016). One prominent factor contributing to suboptimal investigative decision-making is the failure of decision-makers to thoroughly identify all potential alternatives before embarking on the evaluation and integration of information to make a choice (Tversky & Kahneman, 1986). Research conducted by Graham and Lowery (2004) and Smith and Alpert (2007) has indicated that police officers may not necessarily harbour negative sentiments towards minority groups. Nevertheless, they might base their initial decisions on one of two factors: (i) preconceived beliefs, regardless of their accuracy, concerning group criminality, or (ii) assumptions about who is most likely to be involved in criminal activities.

In the current research, both pathways suggested that officers failed to consider all available options, regardless of the suspect's name or race, ultimately leading to choices that were more lenient towards RF than MA. The pathway leading to CWPIS can be seen as the result of a multifaceted causal process, commencing with the activation of unconscious stereotypes, and potentially culminating in more severe punishments for suspects belonging to stigmatised groups.

Limitations

There are a few methodological considerations that may limit the ecological validity and generalisability of this research and its findings. First and foremost, this study has concentrated on investigating the impact of racial stereotypes on investigative decision-making using crisp-set qualitative comparative analysis (csQCA). However, it's important to acknowledge that csQCA, like any analytical method, has its limitations due to data constraints (Coverdill, Finlay, & Martin, 1994). The grounded theory and csQCA employed here identified six key causal conditions associated with two outcomes. It's important to recognise that other factors influencing investigative decision-making may exist within the broader investigative process. These causal conditions, derived from grounded theory analysis, might potentially be influenced by researcher biases, either against the police or the suspects. However, the high Cohen's kappa coefficient of 0.91 between raters suggests that this might not be an issue.

Secondly, the limitations imposed by the dichotomous coding of conditions and outcomes may lead to a loss of information regarding individual cases. Nevertheless, as suggested by Rihoux and Ragin (2008, p. 14), this dichotomous calibration should not be perceived as a limitation, as it is sometimes essential to refer back to cases with all their intricate details and specificity. To address these concerns, the current study complemented analysis with fine-grained qualitative examinations of interview transcriptions and narratives. This approach provided a deeper understanding of how racial stereotypes influence investigative decision-making.

Thirdly, the responses of police officers during interviews may have also been influenced by their training and a tendency towards social desirability (Zerbe & Paulhus, 1987). In some cases, police officers might provide conforming responses rather than expressing their true feelings or opinions.

Lastly, it is important to acknowledge that various other variables, including the age of police officers, their relevant experience, interpretations of presented evidence, and the priorities of their respective police organisations, may exert varying degrees of influence on individual cases. However, it's important to note that these variables do not undermine the actual results or the understanding of the phenomenon under investigation, namely, how a suspect's background can impact the outcome of a criminal investigation. The use of csQCA helped explore the configurations of causal conditions and how multiple influences combine to achieve specific outcomes, rather than assessing the extent to which a single variable, such as age, gender, experience, or training, impacts a dependent variable. Therefore, while these variables may play roles in shaping individual cases, they do not detract from the exploration of how racial stereotypes affect investigative decision-making.

Despite these acknowledged limitations, this research provides valuable new insights into the complexities of policing stigmatised communities within the context of criminal investigations.

Further research

It is worth noting that officers' perspectives were collected in the context of a hypothetical case, and real-life situations may yield different outcomes. Therefore, a study comparing real-life investigations involving indigenous suspects and those from the 'suspect' community could serve two valuable purposes:

(i) To validate the conclusions drawn from the present study in actual practice and assess whether police officers are more inclined to charge a suspect from the 'suspect' community when investigating similar crimes.
(ii) To extend the scope of research to include Crown Prosecution Service (CPS) caseworkers, examining whether a suspect's ethnicity or affiliation with the 'suspect' community plays any role in their decisions regarding whether to press charges.

This approach would provide a comprehensive understanding of how these factors impact decision-making across different stages of the criminal justice system.

Conclusions

The application of csQCA in this study offers unique advantages due to its holistic combinatorial logic and emphasis on causal heterogeneity. It enables a comprehensive exploration of the complexity inherent in investigative decision-making and fosters a dialogue that encourages innovative thinking. In this research, the application of csQCA unveiled two distinct pathways regarding investigation outcomes. These pathways provided compelling evidence that negative stereotypes, rooted in the suspect's group membership, can indeed influence police officers' decision-making when they are deliberating their lines of inquiry and legal elements to establish charges. Both pathways indicate that officers may base their decisions on inappropriate stereotyping, potentially leading to varying outcomes in criminal investigations involving suspects from different community groups who have been subjected to stereotyping. Recognising and addressing the influence of unconscious stereotypes within the context of criminal investigations represents a critical starting point for fostering a more transparent and effective approach to policing stigmatised or stereotyped communities.

Collectively, when considering the findings across all seven chapters of this book, it becomes evident that prejudicial stereotyping based on a suspect's group membership influences both investigative and interviewing processes within the criminal justice system. However, more research is necessary to deepen our understanding of this phenomenon. Specifically, further investigation is needed to assess the potential benefits of police officer training aimed at increasing awareness of the implications of negative (racial/religious) stereotypes. Such training could potentially lead to improvements in interviewing performance, case outcomes, and community cohesion.

In the subsequent chapter, the author delves into a more detailed discussion of the findings presented in this book, exploring their implications and potential applications. It will also contextualise these findings within the broader body of research concerning the criminal investigation process and the impact of stereotyping on the communities.

Notes

1 In England and Wales, the penalties for supplying class A drugs range from up to life in prison, to an unlimited fine, or both (Powers of Criminal Courts [Sentencing] Act 2000).
2 Under Section 18 of PACE (1984) Act, a police officer may enter and search premises occupied and/or controlled by a person under arrest for an indictable offence.
3 Following Ragin's (1987) notation method, the factors within each equation are joined by a multiplication sign (* signifying AND), within each equation, codes in upper-case letters indicate the presence of a factor, while codes in lower-case letters indicate their absence.

References

Banaji, M. R., & Greenwald, A. G. (1995). Implicit gender stereotyping in judgments of fame. *Journal of Personality and Social Psychology*, *68*, 181–192.

Braun, V., & Clarke, V. (2006). Using thematic analysis in psychology. *Qualitative Research in Psychology*, *3*, p.77–101. DOI:10.1191/1478088706qp063oa

Britt, D.W. (1997) *An Introduction to Conceptual Modeling: Integrating Qualitative and Quantitative Perspectives*. Mahwah, NJ: Lawrence Erlbaum.

Chapman, L. J. (1967). Illusory correlation in observational report. *Journal of Verbal Learning and Verbal Behavior*, 6, 151–155.

Charmaz, K. (2006). *Constructing grounded theory: A practical guide through qualitative analysis*. sage.

Correll, J., Park, B., Judd, C. M., Wittenbrink, B., Sadler, M. S., & Keesee, T. (2007). Across the thin blue line: Police officers and racial bias in the decision to shoot. *Journal of Personality and Social Psychology, 92*, 1006–1023. http://dx.doi.org/10.1037

Coverdill, J. E., Finlay, W., & Martin, J. K. (1994). Labor management in the southern textile industry: Comparing qualitative, quantitative, and qualitative comparative analyses. *Sociological Methods & Research*, *23*(1), 54–85.

Coverdill, J. E., & Finlay, W. (1995). Understanding Mills via Mill-type methods: An application of qualitative comparative analysis to a study of labor management in southern textile manufacturing. *Qualitative Sociology*, *18*(4), 457–478.

Cress, D. M., & Snow, D. A. (2000). The outcomes of homeless mobilization: The influence of organization, disruption, political mediation, and framing. *American Journal of Sociology*, *105*, 1063–1104. DOI: 10.1086/210399

Darley, J. M., & Gross, P. H. (1983). A hypothesis-confirming bias in labelling effects. *Journal of Personality and Social Psychology*, *44*, 20–33. http://dx.doi.org/10.1037/0022-3514.44.1.20

Devine, P. G. (1989). Stereotypes and prejudice: their automatic and controlled components. *Journal of Personality and Social Psychology*, *56*, 5. DOI:10.1037/00223514.56.1.5

Fahsing, I., & Ask, K. (2016). The making of an expert detective: The role of experience in English and Norwegian police officers' investigative decision making. *Psychology, Crime & Law*, *22*, 203–223. http://dx.doi.org/10.1080/1068316X.2015.1077249

Fazio, R. H., Jackson, J. R., Dunton, B. C.,&Williams, C. J. (1995).Variability in automatic activation as an unobtrusive measure of racial attitudes: a bona fide pipeline? *Journal of Personality and Social Psychology*, *69*, 1013–1027.

Findley, K. A., & Scott, M. S. (2006). Multiple Dimensions of Tunnel Vision in Criminal Cases, *Wis. L. Rev.*, 291.

Fleiss, J. L. (1981). The measurement of interrater agreement. *Statistical methods for rates and proportions*, 2, 212–236.

Gerring, J. (2001). *Social science methodology: A criterial framework*. Cambridge: Cambridge University Press.

Glaser, B., & Strauss, A. (1967). *The discovery of grounded theory*. Chicago: Aldine de Gruyter.

Graham, S., & Lowery, B. S. (2004). Priming unconscious racial stereotypes about adolescent offenders. *Law and Human Behavior*, *28*, 483–504.

Greenwald, A. G. (1992). New Look 3: Unconscious cognition reclaimed. *American Psychologist*, *47*, 766.

Hall, A. V., Hall, E. V., & Perry, J. L. (2016). Black and blue: Exploring racial bias and law enforcement in the killings of unarmed black male civilians. *American Psychologist*, *71*, 175.

Hamilton, D. L., & Gifford, R. K. (1976). Illusory correlation in interpersonal perception: A cognitive basis of stereotypic judgments. *Journal of Experimental Social Psychology*, *12*(4), 392–407.

Hill, C., Memon, A., & McGeorge, P. (2008). The role of confirmation bias in suspect interviews: A systematic evaluation. *Legal and Criminological Psychology*, *13*, 357–371. doi:10.1348/135532507X238682

Kassin, S. M., Goldstein, C. C., & Savitsky, K. (2003). Behavioral confirmation in the interrogation room: On the dangers of presuming guilt. *Law and Human Behavior*, 27,187–203. Doi.org/10.1023/A:1022599230598

Lammers, J., & Stapel, D. A. (2011). Retracted: Racist biases in legal decisions are reduced by a justice focus. *European Journal of Social Psychology*, *41*, 375–387. DOI:10.1002/ejsp.783

Mackie, D. M., Hamilton, D. L., Susskind, J., & Rosselli, F. (1996). Social psychological foundations of stereotype formation. In C. N. Macrae, C. Stangor, & M. Hewstone (Eds.), *Stereotypes and stereotyping* (pp. 41–78). New York: Guilford.

Macrae, C. N., & Bodenhausen, G. V. (2000). Social cognition: Thinking categorically about others. *Annual Review of Psychology*, 51, 93–120.

Marx, A., & Dusa, A. (2011). Crisp-set qualitative comparative analysis (csQCA), contradictions and consistency benchmarks for model specification. *Methodological Innovations Online*, 6, 103–148. DOI: 10.4256/mio.2010.0037

Maynard-Moody, S. W., & Musheno, M. C. (2003). *Cops, teachers, counselors: Stories from the front lines of public service*. University of Michigan Press. Michigan.

Mears, D.P., Stewart, E.A., Warren, P.Y. & Simons, R.L., (2017). Culture and formal social control: The effect of the code of the street on police and court decision making. *Justice Quarterly*, *34*, 217–247.

Mortimer, A., & Shepherd, E. (1999). Frames of mind: Schemata guiding cognition and conduct in the interviewing of suspected offenders. In A. Memon & R. Bull (Eds.), *Handbook of the psychology of interviewing* (pp. 293–315). Chichester: Wiley.

Mullen, B., & Johnson, C. (1990). Distinctiveness-based illusory correlations and stereotyping: A meta-analytic integration. *British Journal of Social Psychology*, *29*, 11–28.

Musheno, M. C., Gregware, P. R., & Drass, K. A. (1991). Court management of AIDS disputes: a sociolegal analysis. *Law & Social Inquiry*, *16*, 737–774

Peirce, C. S. (1965). *Pragmatism and pragmaticism* (Vol. 5): Harvard University: Belknap Press of Harvard University Press.

Ragin, C. (1987). The comparative method: *Moving beyond qualitative and quantitative methods*. Berkeley: University of California.

Ragin, C. C. (1993). The comparative method. *Moving Beyond Qualitative and Quantita.*

Ragin, C. C. (2004). Turning the tables: How case-oriented research challenges variable oriented research. In H.E. Brady and D. Collier (eds) *Rethinking social inquiry: Diverse tools, shared standards*. 123–138 Lanham, MD: Rowman and Littlefield.

Ragin, C. C. (2008). *Redesigning social inquiry: Fuzzy sets and beyond* (Vol. 240). Chicago: University of Chicago Press.

Ragin, C., & Sean D. (2014). *fs/QCA [Computer Programme]*, Version [3.0]. Irvine, CA: University of California.

Rantala, K., & Hellström, E. (2001). Qualitative comparative analysis and a hermeneutic approach to interview data. *International Journal of Social Research Methodology*, 4(2), 87–100.

Rihoux, B., & Marx, A. (2013). QCA, 25 years after "The comparative method" mapping, challenges, and innovations—Mini-Symposium. *Political Research Quarterly*, *66*(1), 167–235.

Rihoux, B., & Ragin, C. (2008). *Configurational comparative analysis*. Thousand Oaks, London: Sage Publications.

Smith, M. R., & Alpert, G. P. (2007). Explaining police bias: A theory of social conditioning and illusory correlation. *Criminal Justice and Behavior*, *34*, 1262–1283. 10.1177/0093854807304484

Soulliere, D. M. (2005). Pathways to attrition: A qualitative comparative analysis of justifications for police designations of sexual assault complaints. *Qualitative Report*, *10*, 416–438. Retrieved from http://nsuworks.nova.edu/tqr/vol10/iss3/2

Stokke, O. S. (2007). Qualitative comparative analysis, shaming, and international regime effectiveness. *Journal of Business Research*, *60*, 501–511. http://dx.doi.org/10.1016/j.jbusres.2007.01.003

Strauss, A., & Corbin, J. M. (1997). Grounded theory in practice. Sage: London.

Tversky, A., & Kahneman, D. (1986). Rational choice and the framing of decisions. *Journal of Business, 59,* 251–278. Available from www.jstor.org/stable/2352759

Walton, J. (1999). Spirituality of patients recovering from an acute myocardial infarction: A grounded theory study. *Journal of Holistic Nursing,* 17, 34–53.

Ware, L. (2007). A comparative analysis of unconscious and institutional discrimination in the United States and Britain. *Georgia Journal of International and Comparative Law, 36*,89–157.

Winand, M., Rihoux, B., Robinson, L., & Zintz, T. (2013). Pathways to high performance: A qualitative comparative analysis of sport governing bodies. *Nonprofit and Voluntary Sector Quarterly*, 42(4), 739–762.

Zerbe, W.J. and Paulhus, D.L. (1987). Socially desirable responding in organizational behaviour: A reconception. *Academy of Management Review,* 12, 250–264.

Chapter 8

Discussion and conclusions

Tackling prejudicial stereotyping in criminal investigations: the basics

Introduction

This research aims to investigate the extent to which police officers, who may have developed prejudicial stereotypes towards members of a 'suspect' community, use their discretionary authority to act upon such stereotypes and how these stereotypes influence criminal investigations. This book comprises five distinct empirical studies focusing on the role of prejudicial stereotyping in investigative and interviewing processes. The first study, outlined in Chapter 3, examined over 2,100 stop-and-search records and included 20 semi-structured interviews conducted with serving police officers. The objective was to determine whether police officers rely on prejudicial stereotypes to inform their suspicions in day-to-day policing. Building upon the findings of the first study, Chapter 4 introduces the development of an instrument. This instrument explores how prejudicial stereotyping may influence investigative interviews with suspects from certain stigmatised groups.

To further narrow the focus of this research on prejudicial stereotyping within the context of communities perceived as 'suspect' by law enforcement, Chapter 5 delved into the perspectives of real-life Asian Muslim suspects. This chapter aimed to explore their perceptions and determine whether prejudicial stereotyping had an impact on investigative interviews. Building on the insights gained in Chapter 5, Chapter 6 shifted the lens to examine how prejudicial stereotyping within the context of these 'suspect' communities influenced the perceptions of legal representatives regarding investigative interviews and criminal investigations.

Finally, Chapter 7 conducted a qualitative comparative analysis to determine whether prejudicial stereotyping based on a suspect's ethnicity and religious background could influence police officers' decision-making and the outcomes of criminal investigations. Building upon the insights gained in the previous chapters, this chapter brought together the findings from these earlier studies, highlighting their interconnections and connections

DOI: 10.4324/9781003366836-8

with prior research. Additionally, Chapter 7 explored the practical implications of these findings. It also examined how the results can inform the training of investigative interviewers, impact case outcomes, and influence the practices of policing stigmatised groups.

Summary of findings

The first empirical study outlined in Chapter 3 primarily delved into the role of prejudicial stereotypes in stop-and-search practices rather than engaging in the broader discourse surrounding stop-and-searches and their impact on policing BAME communities in the United Kingdom. Within the first study, the investigation revealed that officers often lean on specific stereotype characteristics such as age, race, appearance, location, and social class when forming their suspicions. Through semi-structured interviews conducted as part of Study One, officers conveyed that the issue of disproportionality in stop-and-search statistics might be linked to insufficient and inaccurate information provided when describing a reported offender. Notably, these descriptions tended to focus disproportionately on ethnicity and clothing.

When insufficient and inaccurate information, primarily focusing on certain aspects, combines with an officer's pre-existing suspicions driven by generalised beliefs, it can arguably lead to individuals being subjected to stop-and-search solely based on their ethnicity (Quinton, 2011). This means that prejudicial stereotyping may cause police officers to associate people from specific areas or ethnic backgrounds with particular criminal activities, potentially straining police–community relations. This phenomenon could be one of the reasons why, despite the initiatives implemented by the Home Office, such as the Home Office Stop and Search Action Plan in 2004, individuals from BAME communities still face a higher likelihood of being stopped and searched (HMIC, 2005, 2013, 2015). For instance, the His Majesty's Inspectorate of Constabulary's (HMIC, 2013) report highlighted that there had been no significant improvements in the overall disparities in stop-and-search figures since the inception of the Home Office Action Plan in 1999 and its subsequent update in 2004. In the United Kingdom, as of the year ending March 2021, Black individuals were seven times more likely to undergo stop-and-search procedures under the Police and Criminal Evidence Act and related legislation compared to their White counterparts (Ali, Akintoye, & Agnew-Pauley, 2021).

Chapter Four of this book presents an empirical research study that adopted an innovative approach to examine the impact of prejudicial stereotypes on the police's investigative interviewing of suspects. To achieve this, the author developed utilised the Minhas Investigative

Interviewing Prejudicial Stereotyping Scale (MIIPSS) to gauge the extent of prejudicial stereotyping exhibited by investigative interviewers when dealing with suspects from stigmatised groups. This study involved conducting semi-structured interviews with 20 individuals who had previously been subjects of police interviews in England, along with the participation of eight highly experienced lawyers. This study assessed their views using the MIIPSS and subjected the data to a Guttman analysis. The results of the analysis indicated that the constructs within the MIIPSS met all the criteria for a valid Guttman scale, with a CR (coefficient of reproducibility) value of .92, signifying that the item patterns cumulatively represent a valid measurement instrument. Moreover, all the constructs within the MIIPSS were logically associated with prejudicial stereotyping, particularly within the context of investigative interviewing.

The Guttman scalogram analysis confirmed that the MIIPSS is a valid and reliable model for comprehending the processes and steps involved in identifying instances of perceived prejudicial stereotyping within the context of investigative interviewing. Consequently, the MIIPSS holds promise for future research endeavours, enabling the assessment of the apparent level of prejudicial stereotyping exhibited by interviewers during investigative interviews. It also offers the potential for conducting in-depth evaluations of interviewing practices.

In Chapter 5, the author conducted empirical research to investigate the role of prejudicial stereotyping in the investigative and interviewing processes, focusing on real-life Asian Muslim suspects. As far as it is known, this study represents the first attempt to examine police officers' attitudes towards suspects from the Muslim communities in the United Kingdom. This study revealed that when police officers develop prejudicial stereotypes based on a suspect's ethnicity, it can lead to discriminatory behaviour during suspect interviews. Notably, the majority of the suspects who participated in this study expressed a belief that negative attitudes displayed by police officers towards them were often attributed to their Asian Muslim ethnicity. For instance, one participant remarked, 'There is a certain mindset among some police officers which makes them view people of Asian Muslim background as the enemy or criminals'.

Furthermore, these suspects reported that when they perceived the evidence presented during their police interviews as weak, the interviewers often repeated accusations, a pattern consistent with findings in pre-PEACE studies (Moston, Stephenson, & Williamson, 1992; Baldwin, 1993). Moreover, participants in this study revealed that in cases where the police lacked strong evidence, interviewers tended to pose more guilt-presumptive questions. These individuals felt that during their interviews, interviewers applied undue pressure, seeking confessions even when there was no wrongdoing on their part or when the evidence against them was exceedingly weak or non-existent. Importantly, these interviewees attributed such pressure to their Asian Muslim background. This approach, characterised by a presumption of guilt and a self-fulfilling prophecy, may have contributed to interviewers displaying hostility or discrimination towards suspects, as previously identified in Chapter 4. Notably, one-third of the suspects who participated in this study mentioned instances of interviewers exhibiting hostile and discriminatory behaviour.

Chapter 6 presents a study that delved deeper into the impact of prejudicial stereotyping on investigative and interviewing practices, this time by exploring the perceptions of legal representatives. This study represents pioneering research, as no prior studies (to the best of the researcher's knowledge) have investigated the views of legal representatives regarding police interviews of suspects in England and Wales. The findings of this study revealed that a majority of the legal representatives believed that police interviewers employed various tactics that, if accurate, could potentially contravene both the Police and Criminal Evidence Act (PACE) and the underlying principles of the PEACE model. These tactics included making legal representatives wait unnecessarily and attempting to persuade suspects to undergo interviews without seeking legal advice.

More than half of the legal representatives in this study reported that they perceived police officers as treating suspects from deprived areas, regardless of their ethnicity, less favourably than those from more affluent areas. One-third of these legal representatives also noted instances where the ethnicity and religion of a suspect seemed to play a significant role in officers' decisions to pursue charges against them. Additionally, they observed cases, similar in nature, where a White suspect was released, while a charge was sought against an Asian Muslim suspect. This differential treatment of Muslim suspects was believed by these legal representatives to be influenced by negative portrayals of Muslims in the media. Furthermore, a quarter of these legal representatives recounted instances where they perceived interviewers displaying hostile and discriminatory behaviour towards their Muslim clients, attributing it to their clients' Muslim background.

Chapter 7 presents the final study, which stands as a novel and groundbreaking endeavour, as it delves into the analysis of how prejudicial stereotyping influences the real-life decision-making of police officers concerning investigative and interviewing processes when dealing with Muslim suspects. This study employed an innovative methodological approach aimed at revealing the causal relationship between racial and religious stereotyping and the resulting outcomes of criminal investigations. To investigate whether stereotyping of 'suspect' communities could influence police officers' investigative decision-making, this study conducted semi-structured interviews individually with police officers. Each officer was presented with the same scenario, differing only in the name of the suspect. Half of the sample referred to an indigenous person from the United Kingdom, while the other half referred to a suspect with an obvious Muslim name. To analyse whether a suspect's Muslim background had an impact on the outcomes of a criminal investigation, a crisp-set qualitative comparative analysis (csQCA) was employed.

A comprehensive grounded theory analysis and csQCA revealed a noteworthy pattern among officers. They appeared to make efforts to confirm their initial hypothesis regarding the guilt of Muslim suspects while seemingly disregarding or downplaying conflicting evidence available. This was particularly evident as 60 per cent of the police officers indicated their intention to pursue charges against Muslim suspects. Furthermore, a significant contrast emerged between the two conditions. In the case of indigenous suspects, only half of the sample chose to exercise Section 18 powers as outlined in the PACE Act 1984. However, in the 'Muslim suspect condition', all officers opted to employ these powers. Intriguingly, when the 'Muslim suspect condition' was applied, it was discovered that six times as many officers expressed their intent to charge the suspect with possession and intent to supply class A drugs compared to those in the indigenous suspect condition.

In summary, the findings presented in these studies strongly indicate that prejudicial stereotyping, based on a suspect's group membership, significantly influences both investigative and interviewing processes. These studies shed light on how stereotypes, whether related to ethnicity, religion, or other factors, can impact the decisions and behaviours of law enforcement officers during criminal investigations and interviews.

Theoretical and practical implications

Prejudicial stereotyping and policing

The empirical research, discussed in Chapter 3 of this book, investigated the impact of prejudicial stereotyping on day-to-day stop-and-search practices. The study revealed that police officers often relied on various stereotypes, including age, race, appearance, location, and social class, to inform their suspicions. However, existing research, such as Quinton (2011), suggests that stereotypes, which associate certain factors like age, race, location, time, and appearance with criminal activity, can sometimes offer valuable insights to guide suspicion. Nonetheless, there is a potential risk associated with this approach, as it may lead to the identification of individuals as suspicious even when they do not warrant such attention. Chapter 3 presents the results of the examination of both the analysis of stop-and-search record data sets and interview transcripts. These findings reveal that, in some instances, police officers appeared to be using prejudicial stereotypes in ways that could be considered unlawful and discriminatory. According to the Police and Criminal Evidence Act (PACE) Code of Practice A (1984), individual officers and their supervisors are legally obligated to base their decisions to stop and search on reasonable suspicion that the concerned individual has committed or is about to commit a particular offence. Therefore, it is unlawful to target people based on officers' generalised beliefs concerning factors such as age, race, location, or appearance of a particular group. This raises significant concerns because it may lead police officers to believe that people from a specific area or a certain ethnicity are more likely to engage in criminal activities, potentially damaging police–community relations.

The preceding chapters have discussed the prejudicial stereotypes that police officers tend to rely on when forming suspicions. In the subsequent studies conducted as part of this research:

(i) It was explored whether these prejudicial stereotypes, which are based on a suspect's group membership, influence investigative and interviewing processes.
(ii) It was investigated how such prejudicial stereotyping could impact police officers' attitudes towards Muslim suspects.

Furthermore, within the context of investigative interviews, a detailed analysis was conducted, including the development of the MIIPSS scale as discussed in Chapter 4 of this book. This analysis revealed that when interviewers hold prejudicial stereotypes towards suspects from specific groups, there is a distinct possibility that these stereotypes may result in the interviewer displaying hostility towards the suspect.

Furthermore, the findings from the study on the perception of Muslim suspects, as discussed in Chapter 5, indicate that police interviewers are acutely aware of the importance of adhering to legal and procedural standards imposed by the PACE Act. Failure to do so could risk rendering the interview inadmissible in court. These findings align with earlier research on investigative interviewing (e.g. Clarke & Milne, 2001; Clarke, Milne, & Bull, 2011; Shepherd & Griffiths, 2021), suggesting that the introduction of the PACE Act and the PEACE model has led to an overall improvement in the general standards of police interviewing, particularly concerning legal and procedural matters.

In Chapter 5 of the book, the thematic analysis of interviews with Muslim suspects revealed that two-thirds of the suspects reported experiencing poor communication, including difficulties in building rapport, during their interviews. These interviews may have lacked a solid foundation for open and detailed conversations, which is a fundamental principle of the PEACE model training for police officers in England and Wales. In such interviews, police officers may have obtained incomplete accounts due to the absence of rapport and poor communication with the suspects, leading to a lack of crucial information or evidence that could assist in determining their innocence or guilt. Previous research has consistently suggested that poor communication skills and a failure to build rapport are associated with an increased risk of police interviewers failing to elicit comprehensive and reliable accounts from interviewees (Walsh & Bull, 2012).

In Chapter 6, a thematic analysis of interviews with legal representatives revealed that some of them perceived differences in police officers' attitudes when suspects came from deprived areas. These findings are consistent with previous research, which has shown that police officers tend to view more affluent areas as appreciative and deserving of police service, while poor and decaying areas are often perceived as containing anti-police populations and criminogenic families (Braga, Brunson, & Drakulich, 2019). Several legal representatives reported that police officers treated suspects from deprived areas, regardless of their ethnicity, as inferior to those from more affluent areas. Police officers may hold the belief that individuals from deprived areas are more likely to be involved in criminal activity, and this belief may influence their attitudes towards suspects from such neighbourhoods (Braga et al., 2019).

In Chapter 5, both inductive and deductive thematic analyses of interviews with Muslim suspects revealed that two-thirds of them reported denying their involvement in criminal activity and refuting any accusations of guilt. In such situations, these suspects mentioned that their interviewers tended to repeat the original accusations, which generally led to further denials—a pattern consistent with the pre-PEACE findings of Moston, Stephenson, and Williamson (1992). In their observational study of police practices, Moston et al. (1992) found that suspects typically admitted guilt only when they perceived the evidence against them as strong. Similarly, in Chapter 5, when suspects believed that the evidence against them was strong, they were more likely to confess to their guilt. For instance, six of the suspects who participated in the study described in Chapter 5 stated that they did not attempt to deny their guilt when they perceived the police's evidence as strong.

The studies conducted in Chapters 4, 5, and 6 primarily focused on investigative interviewing of Muslim suspects. In the contemporary United

Kingdom, Muslims are arguably a visible and stigmatised community, especially in the aftermath of the 'war on terror', a phenomenon often referred to as 'Islamophobia' (Abbas, 2019; Awan, 2012; Breen-Smyth, 2014; Pantazis & Pemberton, 2009). Researchers have extensively documented the consequences of 'Islamophobia', including exclusion, discrimination, and prejudice against members of the Muslim community (Abbas, 2019; Awan, 2012; 2014; Hickman et al., 2012; Pantazis & Pemberton, 2009).

The research presented in this book generally aligns with existing research from the perspective of Asian Muslim suspects and the legal representatives who participated in the studies outlined in Chapters 5 and 6. For instance, in Chapter 5, nearly half of the suspects mentioned instances of interviewers displaying hostile and discriminatory behaviour, which they attributed to their Muslim background. However, it's essential to acknowledge that these unsatisfactory findings may not necessarily be linked to race, religion, or Islamophobia. They could instead result from police mishandling or the specific nature of their involvement in certain crimes, concerns that might have been raised regardless of ethnicity or religion. Nevertheless, it's noteworthy that these suspects' views were echoed by the perspectives of legal representatives. In Chapter 6, one-third of the legal representatives reported witnessing instances where a White suspect was released, while charges were sought against an Asian Muslim suspect for an offence of a similar nature.

In the case of individuals under investigation, the initial impression of guilt or innocence is argued to be of significant importance. Earlier studies such as Roach and Trotter (2004) have shown that this initial impression often determines whether an interviewer proceeds with a strong presumption of guilt. Such a presumption can predispose interviewers to ask guilt-presumptive and confirmatory questions, employ persuasive tactics, and seek confessions (Scherr, Redlich, & Kassin, 2020).). In Chapter 5, it was discovered that nearly two-thirds of suspects reported that their interviewers had asked them guilt-presumptive questions. Laboratory studies by Hill et al. (2008) have demonstrated that guilt-presumptive questions triggered a self-fulfilling prophecy effect. Similarly, through deductive analysis of the MIIPSS constructs outlined in Chapter 5 and Chapter 6, it was found that guilt presumption resulted in self-fulfilling prophecy effects. These effects may have ultimately contributed to interviewers demonstrating hostility or discrimination towards Muslim suspects.

These findings present a departure from the perspectives put forth by Greer (2014) and Hargreaves (2015). In their studies, it was postulated that the 'suspect Muslim community' could not be uniformly labelled as 'officially' suspect, as some segments were considered trustworthy by official standards. However, contrasting viewpoints argue that initiatives like Prevent II and intervention projects might inadvertently cast an impression of suspicion within the Muslim community (Abbas, 2019; Choudhury & Fenwick, 2011; Spalek, 2011; Zempi & Tripli, 2023). This, in turn, could lead to the perception of the entire Muslim community as 'suspect' (Awan, 2012).

Consequently, policies such as Prevent II, which have the potential to isolate a community as 'suspect', may result in biased policing practices. Such biases could, in the long run, undermine initiatives aimed at fostering community cohesion (Awan, 2018; Zempi & Tripli, 2023). The overarching concern is that counterterrorism policies and the Prevent Strategy might problematise Islamic religious identities (Spalek, 2011), consequently fostering feelings of racial and religious segregation and promoting ethnic profiling (Awan, 2012). These factors collectively contribute to a climate that may lead to biased policing against members of the Muslim community, as reflected in the studies detailed in Chapter 5, Chapter 6, and Chapter 7.

Suspect community stereotyping and investigative interviewing

Numerous empirical studies have shed light on the concerning tendency of police officers to rely on prejudicial stereotypes, particularly when dealing with suspects. This reliance appears to be influenced by three key factors: whether the suspect is previously known to the police, their ethnicity, or their religious background. Such stereotyping becomes even more problematic when suspects belong to minority communities, often referred to as 'out-groups'. Previous studies, including the works of Devine (1989), Tajfel (2010), and Tajfel and Turner (1979), have demonstrated the negative consequences of these biases, especially during investigations involving minority suspects. Notably, a significant portion of the suspects involved in the research study presented in Chapter 5 expressed concerns. They reported that police interviewers frequently asked them repetitive questions that seemed to presume guilt and employed coercive tactics.

Despite these findings, the existing literature on investigative interviewing (e.g. Bull, 2014; Williamson, 2006), consistently highlights the importance of conducting police interviews, whether with witnesses or suspects, in an ethical manner. Ethical interviews are characterised by avoiding coercive questioning and hostile techniques. Instead, the primary goal of these interviews should be to gather comprehensive and relevant information from the interviewees. Coercive tactics have been found to be both unethical and ineffective in terms of gathering accurate information, as indicated by research such as Oxburgh (2011) and Williamson (2006).

Furthermore, in Chapter 6, the researcher explored the application of five constructs from the MIIPSS during interviews conducted with 15 legal representatives. The results revealed a concerning trend, with nearly two-thirds of these legal representatives reporting instances where they observed negative attitudes exhibited by police interviewers towards Muslim suspects. These negative attitudes included the presumption of guilt and the use of coercive and guilt-presumptive questions. In Chapters 5 and 6, the research unveiled the repercussions of such guilt presumption, notably its contribution to a self-fulfilling prophecy. In essence, this phenomenon can be described as a 'false definition of the situation evoking a new behaviour which may make the originally false conceptions come true' (Merton, 2016, p. 477). To illustrate, it occurs when individuals fail to recognise how their own beliefs have shaped a distorted reality (Biggs, 2009). Consequently, they become fixated on specific individuals or incidents, often disregarding any alternative perspectives (Findley & Scott, 2006). Importantly, this self-fulfilling prophecy is not limited to just one group; it can also affect researchers, legal representatives, and suspects. Therefore, it should be acknowledged as a limitation of this research, which is further discussed in the limitations section.

The results presented in Chapters 5, 6, and 7 have highlighted instances where police officers have exhibited certain investigative behaviours. These behaviours include (i) asking repetitive questions, (ii) exaggerating the strength of evidence, or (iii) becoming overly focused on charging the suspect to the extent that they overlooked evidence that could have favoured the suspect. Such investigative approaches have been identified as contributing to tunnel vision, a phenomenon influenced by various processes, including cognitive distortions such as confirmation bias. This tunnel vision can lead to discriminatory behaviours towards suspects (Findley & Scott, 2006), particularly those from specific demographic groups (Giani & Merlino, 2021). The study findings described in Chapter 5 further support these concerns. The data revealed that nearly half of the Muslim suspects reported experiencing discriminatory treatment during interviews. These reports were corroborated by legal representatives, with a quarter of them noting instances of perceived discriminatory behaviour towards Muslim suspects. These legal representatives believed that such discrimination was often linked to their clients' Muslim background.

As explored in Chapter 7, the research delved into the impact of prejudicial stereotyping on police interviewers' decision-making within the context of communities labelled as 'suspect'. These findings were cross-referenced with insights from suspects and legal representatives involved in the process. Chapter 7 revealed a noteworthy discovery: the presence of a Muslim name among the suspects significantly influenced police officers' subsequent decision-making. It's crucial to acknowledge that besides the suspect's name, other variables, such as the age and relevant experience of police officers, may also exert varying degrees of influence on their investigative decision-making.

However, it became evident that officers exhibited a tendency to confirm their initial hypothesis regarding the guilt of Muslim suspects while seemingly disregarding or minimising conflicting evidence available. This behaviour could be attributed to unconscious racial stereotypes, which may lead individuals within the criminal justice system to 'focus on a suspect, select and filter the evidence that will "build a case" for conviction while ignoring or suppressing evidence that points away from guilt' (Findley & Scott, 2006, p. 292). When considering the 'Muslim suspect condition', a striking contrast emerges. In this scenario, six times as many officers indicated that they would charge the suspect with possession and intent to supply class A drugs compared to those in the indigenous suspect condition.

Furthermore, in the study outlined in Chapter 7, a significant contrast emerged. While only half of the sample in the indigenous suspect condition decided to exercise Section 18 powers as stipulated in the PACE Act of 1984, a noteworthy difference emerged in the 'Muslim suspect condition'. In this scenario, all the officers chose to invoke these powers, even though, in name alone, the two conditions did not differ. Previous research has identified confirmation bias as a prominent factor during police interviews, leading to an 'accusatorial' style of questioning. In such cases, police officers employ a confirmatory strategy to elicit confessions (Mortimer & Shepherd, 1999), which, in turn, can contribute to or result in false confessions (Scherr, Redlich, & Kassin, 2020). Consequently, investigations may be susceptible to miscarriages of justice when officers become overly fixated on charging the suspect, expending more resources to confirm their initial hypotheses regarding the suspect's wrongdoing.

These findings lend credence to the assumption that the Muslim community in contemporary UK society is often viewed as a suspect community, as previously argued by scholars like Abbas (2019), Awan (2012), Breen-Smyth (2014), Hickman et al. (2012), and Pantazis and Pemberton (2009). This, in turn, can result in police bias, echoing the concerns initially raised by Hillyard (1993) in the context of Ireland.

Furthermore, prior research has demonstrated that unconscious racial stereotypes can play a role in biased decision-making, especially when dealing with members of stigmatised minority groups (Mears, Stewart, Warren, & Simons, 2017). These prejudicial stereotypes are believed to be automatically activated when individuals encounter members of stigmatised groups (Devine, 1989), potentially influencing the decisions made by police officers (Hall, Hall, & Perry, 2016). The empirical research presented in the preceding chapters appears to corroborate these findings. For instance, in Chapter 5, a noteworthy observation emerged: a quarter of legal representatives reported instances where a White suspect was released without charge, while a charge was sought from the Crown Prosecution Service (CPS) in the case of a Muslim suspect (in what was considered a comparable situation). During criminal investigations, the initial stage of abductive reasoning entails comprehensive problem recognition, problem framing, and option generation (Fahsing & Ask, 2013). One prominent cause of suboptimal investigative decision-making is the decision smaker's failure to identify all potential alternatives before embarking on the evaluation and integration of information, which is essential for reaching a final decision (Tversky & Kahneman, 1986).

Research, as demonstrated by Graham and Lowery (2004), has shown that police officers may not harbour negative feelings towards minority groups. Nevertheless, their initial decisions can still be influenced by either (i) beliefs about group criminality, regardless of their accuracy, or (ii) perceptions of who is most likely to be involved in criminal activity. Chapter 7 of this book sheds light on how police officers' perceptions of the suspect's name may have led to such decision-making. Consequently, officers often failed to consider all available options, regardless of the suspect's name, and arrived at decisions, such as whether to issue a caution or seek a charge for intent to supply class A drugs, which were more lenient when dealing with indigenous suspects as compared to Muslim suspects.

These findings not only align with Hillyard's work from 1993 (which suggested that stereotyping of suspect communities could contribute to failures in criminal investigations) but also indicate that perceived prejudicial stereotyping based on the suspect's group membership can indeed influence officers' decision-making during investigations. Several legal representatives expressed the belief that such outcomes might be attributed to the negative portrayal of the Muslim community in the media. This observation aligns with the findings of Awan and Rahman (2016), who noted that the negative portrayal of British Muslims may have contributed to the framing of these communities as 'othered' and could also impact people's perceptions of Muslims due to the dominant type of headlines and stories they encounter. These findings find further support in recent research conducted by scholars such as Abbas (2019), Awan and Rahman (2016), and Baker, Gabrielatos, and McEnery (2013). Their work consistently reveals that post-the 'war on terror', stories about Islam and Muslims primarily revolved around terrorism, perpetuating negative stereotypes about this community.

Such prejudicial stereotyping has arguably contributed to human rights violations with dire consequences, as observed in the Irish context (Hillyard, 1993), and arguably continues in the context of Muslims (Awan & Rahman, 2016). This implies that the circumstances witnessed in the past in the Irish context, including miscarriages of justice involving cases like the 'Birmingham Six' and the 'Guildford Four', persist in recent times in the context of Muslims, exemplified by incidents such as 'Forrest Gate' and 'Nottingham Two'. The results from the studies detailed in Chapters 5, 6, and 7 align with existing research (Abbas, 2019; Breen-Smyth, 2014; Hickman et al., 2012). This body of research consistently suggests the presence of police bias against Muslims in the United Kingdom, thereby identifying the existence of a Muslim 'suspect' community.

To mitigate the influence of prejudicial stereotyping within police investigative and interviewing processes, this book introduced the MIIPSS, which resulted from innovative and groundbreaking research outlined in Chapter 4. In England and Wales, self-evaluation of interviews conducted by police interviewers is a fundamental aspect of the PEACE model of investigative interviewing, driving their professional development. The MIIPSS serves as a valuable tool during self-evaluations, offering interviewers the means to monitor their own attitudes or providing police supervisors with a way to assess interviewers' attitudes towards suspects from certain groups. As discussed in Chapter 4, the argument was made that by identifying (i) the sources that contribute to interviewers' negative perceptions of stigmatised groups and individuals suspected of specific offences, and (ii) by tracking the development of explanations that support such negative perceptions, interviewers can refrain from prematurely presuming suspects' guilt before the interview. This approach can effectively help prevent tunnel vision and confirmation bias, which could otherwise compromise the integrity of the investigative process.

Through the use of the MIIPSS, it becomes possible to identify the sequential factors that lead interviewers to develop negative attitudes towards suspects. It was revealed that the MIIPSS not only allows researchers and police supervisors to gauge potential negative stereotypes held by police interviewers towards suspects but also offers insights into why interviewers may prematurely presume suspects to be guilty before conducting interviews. Furthermore, the MIIPSS provides researchers with a scientific tool to assess police officers' prejudicial stereotyping, whether in controlled experimental settings or naturalistic research environments.

In summary, the findings from the empirical studies lend support to the concept of suspect community stereotyping, suggesting that such stereotyping may lead to biased attitudes among police officers towards members of these communities, in line with Hillyard's (1993) earlier research. These biased attitudes, as observed in this book, can result in self-fulfilling prophecies and the use of hostile techniques during investigative and interviewing processes. It's worth noting that the studies within this book focused predominantly on Muslim suspects. In future research, it would be valuable to compare and contrast the experiences of suspects from different communities to gain a more comprehensive understanding of the implications of prejudicial stereotyping for police officers' attitudes.

Limitations and future research

Several limitations in the studies conducted for this book were anticipated due to the research paradigms employed. One such limitation pertains to the ecological validity of Chapter 7. In this chapter, officers' perspectives were gathered based on a hypothetical case scenario. Responding to a hypothetical crime scenario could differ from participating in the investigation of real-life crimes, and it's plausible that officers' judgements could vary in actual situations. The results presented in Chapter 7 might have differed had the study focused on comparing real-life investigations involving indigenous suspects and suspects from 'suspect' communities. However, it's essential to acknowledge that examining real-life criminal investigations concerning Muslim suspects and indigenous suspects was beyond the scope of this book and often poses practical challenges for researchers. Consequently, conducting large-scale research that directly compares real-life investigations involving indigenous suspects and those from 'suspect' communities is a critical step to determine whether the findings outlined in this book hold true in practical scenarios. Additionally, similar research involving CPS caseworkers would be beneficial to assess whether a suspect's ethnicity plays any role in their decisions regarding whether or not to charge the suspect.

Another limitation stemming from methodological decisions pertains to the generalisability of the findings, particularly in Chapters 5 and 6. Chapter 5 exclusively focused on suspects from a Muslim background, and Chapter 6 gathered the views of legal representatives concerning investigative and interviewing processes for Muslim suspects. It is important to acknowledge that these studies may not be fully representative of suspects from all ethnic groups. However, it's worth noting that these studies are among the first to delve into police officers' attitudes towards suspects from stigmatised communities, as well as legal representatives' perceptions in the context of police interviews in England and Wales. As such, the findings presented in this book make a valuable contribution to the existing body of literature that explores investigative and interviewing processes, specifically regarding suspect community stereotyping and issues related to Islamophobia.

Unforeseen limitations emerged during the research, particularly related to the sample sizes in Chapters 4, 5, and 6. Recruiting both Muslim suspects and legal representatives proved to be a challenging aspect of this study, as these groups are traditionally hard to reach for research purposes. The difficulties encountered in recruiting suspects from the Muslim communities and legal representatives were more substantial than initially anticipated. The second study, outlined in Chapter 4, was originally designed to serve as a foundational element for subsequent studies. While data collection yielded responses from over 20 suspects, achieving a similar sample size from legal representatives proved to be more challenging. While initial agreements were secured from several legal representatives, only eight of them participated in the study. Consequently, the research was conducted with a sample comprising 20 suspect participants and eight legal representatives.

For the follow-up study outlined in Chapter 6 (which represents the first study to gather legal representatives' views within the context of investigative and interviewing processes concerning Muslim suspects), additional agreements were sought from several legal representatives. Over three years of data collection, views from 15 legal representatives were successfully gathered. It is important to note that the researcher did not pursue further interviews with legal representatives. Data collection was halted when the analysis of interview transcripts indicated thematic saturation, signifying that no new codes or themes emerged from the last four interviews. Despite the relatively small sample size, these studies have yielded novel findings, as detailed in Chapters 4, 5, and 6, contributing to our understanding of investigative interviewing in both general terms and specific factors that can influence investigative and interviewing processes.

In hindsight, certain aspects could have been included in the research to further enrich its comprehensiveness. For instance, following the development of the MIIPSS in Chapter 4, an experimental study could have been conducted to investigate the use of potential prejudicial stereotyping during investigative interviews by employing the MIIPSS. Such an experiment would have allowed for an examination of the accuracy and validity of the MIIPSS in a controlled experimental setting, shedding light on its effectiveness.

Additionally, a more in-depth analysis and evaluation of the beliefs and attitudes of interviewers during interviews with suspects from specific groups could have been included. This could have provided a deeper understanding and determined whether extreme negative attitudes might lead to coercive forms of interviewing. It is worth noting that the MIIPSS was developed using real-life suspects and legal representatives' views, which could have been influenced by social desirability biases. Conducting controlled experimental studies to scrutinise the five constructs of MIIPPS would have offered a more detailed understanding of the factors that potentially influence the attitudes of investigative interviewers.

Throughout this book, potential avenues for future research have been suggested after each chapter. To consolidate these areas, the following key research directions are highlighted:

(i) Comparative Analysis: Future research should involve a comparison of investigative interviewing practices across suspects from various ethnic groups to ascertain whether racial and religious stereotypes exert an influence on real-life investigative and interviewing practices. This comparative study can offer valuable insights into the impact of stereotypes on law enforcement processes.
(ii) MIIPSS Experiment: Conducting an experiment involving a controlled group of interviewers using the MIIPSS could help uncover why interviewers tend to presume a suspect's guilt before conducting an interview. Such research can provide practical guidance and clear training recommendations for police officers, aiming to prevent premature guilt presumptions and promote fair trials and non-coercive investigative interviewing practices.

These future research areas hold significant promise for advancing our understanding of the complex dynamics within investigative interviewing and enhancing the fairness and effectiveness of the criminal justice system. Future research should encompass comparative analysis studies that examine investigative and interviewing practices involving suspects from various ethnic groups, those suspected of committing different types of crimes, and individuals from both affluent and deprived areas. Such studies are essential to determine whether prejudicial stereotyping influences police practices uniformly across these diverse groups, as it may affect suspects from 'suspect' communities.

Furthermore, it would be valuable to conduct a comprehensive Study Space Analysis (as proposed by Malpass et al., 2008) on the current Prevent II strategy. This analysis could shed light on whether the existing body of literature provides sufficient empirical support for the Prevent policy or whether it warrants reconsideration or revision based on empirical evidence. Given the widespread debate and concerns surrounding Prevent, such an analysis could be instrumental in shaping future policies and practices. These research directions hold significant potential to advance our understanding of the complex dynamics involved in policing practices and their implications for different communities, ultimately contributing to a more equitable and effective criminal justice system.

Conclusions

The studies presented in this book reveal a connection between the stereotyping of certain communities and the attitudes held by police officers towards individuals from these communities. This connection implies that preconceived notions and biases can influence the behaviour of law enforcement officers. Importantly, this discovery has significant implications for investigative and interviewing procedures employed by law enforcement agencies. This suggests that these procedures may not consistently maintain impartiality or remain free from bias. Prejudicial stereotyping often results in a presumption of guilt when dealing with individuals from suspect communities, leading to individuals being treated as suspects before any evidence or facts are considered. This treatment can potentially violate their rights. Stereotyping, in turn, often leads to confirmation bias, a cognitive bias that influences officers' behaviour. Once officers form a particular view of a suspect, they may subconsciously seek out information that confirms their preconceived notions while disregarding evidence to the contrary.

The presence of these biases, especially the presumption of guilt and confirmation bias, can lead to coercive interviewing techniques and tunnel vision. These techniques may involve pressuring individuals or using tactics that could lead to false confessions. Tunnel vision, on the other hand, can cause officers to become so fixated on their initial assumptions that they overlook alternative explanations or suspects. Tunnel vision can significantly hinder a thorough and unbiased investigation. These biases, along with their associated consequences, can be underlying factors contributing to miscarriages of justice, leading to wrongful convictions and other legal injustices. In other words, they can result in severe failures within the legal system. Overall, the studies presented in this book highlight the intricate relationship between bias, policing attitudes, and the criminal justice system. This underscores the critical need for awareness and strategies to address these issues and ensure fairness and justice in law enforcement and the legal process.

The PEACE model of investigative interviewing, a well-established approach, aims to mitigate the risk of fundamental human errors such as guilt presumption, confirmation bias, and tunnel vision. It does so by encouraging interviewers to maintain open-mindedness throughout the process. It's important to emphasise that operationalising the burden of proof involves systematically eliminating all alternative explanations for guilt, which is essential for meeting the legal threshold of 'beyond reasonable doubt', as stipulated by the Convention on Civil and Political Rights (ICCPR) Article 14. This article underscores the importance of presuming suspects innocent until proven guilty. However, when dealing with the presumption of innocence, especially within the context of criminal investigations, challenges arise. These challenges can become even more pronounced when dealing with suspects from stigmatised communities, where the likelihood of confirmation bias and tunnel vision is higher, as revealed in this book.

In Chapter 4, a novel approach was undertaken to develop the MIIPSS, a purpose-built tool aimed at countering the presumption of guilt in investigative interviews. The MIIPSS is a purpose-built tool aimed at countering the presumption of guilt in investigative interviews. Its primary goal is to assist interviewers, including police officers, in refraining from prematurely jumping to conclusions about a suspect's guilt before conducting an interview or gathering evidence. Another pivotal objective of the MIIPSS is to minimise the influence of prejudicial stereotyping. To achieve these goals, the MIIPSS introduces a set of strategies and techniques that empower interviewers to maintain impartiality and objectivity when interacting with individuals from stigmatised groups. A fundamental aspect of the MIIPSS involves identifying the sources contributing to interviewers' negative perceptions of these groups. This process often entails recognising and addressing biases or preconceived notions that interviewers may hold. Moreover, the MIIPSS emphasises the importance of tracking the development of explanations that support these negative perceptions, encouraging interviewers to critically evaluate and challenge their own assumptions regarding certain behaviours or situations.

Ultimately, the MIIPSS is structured as a comprehensive tool designed to enhance the fairness and objectivity of police interviews and investigations. Its focal points encompass addressing issues related to bias, stereotyping, and the presumption of guilt. By helping interviewers identify and manage their own biases and perceptions when dealing with stigmatised groups, the MIIPSS aligns with the broader aim of ensuring equitable and unbiased investigative procedures.

Counterterrorism policies and intervention projects, such as Prevent II, appear to be founded on a pervasive sense of suspicion, which can inadvertently cast Muslim communities, especially in the eyes of law enforcement and security agencies, as a 'suspect' group. This portrayal has the potential to transform the Muslim communities into a visibly stigmatised one, possibly fostering an environment of 'Islamophobia'. Such an environment may lead Muslim communities to perceive themselves as unfairly targeted and treated as a 'suspect' group, primarily because counterterrorism policies have predominantly focused on identifying potential extremists within their ranks. Within the context of criminal investigations, these policies rooted in an underlying sense of suspicion can result in biased policing practices directed at members of the Muslim communities. This bias, in turn, may give rise to the presumption of guilt, self-fulfilling prophecies, and the employment of hostile investigative techniques by the police when dealing with members of the Muslim community, as evidenced in this book.

Prevent II is fundamentally rooted in an 'impression of suspicion'. This implies that the policy operates on the presumption that certain individuals or communities are inherently suspicious or potentially involved in activities requiring monitoring or intervention. Consequently, Prevent II has the potential to stigmatise Muslim communities, as this approach may give rise to negative perceptions and biases against their members. This stigmatisation can have far-reaching consequences, and one of the most concerning outcomes is an increase in discriminatory acts against Muslim communities. These acts of discrimination can originate from both the broader public and law enforcement agencies. It is essential to recognise that this phenomenon is not limited to societal biases; even law enforcement personnel may be influenced in ways that negatively impact Muslim communities.

The studies presented in this book underscore the critical concerns surrounding Prevent II, especially its potential impact on Muslim communities. These studies suggest that if the programme's foundation of suspicion leads to stigmatisation, it could exacerbate discrimination against Muslim communities. Both the general public and law enforcement agencies may play roles in contributing to this troubling issue.

Moreover, to safeguard the integrity of the justice system and foster non-coercive investigative and interviewing practices, the imperative is clear: police officers must undergo additional training. This training should be designed to equip officers with the essential skills, knowledge, and awareness necessary for conducting interviews and investigations in an equitable and non-coercive manner. Its primary focus should be on deepening officers' understanding of the far-reaching implications of prejudicial stereotyping, particularly concerning race and religion. This implies that officers should receive education on recognising and addressing the biases and stereotypes that may influence their attitudes and behaviours. By providing such training, we not only elevate the performance of police officers in interviews and investigations but also pave the way for improved case outcomes. It underscores the idea that fair and unbiased procedures are more likely to yield positive and just results. Beyond its direct impact on law enforcement practices, such training holds the potential to contribute significantly to community cohesion. By addressing biases and promoting fairness, it can help establish trust and positive relationships between law enforcement agencies and the communities they serve. This, in turn, can foster lasting community cohesion and a sense of security. Therefore, the investment in additional training for police officers, with a focus on combating prejudicial stereotyping and cultivating non-coercive procedures, is indispensable. It not only upholds the integrity of the justice system but also enhances law enforcement outcomes and strengthens the bonds between communities and those who serve them.

Nevertheless, it is important to recognise that training represents just one facet of a far-reaching and holistic strategic framework. This overarching strategy must encompass a profound exploration of the origins and endurance of prejudice. Prejudice, deeply ingrained in societal structures, often operates on multiple levels, and addressing it necessitates a comprehensive approach. This approach should extend beyond training programmes and delve into the complexities of how bias and stereotyping are sustained within suspect communities. Recognising the influence of these stereotypes on the criminal investigation process is not merely a valuable insight but a pivotal starting point for fostering transparent and effective policing in stigmatised communities.

To operationalise this comprehensive strategy, tangible actions are essential. For instance, it could involve community engagement initiatives, collaboration with social scientists for in-depth research on bias, and the development of policies that prioritise fairness, impartiality, and the protection of civil rights. Moreover, research should play a central role in this effort. Understanding the multifaceted roots and the perpetuation of prejudice requires rigorous investigation. This research can serve as a compass, guiding the development and refinement of strategies aimed at dismantling prejudicial stereotypes. Furthermore, this broader strategy resonates with the overarching objectives of promoting inclusivity, diversity, and equity within law enforcement agencies and society as a whole. By addressing the deep-seated issues of prejudice and bias, we pave the way for a more just, equitable, and harmonious coexistence between law enforcement and the communities they serve.

Therefore, it is imperative to recognise that while training is a crucial component of these endeavours, it cannot singularly offer a complete solution to this deeply entrenched systemic issue. Confronting this endemic problem necessitates a multifaceted approach that encompasses various dimensions. Central to this approach is the need for further research into the roots of prejudice, as a comprehensive understanding of its origins is fundamental to informed action. In parallel, we must call for sincere, sustained, and decisive efforts from senior police managers. These leaders must commit to proactive steps that extend beyond training programmes. For instance, they can take the lead in policy development, crafting directives that underscore the principles of fairness, impartiality, and the safeguarding of civil rights in all policing activities. Moreover, community engagement should become a cornerstone of their strategy, fostering open dialogue and cooperation between law enforcement and the communities they serve.

Equally important is the cultivation of a culture within law enforcement agencies that champions fairness and equity. This culture should permeate every aspect of their operations, from recruitment and training to daily interactions with the public. The urgency of addressing this issue cannot be overstated. Failure to act decisively may perpetuate discrimination, erode public trust, and undermine the very foundations of justice and security. Therefore, it falls upon all stakeholders—police leaders, policymakers, researchers, and the community—to collaborate in dismantling prejudice and building a just and inclusive future.

References

Abbas, M. S. (2019). Producing 'internal suspect bodies': divisive effects of UK counter terrorism measures on Muslim communities in Leeds and Bradford. *British Journal of Sociology*, *70*(1), 261–282.

Ali, A., Akintoye, B., & Agnew-Pauley, W. (2021). *Stop and search: New data shows continued ethnic disproportionality.* The Conversation. https://theconversation.com/stop-and-search-new-data-shows-continued-ethnic-disproportionality-172260tim

Awan, I. (2012). 'I Am a Muslim Not an Extremist': How the Prevent Strategy Has Constructed a 'Suspect' Community. *Politics & Policy*, *40*, 1158–1185. Doi:10.1111/j.1747-1346.2012.00397.x

Awan, I. (2014). Islamophobia and Twitter: A typology of online hate against Muslims on social media. *Policy & Internet*, 6, 133–150.

Awan, I. (2018). 'I never did anything wrong'–Trojan Horse: a qualitative study uncovering the impact in Birmingham. *British Journal of Sociology of Education*, *39*, 197–211.

Awan, I., & Rahman, M. (2016). Portrayal of Muslims Following the Murders of Lee Rigby in Woolwich and Mohammed Saleem in Birmingham: A Content Analysis of UK Newspapers. *Journal of Muslim Minority Affairs*, *36*, 16–31.

Baker, P., Gabrielatos, C., & McEnery, T. (2013). *Discourse analysis and media attitudes: The representation of Islam in the British press.* Cambridge: Cambridge University Press.

Baldwin, J. (1993). Police interview techniques: Establishing truth or proof?. *British Journal of Criminology*, *33*, 325–352.

Biggs, M. (2009). Self-fulfilling prophecies. In P. Bearman & P. Hedstrom, (Eds.) *The Oxford handbook of analytical sociology* (pp. 294–314), Oxford University Press, Oxford, UK.

Braga, A. A., Brunson, R. K., & Drakulich, K. M. (2019). Race, place, and effective policing. *Annual Review of Sociology*, *45*, 535–555.

Breen-Smyth, M. (2014). Theorising the 'suspect community': counterterrorism, security practices and the public imagination. *Critical Studies on Terrorism*, 7(2), 223–240. Doi:10.1080/17539153.2013.867714

Bull, R. (2014). Investigative interviewing. New York, NY: Springer. http://dx.doi.org/10.1007/978-1-4614-9642-7

Choudhury, T., & Fenwick, H. (2011). The impact of counter-terrorism measures on Muslim communities. *International Review of Law, Computers & Technology*, *25*, 151–181.

Clarke, C., & Milne, R. (2001). *National evaluation of the PEACE investigative interviewing course*. Police Research Award Scheme Report No. PRAS/149. London: Home Office.

Clarke, C., Milne, R., & Bull, R. (2011). Interviewing suspects of crime: The impact of PEACE training, supervision and the presence of a legal advisor. *Journal of Investigative Psychology and Offender Profiling*, *8*, 149–162. DOI: 10.1002/jip.144

Devine, P. G. (1989). Stereotypes and prejudice: their automatic and controlled components. *Journal of Personality and Social Psychology*, *56*, 5. Doi:10.1037/0022-3514.56.1.5

Fahsing, I., & Ask, K. (2013). Decision making and decisional tipping points in homicide investigations: An interview study of British and Norwegian detectives. *Journal of Investigative Psychology and Offender Profiling*, *10*, 155–165. DOI:10.1002/jip.1384

Findley, K. A. & Scott, M. S. (2006). The Multiple Dimensions of Tunnel Vision in *Criminal Cases. Wisconsin Law Review,* Vol. 2, 2006; Univ. of Wisconsin Legal Studies Research Paper No. 1023. Available at SSRN: https://ssrn.com/abstract=911240

Giani, M., & Merlino, L. P. (2021). Terrorist attacks and minority perceived discrimination. *British Journal of Sociology*, 72(2), 286–299.

Graham, S., & Lowery, B. S. (2004). Priming unconscious racial stereotypes about adolescent offenders. *Law and Human behavior*, *28*, 483.

Greer, S. (2014). Reply to Marie Breen-Smyth, 'Theorising the "suspect community": counterterrorism, security practices and the public imagination'. *Critical Studies on Terrorism*, 7, 468–471.

Hall, A. V., Hall, E. V., & Perry, J. L. (2016). Black and blue: Exploring racial bias and law enforcement in the killings of unarmed black male civilians. *American Psychologist*, *71*, 175.

Hargreaves, J. (2015). Half a story? Missing perspectives in the criminological accounts of British Muslim communities, crime and the criminal justice system. *British Journal of Criminology*, *55*(1), 19–38.

Hickman, M. J., Thomas, L., Nickels, H. C., & Silvestri, S. (2012). Social cohesion and he notion of 'suspect communities': a study of the experiences and impacts of being 'suspect'for Irish communities and Muslim communities in Britain. *Critical Studies on Terrorism*, *5*, 89–106.

Hill, C., Memon, A., & McGeorge, P. (2008). The role of confirmation bias in suspect interviews: A systematic evaluation. *Legal and Criminological Psychology*, *13*, 357–371. doi:10.1348/135532507X238682

Hillyard, P. (1993). *Suspect Community: People's Experiences of the Prevention of Terrorism Acts in Britain*. London: Pluto Press.

HMIC (2005) *Community and race relations: Policies and practices within the police service*. London: Home Office.

HMIC. (2013). *Stop and search powers*: Are the police using them effectively and fairly? London: HMIC.

HMIC. (2015). *Stop and search powers 2:* Are the police using them effectively and fairly? London: HMIC.

Malpass RS, Tredoux CG, Schreiber Compo N, McQuiston-Surrett D, Maclin OH, Zimmerman LA, & Topp LD. (2008). Study space analysis for policy development. *Applied Cognitive Psychology* 22: 789–801. https://doi.org/10.1002/acp.1483.

Mears, D.P., Stewart, E.A., Warren, P.Y. & Simons, R.L., (2017). Culture and formal social control: The effect of the code of the street on police and court decision making. *Justice Quarterly*, *34*, 217–247.

Merton, R. K. (2016). The self-fulfilling prophecy. *The Antioch Review*, *74*, 504–521.

Mortimer, A., & Shepherd, E. (1999). Frames of mind: Schemata guiding cognition and conduct in the interviewing of suspected offenders. In A. Memon & R. Bull (Eds.), *Handbook of the psychology of interviewing* (pp. 293–315). Chichester: Wiley.

Moston, S., Stephenson, G. M., & Williamson, T. M. (1992). The effects of case characteristics on suspect behaviour during police questioning. *British Journal of Criminology, 32,* 23–40.

Oxburgh, G. E. (2011). *Developing a more effective framework for the investigative interviewing of suspected sex offenders* (Unpublished doctoral dissertation, University of Portsmouth).

Pantazis, C. & Pemberton, S. (2009). From the 'old' to the 'new' suspect community examining the impacts of recent UK counter-terrorist legislation. *British Journal of Criminology*, *49*, 646–666. DOI: 10.1093/bjc/azp031

Quinton, P. (2011). The formation of suspicions: police stop and search practices in England and Wales. *Policing and Society,* 21, 357–368.

Roach, K., & Trotter, G. (2004). Miscarriages of Justice in the War against Terror. *Penn State Law Review*, *109*, 967.

Scherr, K. C., Redlich, A. D., & Kassin, S. M. (2020). Cumulative disadvantage: A psychological framework for understanding how innocence can lead to confession, wrongful conviction, and beyond. *Perspectives on Psychological Science*, *15*(2), 353–383.

Shepherd, E., & Griffiths, A. (2021). Investigative interviewing. In Oxford University Press eBooks. https://doi.org/10.1093/oso/9780192843692.001.0001

Spalek, B. (2011). New terrorism and crime prevention initiatives involving Muslim young people in the UK: Research and policy contexts. *Religion, State and Society*, *39*, 191–207.

Tajfel, H. (2010). *Social identity and intergroup relations*. Cambridge: Cambridge University Press.

Tajfel, H., & Turner, J. C. (1979). An integrative theory of intergroup conflict. In W. G. Austin & S. Worchel (Eds.), *The social psychology of intergroup relations* (pp. 33–47). Monterey, CA: Brooks/Cole.

Tversky, A., & Kahneman, D. (1986). Rational choice and the framing of decisions. *Journal of Business, 59,* 251–278. Available from www.jstor.org/stable/2352759

Walsh, D., & Bull, R. (2012). Examining rapport in investigative interviews with suspects: Does its building and maintenance work? *Journal of Police and Criminal Psychology* 27, 73–84. Doi:10.1007/s11896-011-9087-x

Williamson, T. (2006) *Investigative interviewing: Rights, research, regulation.* Devon: Willan Publishing.

Zempi, I., & Tripli, A. (2023). Listening to Muslim students' voices on the Prevent Duty in British universities: A qualitative study. *Education, Citizenship and Social Justice*, *18*(2), 230–245.

Index

Note: Page numbers in **bold** refers to Tables.